T0386743

The growth of Superbikes and
Superbike racing 1970 to 1988

www.veloce.co.uk

Front cover picture: Freddie Spencer's assault on the 1981 Daytona Superbike race faltered in a sheet of flame during a bungled fuel stop. He abandoned ship but got going again to put his 1023cc Honda into third behind the Suzukis of winner Wes Cooley and Graeme Crosby. (Courtesy Mortons Media Archive)

First published in February 2020 by Veloce Publishing Limited, Veloce House, Parkway Farm Business Park, Middle Farm Way, Poundbury, Dorchester DT1 3AR, England. Tel +44 (0)1305 260068 / Fax 01305 250479 / e-mail info@veloce.co.uk / web www.veloce.co.uk and www.velocebooks.com.
ISBN: 978-1-787113-16-9; UPC: 6-36847-01316-5.

The growth of Superbikes and Superbike racing 1970 to 1988

Bob Guntrip

VELOCE PUBLISHING
THE PUBLISHER OF FINE AUTOMOTIVE BOOKS

CONTENTS

INTRODUCTION

AIDE MEMOIRE

During an interval between speeches at a recent wedding reception, our table fell silent as a fellow guest explained how Yuri Gagarin became a television star in the '70s because he could bend spoons. None of the half-dozen of us within earshot contradicted him, no doubt thinking the error a simple and forgivable blurring of memory typical among people passing reluctantly through their sixties. But I was saddened that Gagarin's status as a pioneering figure of the Soviet space programme wasn't enough to protect him from being mistaken for an illusionist.

Still, I should be generous: my own head is so crammed with numbers, names and addresses – and let's not forget the modern blight, passwords – that there is diminishing room for more interesting stuff. So now, after half a lifetime spent scrutinising motorcycles and motorcycle sport in some detail, I find the corner of my memory that once stored details of the 1959 Triumph Bonneville is now full of junk about social media and the benefits of a low-carb diet.

Hence this book. After the excitement of racing during the '60s – largely provided by Hailwood and Ago – I wondered for a time if there would ever be anything as good. But then came Jarno Saarinen and Kenny Roberts, and when Yamaha's TZ750 got into its stride I witnessed the world's first 10-second, 180mph Production motorcycle with something akin to shock. After F750 died and the four-stroke began its comeback, more exciting developments began to take the sport in new directions. Most of the money, the technology, the resources were drawn into grand prix racing, which is as it should be – but since America came to European racing in the early '70s, something more democratic developed alongside the world championships, something we now understand as Superbike racing. The FIM grand prix world championships are no longer the only game in town.

So, lest we forget under the weight of oppressive rubbish apparently essential to modern life, this book is my own take on how racing of the 1970s eventually became what we now know as the Superbike World Championship. And while I stress that the following pages contain, warts and all, my own deeply flawed attempt to explain who did what and when, this is by no means a solo effort. Many learned and enthusiastic folk have shared their wisdom with me and deserve my unstinting thanks. First and foremost must be Steve McLaughlin, who has perhaps more claim on the concept of Superbike racing than anyone. I badgered him for months for his memories of the time, pestered him to scrutinise what I'd written and generally got in his way while he wanted to be doing other things. To Mr Superbike then, my abiding thanks. There were more, many more who consented to interviews: in the UK, Paul Smart, Mick Grant, Tony Jefferies and John Cooper. Also in Britain, John Froude is proof of what can be achieved with enthusiasm and social media – his Facebook page on US Superbike racing of the early '80s is a living museum of treasures. Richard Peckett took time out of his still-crowded day to humour my enquiries about the early days of TT-F1, and after starting the hunt for him in Scotland, I finally tracked down Britain's first TT-F1 national champion, John Cowie, on the east coast of Australia. Paul Boulton, a loyal servant of Suzuki for many years, put me straight on Heron Suzuki's machinery during the 1980s, as did Mick Smith, who, along with Barry Symmons, former team boss at Honda Britain, also helped with the details of in-line and V4s. I also owe thanks to two other prominent Honda men, Melburnian brothers Rex (air-cooled) and Clyde (water-cooled) Wolfenden. And in a part of Australia where the grass will always be greener, father and son Neville and Peter Doyle, Kawasaki builders par excellence, offered a glimpse of their wealth of experience that spans decades. For Suzuki – and Superbike racing generally – down under, no one speaks with more passion than Mick Hone, no one with more understated wisdom than Alan Pickering. Ross Hannan, who's forgotten more about Superbike racing than I'll ever know, and Tony Hatton, perhaps the most engaging conversationalist on motorcycle racing I've ever met, were both found in Sydney and still in world championship form. I also bumped into Kiwi Richard Scott during the Long Lunch in Sydney, and he steered me in the right direction about Ron Grant's contribution to Superstock and TT-F1 during 1986-7. Valued comrades Peter Clifford, Don Cox and Fraser Stronach fielded my enquiries with good humour. Also Down Under, veteran TZ750 punters Bob Rosenthal and Jeff Sayle shared their memories, as did Jeff's brother, Murray, while for Ducati my old colleague Ian Falloon and, in leafy Vermont, Cook Neilson both gave me their time, along with Pat Slinn, who was at Sports Motor Cycles during the great days of 1978. Finally, and also on the east coast of the US, the great Kevin Cameron, who answered my questions with courtesy and patience. To all, my gratitude.

Photographers: Mary Grothe generously allowed me access to her portfolio, and, in Britain, Elwyn Roberts once again opened his collection to me. Rob Lewis turned the clock back to the early days of Australian Superbike, and in California Stuart Rowlands allowed me access to his Honda PR portfolio. Bill Snelling at TTracepics.com, Phil Aynsley, Jacqui Harris at Bauer Media and Jane Skayman at Mortons Archive all helped with images. Many hours, too, were spent poring over the printed word, and again I must thank Pete, Vicky and Roz – and of course Pam – at the VMCC in Burton Upon Trent, and the staff at the NSW State Library. The pages of *Motor Cycle News*, *Motor Cycle Weekly* and in the US, *Cycle News*, were essential reading, as were *Team Suzuki* by Ray Battersby, *Yamaha Two-stroke Racing Motorcycles* by Greg Bennett, Kevin Cameron's *Classic Motorcycle Race Engines*, *Triumph Experimental* by Mick Duckworth, Ian Falloon's *Ducati Racers* and *Kawasaki Racers*, *Race Across the Great Divide* by Darryl Flack and Don Cox, *Yamaha* by Colin MacKellar, *Ducati & the TT* by Greg Pullen, *Suzuki GSX-R750* by Gary Pinchin and *Honda's V-Force* by Julian Ryder.

Thanks again to Rod Grainger and his talented tribe at Veloce Publishing, particularly Becky Martin and Emma Shanes for their calm professionalism, and, last but by no means least, thanks to my dear wife Sandy for her skills as agent provocateur and proof-reader, and for her forbearance: I've woken her in the middle of the night shouting in my sleep about Daytona qualifying times, and have sadly neglected my house maintenance duties, but she's still addressing me by name. Most important of all, thanks to you, honoured reader, for your interest.

Bob Guntrip
Wentworth Falls

1

SUNRISE

The first photos began to appear in the summer of 1968. The British press had at first to be content with long shots of a chunky rear tyre, four exhausts canted rakishly upwards, an impressive breadth of crankcase; but in the US sometime Honda dealer, racing chief and, later, national parts manager Bob Hansen received a set of black and whites depicting a late prototype of Honda's ground-breaking newcomer, albeit with a drum front brake. It had been an open secret that Honda was up to something, that amid all the headlines about BSA-Triumph's new triples, the Norton Commando and Kawasaki's new 498cc three-cylinder two-stroke, Japan's biggest was about to trump them all with a four-cylinder roadster bearing echoes of the marque's exploits in grand prix racing of the 1960s.

The grainy images and rumours finally assumed substance in November, when Honda gave the Dream CB750 its world première at the Tokyo show. True, the new bike had single-overhead-cam valve actuation instead of the racers' double overhead cams, and lacked the four-valve heads and geared primary drive of its supposed racetrack predecessors, but it was impressive enough. Its claimed 67bhp gave it an edge over everything else in volume production (the power output chosen in part to surpass the Honda's closest rival, Harley-Davidson's then new 66bhp 1210cc Shovelhead engine), and at 218kg dry it was just 10kg heavier than BSA/Triumph's new Rocket 3 and Trident. The age of the Superbike had arrived.

Had Britain's tottering giant managed to get its 741cc triples on sale as early as 1965, as former deputy MD Bert Hopwood had reflected on in his memoirs, *Whatever Happened to the British Motorcycle Industry?*, they might have been established in time to counter the allure of the CB750's electric start, front disc, five-speed transmission, and additional nine horsepower. As it was, the British bikes were launched in the USA just as Honda's big news broke; and when the CB750 went on sale in the USA it undercut the $1800 Trident/Rocket 3 by $300. In their first year of production

Honda's Saitama (engine) and Hamamatsu (chassis) plants turned out nearly twice as many CB750s as Small Heath and Meriden made in their full seven years of triples production – and by the end of its production life in 1978, Honda had built some 550,000 CB750s, while BSA-Triumph totalled around 33,000 Trident/Rocket 3s.

Britain wasn't quite ready to throw in the towel, however, and when the AMA opened its premier racing class to all 750cc production engines, BSA-Triumph, at the urging of its North America President Peter Thornton, decided that racing might be the means of demonstrating to America the merits of its triples. And it had just the people for the job.

Triumph's Chief Developmental Engineer, Doug Hele, already thinking about developing the threes to relieve Triumph's hard-pressed Bonneville in domestic Production racing, now had an additional deadline, and inspired his small team at Triumph Experimental to work on the bikes through the winter of 1969-70 in preparation for the Daytona 200 in March.

For a time, Daytona's 200-mile season opener (then run over a 3.81-mile circuit that combined part of the car-racing speedbowl with a sequence of infield bends) ranked among the most important races in the motorcycle world, and for 1970 it soon became clear that the BSA-Triumph team would have more to contend with than buzzing hordes of 350 Yamahas. Added spice among the two-stroke lobby came from Kawasaki's new three-cylinder H1-R, to be campaigned by New Zealander Ginger Molloy, reputedly pumping out 75bhp and weighing a trim 136kg. And Suzuki would field TR500 twins, lighter and more powerful at 68bhp than Art Baumann's 1969 Sears Point winner – this year to be ridden by Baumann again, along with Jody Nicholas, Ron Grant, and New Zealander Geoff Perry. Norton, on the other hand, was busy developing its new 68bhp Commando Production racer and pushing for its eligibility for UK competition, and so had nothing to spare for Daytona.

For the home team, Harley-Davidson had pensioned off its old side-valve

The way we were: TR500-mounted Ron Grant leads US Suzuki team-mate Art Baumann in 1970. (Courtesy Elwyn Roberts)

KR750 for a new overhead-valve engine derived from the 883cc (55 cubic inch) XLR-TT dirt-tracker, using a shorter stroke but keeping the older bike's iron barrels and heads. Dubbed the XR, the newcomer was developed by a team led by H-D's gifted racing manager Dick O'Brien, and its 70bhp and 150kg would be employed by an abundance of talent in a team headed by the great Cal Rayborn, who'd won six of the nine AMA National road races leading up to the 1970 Daytona meeting. It got better: word had it that during discreet tests early in the New Year, Rayborn had run the XR up to better than 160mph around Daytona's mighty tri-oval, the bike's barking exhaust note echoing among the empty grandstands to offer the Harley faithful some welcome seasonal cheer.

And that, according to Thornton, was right on the money. At a press conference in February he suggested that the 1970 Daytona-winning bike would have to have 160mph in it, with a 155mph qualifying lap also on the list of desirable attributes.

Hele did his best. His small team, which included mechanics and fitters Bill Fannon, Norman Hyde, Arthur Jakeman, Jack Shemans, Fred Swift and foreman Les Williams – all to become known in their own right – worked long winter nights to have six bikes ready for shipping to the States: three Triumph Tridents and three BSA Rocket 3s – plus an additional bike for Triumph's veteran development rider Percy Tait.

Key elements of the three-cylinder engine's development were rooted in Hele's experience of racing the marque's 500cc twin during the second half of the 1960s. Compression was lifted from the standard triple's 9:1 to 11:1; TH6 cam profiles were used to give longer duration and higher lift than stock, and the roadster's 26/27mm Amal Concentric carburettors were initially replaced with 1$\frac{3}{16}$ in Amal GPs. Early experimentation with the production engine had given it aluminium alloy conrods, with plain bearings for the big ends and the central main bearings. There were, too, American-made S&W valve springs and cam lobes hardened by nitriding. It would all help to cope with the engine's capacity to rev (safe to 9500rpm, compared with the roadster's 8000). The exhaust system caused a little head-scratching, but after some experimentation Hele opted for a three-into-one that yielded more power than its competitors and gave smooth running. The resulting power figures were, as ever, open to wild speculation, but the reality of 78-80bhp at the crankshaft was gratifying enough, particularly when allied to the race bike's all-up weight of 175kg, some 40kg lighter than the roadster. The five-speed gearbox (the street bikes had four gears) was the work of specialist Rod Quaife, and mated to a standard single-plate clutch modified to reduce width and weight. Another notable import was the 250mm double twin-leading-shoe front brake from Italian manufacturer Daniele Fontana, with a 230mm hydraulic disc at the rear.

The BSA/Triumph racing triple's trademark angular look belongs largely to Rob North, a freelance engineer Hele commissioned to design and build the frames after Ken Sprayson at the Reynolds Tube Company had turned him down for want of time. North accepted the commission, building and delivering the duplex frames (based on a one-off he'd done for Percy Tait's 650 twin) when he could. Because of the rush nature of the job, each frame differed slightly from the others, but the principal attributes were common to all: the engine was higher and further forward than stock to improve cornering clearance and aid steering; the steering head was rigid and sturdily braced, and the oval-section swinging arm likewise boasted plenty of strength.

The last piece of the puzzle, the fairing, was the design of the BSA-Triumph research unit based at Umberslade Hall, a 17th century house at Tanworth-in-Arden, Warwickshire. Wind-tunnel testing went well and, finally, tests on the runway of snow-laden Elvington airfield in Yorkshire, with Tait aboard, yielded a top speed of 164mph. So far, so good.

Which left Honda and its CB750. The bike was gathering accolades on the racetrack even as it went on sale. In September 1969, Frenchmen Michel Rougerie and Daniel Urdich had taken a race-prepped CB750 to victory at the Bol d'Or. By January, rumours were circulating that the bike's next appearance would be at Daytona, and in the third week of the New Year a British-based team was announced under the leadership of TT veteran Bill Smith, riding alongside former Honda GP stalwarts Ralph Bryans and Tommy Robb.

Before February was out, the first batch of CB750s to reach the UK – some 140 bikes – had been snapped up, while the Daytona team had been testing at Oulton Park to the apparent satisfaction of all. And now it seemed there would be a fourth bike for Daytona, to be ridden by 1963 AMA Grand National Champion, 35-year-old Dick Mann.

Roll your own

All four Daytona bikes, variously to become known as the CB750 Racing Type, CB750R and CR750, were built in Japan. Not long after the Daytona meeting, Honda offered a limited number of kits that gave the well-heeled buyer (US$10,000 in 1970) the hardware necessary to convert his or her mild-mannered CB750 tourer into a CR750 monster. The list of components reveals in part how Honda coaxed a claimed 90bhp from its 67bhp street bike: high-lift, long-duration cams opening larger-diameter intake valves, and smaller exhausts; slipper pistons that boosted the compression ratio from 9 to 10.5:1; 31mm Keihin racing carburettors (the street bike had 28mm Mikunis); a close-ratio gearbox, and a black-finished, dyno-tuned exhaust system that bellowed as it should at a redline of 10,500rpm, a hefty boost from the street bike's 8500.

Weight reduction posed a bigger problem for Honda's race engineers than for BSA-Triumph's men, but no more intractable. Using magneto ignition in place of alternator and battery was a good start. The frame, similar to stock though made of chrome-moly rather than mild steel, lost any unneeded lugs and brackets. There were 18-inch alloy wheels, the

Dick Mann's CB/CR750 was the sole survivor of a four-bike Honda team at Daytona in 1970. Bugsy won a shrewdly-judged race.
(Courtesy Mike Ricketts/ Wikipedia Commons)

rear laced to a magnesium hub. Alloy fuel and oil tanks, and a lightweight fairing kept weight down. Extra weight was added where necessary: a second front brake disc, more durable primary drive and camchains. Ultimately, the CR750 was pared from the CB750's 218kg dry weight to around 175kg.

That was what the kit gave its buyers. Smith, Robb, Bryans and Mann got a little extra, including a lightened and balanced crankshaft, and costly Keihin 35mm carburettors. Also, never confirmed but widely believed, the factory bikes were said to have magnesium crankcases that were illegal under AMA rules. The final piece of the Honda puzzle fell into place with the arrival of Yoshio Nakamura, who had overseen Honda's F1 car team when John Surtees and Richie Ginther drove the company's cars in the mid-1960s. Now he was at Daytona to supervise the team whose bikes he'd tweaked back in Japan.

A month before the big event BSA-Triumph announced its team. Gary Nixon, Gene Romero and Don Castro would ride Triumphs, while Dave Aldana and Jim Rice would fly BSA's colours together with nine-time world champion Mike Hailwood, who happened to be in Florida to share a Lola T70 with Mike De Udy in the Sebring 12-hour car race (DNF).

Peter Thornton's musings about the speeds necessary to win soon proved correct. Romero opened what would become his year by taking his Pat Owens-tuned Trident around the speed bowl to qualify fastest at 157.34mph with a top speed of 165.44mph. A year later Paul Smart, new to the Triumph team, and perhaps a little intimidated by the dazzling grandeur of Daytona after plying his trade at Castle Combe and Snetterton, received some useful advice from team-mate Romero about qualifying on the speed bowl.

"You did one warm-up lap, one fast lap and a slowing lap," Smart recalls. "Gene said to me: 'You've got to ride round the bottom. Run a front tyre on the back, and very, very high poundage in both. Hang on like grim death, and run with your wheels in the groove in the bottom of the track like a train'."

Romero headlined a promising start for BSA-Triumph. Hailwood qualified second fastest, though well adrift of Romero at 152.90mph, with Nixon third at 152.82. Still, all was not quite well. Design faults combined with high ambient temperatures were causing overheating and misfires: a "maze of ducting" (Hele) inside the Umberslade-designed fairings directed hot air onto the carburettors; oil coolers, mounted in front of the exhaust rocker box and above the header pipes, struggled to perform. There were ignition problems, too, with the contact breakers themselves, and with settings slipping because the ignition cam didn't fit firmly enough into the exhaust camshaft, as Mick Duckworth explains in his fine book, *Triumph Experimental*. Now there were more misfires – and pistons were beginning to fail.

Mann qualified fourth at 152.67mph, but Honda, too, had its log of problems. Ralph Bryans crashed on the banking, his CR750 catching fire from spilt fuel as it ground along the track. The bike burnt for so long it prompted shrewd smiles from opposing teams, accompanied by more ripe comments about magnesium cases.

As the British team set about rebuilding Bryans' bike, Hansen pointed out the dangers inherent in re-using a frame that had undergone prolonged exposure to fire. After the pointed exchange of views that followed, the American arm of the operation decided to keep its advice to itself. Mann, meanwhile, was trying to practise on a bike suffering something akin to a misfire. Chief mechanic Bob Jameson discovered fragments of a black, rubber-like material in the bike's oil, and quickly diagnosed a disintegrating camchain tensioner. Hansen invoked a temporary perestroika to explain the problem to Bill Smith's men, and then went to work, replacing the stock camchain tensioner with one from a CB450.

While the BSA-Triumph team was stripping the inefficient ducting from its fairings in an effort to address its overheating problems, Harley-Davidson was resorting to more extreme measures. Massive heat dissipation difficulties were causing a spate of burnt rear pistons. Already low on power compared with the opposition, O'Brien had no choice but to fit pistons that dropped compression from 8.5 to 7:1. H-D's best qualifier was Bart Markel in 15th at 147.50mph; Rayborn's best was slower than his 1969 time on the old side-valve KR. The future, meanwhile, arrived by stealth, with Kel Carruthers qualifying fifth on his 350 Yamaha.

Mann said his rebuilt bike ran better than ever, and made good use of it by taking an early lead at the start of the 53-lap, 200-mile race. But Romero,

Ralph Bryans rode alongside Bill Smith and Tommy Robb on the British-entered Hondas at Daytona in 1970 …

… but it all went wrong for Bryans in practice. (Both photos courtesy Ian Falloon)

Nixon and Hailwood were quickly with him, and used their better-handling British bikes to pass him in the infield on the opening lap. By lap five Romero had run off the track and was now working through the field while Nixon and Hailwood swapped the lead, the Brit giving a masterclass through the infield turns while Nixon passed him on the banking. Mann, plugging along in third, had Rayborn immediately to his rear, the Harley man apparently doing the impossible from a lowly starting position. Behind them came the best of the two-strokes: Grant's Suzuki and Carruthers' Yamaha.

Retirements began to mount. With scarcely a lap on the board, Art Baumann was involved in a turn 2 crash that left him with a dislocated elbow. Bill Smith hadn't got that far, his Honda breaking a camchain in final practice, and team-mate Bryans rolling to a stop with the same ailment after just three laps. Meanwhile, Grant hustled through the field, taking on Nixon for the lead, and matching the Triumph on acceleration. Hailwood came under pressure from Mann for third, and the pair scrapped for a lap until Hailwood's bike belched flame and stopped with a broken valve.

Before half distance, Tommy Robb, after circulating in 11th place, had joined his team-mates, the last British Honda having broken its camchain. Rayborn, striving to uphold Harley's honour, got the better of both Carruthers and Mann, before he retired with a broken valve. Carruthers went out with crankshaft failure, and Grant was next. The Suzuki rider began lap 26 with his nose in front, but, running dangerously low on fuel, the TR500 seized its left-hand piston, leaving Nixon in the lead until the Triumph holed a piston on lap 30.

Enter Dick Mann, never quite fast enough for comfort, but now leading. Bob Hansen later suggested that Mann's rebuilt CR750 was well advanced in the destruction of its new camchain tensioner as early as half distance, but Mann, shrewd and capable to the last, knew how to nurse an ailing engine, and did just that, while dirt-tracker Romero tore through the field on the fastest of the remaining triples, gaining on his quarry hand over fist. With 15 laps to run, Mann led Romero by 21 seconds. Hansen calculated that Mann could drop a second a lap on his pursuer and still get home in some comfort. Team chief Nakamura thought otherwise, and the ensuing argument, Hansen later thought, cost him his job. But Mann ran his own race, his poor Honda increasingly off-song, smoking and misfiring, and he took the chequered flag with 10 seconds to spare over Romero. During its post-race strip, Hansen's men found less than a pint of oil in the engine.

Honda's single survivor of a four-bike team had won, BSA-Triumph had three finishers from seven bikes: Romero and Castro taking second and third, and Dave Aldana, having crashed and remounted, bringing his BSA into 12th place.

Yvon Du Hamel had bustled his way into fourth place on the best of the Yamahas, ahead of New Zealander Perry's Suzuki. The pick of the Harleys was one of the old side-valve KR750s, cajoled into sixth place by veteran Walt Fulton; the best of the 'new' XRs was Mert Lawwill's, finishing 15th.

Mike Hailwood rode a BSA Rocket 3 at Daytona in 1970 and (shown here) 1971, going superbly in both races until stopped by mechanical failure. (Courtesy Elwyn Roberts)

America had a good race to savour and, more importantly, a long-overdue win by one of its favourite sons, a veteran who embodied the competitive toughness of his sport. Few riders were better liked on the gruelling ten-month AMA Grand National Championship than 'Bugsy' Mann, and few more deserving.

Across the Atlantic, news from Daytona 1970 blew fresh stimulus into the immutable landscape of British racing. Doug Hele, though disappointed at not having won the big race, was enthusiastic about the future and started work on improving his bikes with the full support of BSA-Triumph. Indeed, the group soon announced it was pulling out of British racing to concentrate more fully on events the other side of the pond. The decision soon paid off. The 1970 AMA season included just a handful of road races, but these were well sponsored and heavily cashed up. The prize fund for Daytona was around $15,000, and a similar sum was on offer at Seattle International Raceway (a drag strip/road race circuit, rather than a speed bowl), 3000 miles away on the other side of the country, three weeks later. There, Ron Grant made good his Daytona threat, winning the 125-mile race for Suzuki while Du Hamel (Yamaha) fended off Nixon's Triumph for second place in another edge-of-the-seat thriller. A month later it was Dave Aldana's turn in the spotlight, using Mike Hailwood's Daytona BSA, rebuilt and rejetted, to win at the Talladega Superspeedway after a long duel with Nixon – until

Nixon's throttle jammed open, forcing him to surrender second place to Jody Nicholas' Suzuki.

Rules for the world
This was stirring stuff from a nation that had little road racing in its cultural DNA, and added weight to the cause of those in Britain who championed American-style racing. *Motor Cycle*'s racing man, Mick Woollett, came back from Daytona to stress again the low cost and basic equalities of the formula. Mike Nedham, Engineering Director of BSA-Triumph, spoke with admiration of a contest that allowed "virtually any change" to a bike's chassis, while using what were "basically roadster engines." What was needed, he said, was "one set of rules for the world."

Honda, meanwhile, had packed up its tents and gone. The company had no interest in pursuing glory within the AMA series, dispatching two of its four CR750s to France for endurance racing. As for the others, well, no-one quite seemed to know where they'd gone. Meanwhile, its principal ambition in UK racing seemed to be for a good showing in the Production TT.

For the moment, at least, Production racing remained the major form of big-bore racing in the UK, with the first round of the season going to Norton. In May, Peter Williams and Charlie Sanby won the Thruxton 500-mile race, ending Triumph's five-year winning streak and giving the factory's so-called Commando Production Racer, the 'Yellow Peril,' its first major victory. Triumph turned the tables in the Production TT, with Trident-mounted Malcolm Uphill getting home by just 1.6 seconds from Williams' Commando. The best Hondas – "outsped and outsteered," said *Motor Cycle* – were eighth (Robb) and ninth (John Cooper).

Change was on its way. In July, word came that the AMA would be granted full membership of the FIM at its October congress. Meanwhile, Brands Hatch began making plans to run the first AMA-style 750cc race in Britain, at its season-ending international Race of the South meeting in October, while Triumph-mounted Nixon won his single AMA national road race of the season at Loudon in New Hampshire.

Not that BSA-Triumph was starved of headlines. The next conquest came at the Bol d'Or, France's leading 24-hour race for motorcycles, in 1970 running at Montlhéry for the last time. Honda was making a major effort here, with five CB750s entered alongside factory bikes from Moto Guzzi, Laverda, and BMW. Triumph's leading hope lay in the bike shared by Paul Smart and Tom Dickie, which slipped into the lead at the fifth hour and then spent much of the race fending off the CB750 ridden by Bill Smith and John Williams until, after 19 hours, the Honda stopped with suspected piston failure. Norton's best entry, the Commando of Peter Williams and Charlie Sanby, went out with a failed main bearing, and the Smart/Dickie Trident took the flag nine laps clear of the runner-up, a stock Honda CB750 shared by Peter Darvill and Olivier Chevallier.

The climactic races of the British season highlighted the excitement implicit in 'Daytona-style' 750cc racing, and the capacity of a well-ridden Yamaha two-stroke twin to spoil anyone's party. The second point was borne out first when John Cooper took the second of his three Mallory Park Race of the Year victories, this one on his Seeley-framed TR2, from Phil Read on a 250 Yamaha and a pack of 750s led by Smart, who'd made a poor start on his Triumph Trident, Gary Nixon, also on a Trident, then Tony Jefferies and Ken Redfern on Norton twins. Two weeks later at Brands Hatch the 750s got their own back in the 'Daytona' race, Smart leading a Triumph 1-2-3, with Ron Chandler the best 350 Yamaha in fourth place. Even at this early stage of the new era, it was clear that the two-strokes weren't going away.

The closing weeks of 1970 belonged largely to the sport's administrators. At the FIM Autumn Congress the AMA was duly granted its place at the high table, but, to the open exasperation of many, the sport's premier governing body passed up the opportunity for a formal discussion of 750cc racing in any of its steadily evolving forms. The AMA did a little better at its Competition Congress, also in November, by agreeing to accept the FIM's regulations for its events, and endorsing seven national road races for the 1971, including a newcomer at Ontario in California, which would offer a staggering $50,000 (then £20,000) prize purse. Meanwhile, Gene Romero, the dirt-tracker with the flashing smile, had become America's Grand National Champion with a come-from-behind win in the dirt at the famous

John Cooper had a good '71 season that culminated in his third Race of the Year win, borrowing a Rocket 3 to beat Ago's 500 MV. (Courtesy Elwyn Roberts)

Sacramento Mile. At season's end he was some 93 points clear of BSA man Jim Rice in second place, and neither man had won a single national road race – there had been only four, after all.

Work on the 1971-spec Daytona Tridents was well advanced before the end of the 1970 British season. The bikes Smart and Nixon had ridden in the Race of the Year and at Brands Hatch each had a new frame, which mounted the steering head 50mm lower, and altered the steering-head angle to make the bike a better proposition for British circuits. This was the so-called 'lowboy' frame.

In the depths of the northern winter, Smart and Ray Pickrell (who'd been recruited by BSA-Triumph after he'd left Paul Dunstall during the autumn) were packed off to Pietermaritzburg with 1970-spec bikes for the South African TT. There, Smart had the temerity to lead Ago's 500 MV for a time before settling for second, while Pickrell ran third until his BSA broke a chain. Meanwhile, Hele and his team were putting the final touches to the bikes that would make such a name for themselves during the season ahead. Many of the changes were intended to counter the problems encountered at Daytona the previous spring. The oil cooler was moved in front of the steering head with a slot cut into the new fairing – dubbed the 'letterbox' – to ensure it received maximum airflow. Compression ratio was pegged at 11.4:1, with new squish cylinder heads on some engines, and ignition timing attained a new reliability with Doug Hele's new 'quill' system, which mounted the ignition plate on a shaft anchored deep inside the engine's hollow exhaust camshaft.

The steering head was widened to accommodate twin-disc front brakes. The discs themselves were aluminium sprayed with steel, running in magnesium alloy Lockheed callipers. Detail changes that gave engine components a simpler life included strengthened pushrods. Some engines had Amal Concentric carburettors in place of the Amal GPs. These were held to run cleaner throughout the rev range, and fitted with Jack Shemans' bellmouths that were themselves said to give better than 5bhp. A new, longer-duration, higher-lift inlet cam profile was developed, and oil supply to both camshafts improved. Finally, there was a new, simpler fairing.

As February began, BSA-Triumph's bikes, now rated at around 84bhp, were nearing readiness for the Florida season opener, which was more than could be said of the meeting itself. The AMA had applied to the FIM in good time for its international permit to run the Daytona race, asking if it might use AMA regulations for the occasion as there wasn't the time before March to get everyone into line with FIM requirements. FIM Secretary-General Raymond Trost replied that the AMA might indeed use its own regulations, but the meeting would then be a national, and any European FIM licence holder to ride in such an event would face possible suspension.

A groan went up on both sides of the Atlantic. 'Scoop' Woollett thundered in *Motor Cycle* that the FIM had "vaulted onto their high horse," pointing out that the body that had "virtually no 750cc racing" under its control. Britain's ACU weighed in next, sending a delegation to America with the intention of mediating in a prickly situation. Norman Dixon and Neville Goss from the ACU, together with Mike Nedham of BSA-Triumph, headed for Cincinnati, and disappeared into conclave for three days with the AMA and American motorcycle industry heavyweights from the four Japanese manufacturers, plus Harley-Davidson and BSA. Then the Canadians popped up, offering CMA licences to Hailwood and Smart, and so enabling them to ride in American events without invoking the wrath of the FIM.

FORMULA FUTURE

In the end the AMA, via the France family, decided to run Daytona the way it always had, while the British party came back from the USA with the blueprint of AMA 750cc racing to apply within its own jurisdiction. The AMA-ACU talks had yielded an Anglo-American agreement on something that would be known as Formula 750. It would follow the AMA's rules in all but three major requirements: for a given bike to be eligible for the class, its manufacturer need only have made 100 examples (200 for AMA events), but it was required to have the stock model's transmission type and number of gears (the AMA stipulated a maximum of five); and it must have the cooling system of the original bike (the AMA proscribed liquid cooling). All else was as per AMA: stock components to include cases, cylinders, heads and gearbox castings. Major accessory components – frames, for example, to be approved by the bike's manufacturer.

Britain's first F750 race would be a 200-miler to run concurrently with the Thruxton 500-mile Production race in May, followed by a three-lap F750 TT on the Saturday of race week. But there was plenty to be getting on with. First, there was something new to consider, an innovation with the working name of the UK-US match races. The idea came from California-based Brits, Bruce Cox and Gavin Trippe, with later help from Chris Lowe of Motor Circuit Developments, Britain's biggest track combine. It been given the go-ahead of the ACU and AMA (now the FIM accepted AMA licences), to be billed as the first Anglo-American Match Races, contested by teams of five riders from Britain and the USA over two races at each of the three major meetings at Easter: Brands Hatch on Good Friday, Mallory Park on Sunday, and Oulton Park on the Monday.

There was also the British 750cc Championship, newly established for 1971, to consider. Sparsely supported to begin with, its fields thickened quickly as fancied runners found themselves competitive mounts. After the first three rounds, Percy Tait, with wins at Oulton Park and Thruxton, found himself well in control for BSA-Triumph, though with stiffening resistance from Charlie Sanby on a Gus Kuhn Norton, and Mick Grant, winner of the Cadwell Park second round, on Jim Lee's Commando.

If numbers counted for anything, the 1971 Daytona 200 would run to a similar script. Altogether, BSA-Triumph would field 10 bikes: four of them

*Dick Mann won the Daytona 200 in 1970 for Honda, and in 1971 for BSA. He led
a much-reduced Triumph effort in 1972, and was dogged by ignition problems.
(Courtesy Elwyn Roberts)*

new (BSAs for Hailwood and Dick Mann, Triumphs for Romero and Smart),
and the six from 1970 (BSAs for Aldana, Rice and Don Emde, Triumphs for
Nixon, Castro and Tom Rockwood).

There was no official Honda presence at Daytona in 1971, but the nod
for the fastest bike of the meeting went to the CR750 ridden by Gary
Fisher and prepared by Hideo 'Pops' Yoshimura. Essentially a race-kitted
bike, it weighed a claimed 168kg, but had the power – said to be around
94bhp – to compensate. Among the two-strokes, the fastest Yamaha
again belonged to Kel Carruthers, who nudged his TR2B into seventh on
the grid. Porting changes, increased compression ratio and new conrods
helped the 111kg air-cooled twin maintain its competitive edge, and
boosted power a little over the 1970 bike, to 56bhp at 10,000rpm. But
if Yamaha went quietly about its business, confusing signals came from
Kawasaki. At the close of 1970, the factory announced it would build no
more H1R triples; the last batch of 15 was then being made, of which a
dozen would go to the US, two to France, and the last to Italy. But this was
not, it seemed, a sign that Kawasaki was losing interest in racing. Weeks
later, its US subsidiary signed Yvon Du Hamel for a new team to contest
all seven AMA national road races in '71, riding factory-supported H1Rs.

Suzuki meanwhile had lightened and lowered its TR500s and boosted power to around 72bhp. New for the year was CDI electronic ignition, but there were problems ranging from misfires to melted pistons.

Harley-Davidson's XR750s were again down on power – 66bhp at 7600rpm, according to some – but a switch to over-bored Mikuni carburettors helped acceleration. And the Milwaukee outfit still had Cal Rayborn's signature, which, said his legion of admirers, was worth a lot more than mere horsepower.

Qualifying now took place on the full circuit, and Paul Smart heeded Gene Romero's advice – if not on the matter of tyres, because Romero ran Goodyears and Smart was on Dunlops. But the Maidstone boatbuilder had the right tyre for the job: "I still ran triangulars and I got on well with them. I don't think Gene was too keen on me telling Dunlop what he'd said, but we ran much higher tyre pressures, and I rode round the bottom and qualified on pole. Considering what the speeds were you weren't going to gain anything anywhere else. I ended up making more money out of qualifying than I ever made in any one race before."

Not that practice and qualifying were entirely plain sailing for those on BSA-Triumph's '71-spec bikes. The front aluminium brake discs expanded dramatically when hot, and would jam in the callipers, calling for a prompt change to cast iron rotors. Still, Smart qualified at 105.8mph, a whisker in front of the Harleys of Rayborn (105.68mph) and Mark Brelsford (105.61mph). Yet it was Fisher's Honda that bolted in the race, if passed smartly by Rayborn's Harley. Both were soon sidelined, Rayborn with gearbox failure, Fisher with that familiar Honda bogey, a broken camchain. Smart and Hailwood then headed for the flag, swapping the lead, but with Smart usually in front at the line to collect his $125 lap leader's money. Gradually, the field thinned … Du Hamel fell, Carruthers stopped with oil coming from a gearbox breather, and, one by one, the Suzuki team fell by the wayside with ignition problems, Ron Pierce the last to stop after 27 laps.

Smart surged on, alone after Hailwood's BSA broke a pushrod on lap 15. He led until lap 40 of 53, by which time his engine was smoking heavily: "There wasn't the slightest indication it was going to let go," he recalled. "In fact, it wasn't until I looked behind me and saw clouds of smoke I realised there was a major problem."

Smart's bike had holed a piston. A technician from Champion spark plugs had warned about the 12:1 compression of Smart's engine, but it had given no trouble in practice. Now, though, he joined team-mates Aldana, Castro and Nixon in retirement. Then there was Dick Mann, never quite fast enough for comfort but now leading, almost a minute down on Smart when the Brit had retired, riding his tall-geared BSA as if he'd paid for every last nut and bolt himself; and there too was Gene Romero, hustling his Triumph into second place from Roger Reiman's home-built XR Harley and Don Emde's BSA. In the closing stages Emde got into third, and that's how they finished, Mann taking a second finely-judged win and collecting $5000 first prize plus contingency money, Smart earning $3875 in lap leader's money alone – more than he'd earned during the whole of his best season's racing in Britain.

There was little qualification to Hele's delight this time around: his bikes had taken the first three places, with '71-spec bikes first and second. There was still work to be done, but not yet. First, there were bikes to be readied for the Anglo-American Match Races. As this was a BSA-Triumph affair it couldn't rightly be considered an F750 series, but it was hardly less enticing for that. The Americans would draw their team from a pool of six under the captaincy of Gary Nixon – now aged 31 but with two Grand National Championships behind him, the hard-school experience he shared with the senior member of the team, Dick Mann. BSA stalwarts Dave Aldana, Don Emde and Jim Rice, and sole Triumph representative Don Castro, added competitive weight to the squad.

The UK captain was Triumph test rider and current leader of the British 750 Championship, Percy Tait, with 750 aces Pickrell, Smart, and Tony Jefferies ranged alongside him, together with the incomparable John Cooper. True, the Americans were without Rayborn as the British lacked Hailwood's services; but the two teams were strong enough to attract a crowd of 66,000 over the weekend to endure some truly vile weather – and enjoy some fine racing, all of which Nixon missed. To a broken leg, sustained during off-road training in January (he rode the Daytona 200 with a steel pin in his thigh), he now added a broken wrist after a Brands practice fall.

Leaderless the Americans might have been, disgraced they were not. True, Pickrell won both Brands Hatch races from Smart, both of whom knew the short circuit down to the last square inch. Yet Mann got home third in the first race – battling gearbox gremlins – from British captain Tait, with Castro third in the second race. In the supporting round of the British 750 Championship, Charlie Sanby took his Kuhn Norton Commando to a solid win from Tait's triple, and this just days after Gus Kuhn Motors boss, Vincent Davey, had said how pleased he was with the performance of the bike, given that the team was getting no support from the Norton factory.

At Mallory Park the BSA-Triumph cavalcade found more filthy weather. Pickrell, defying augury, scorched away at the start of race one, taking Smart with him. Tait was handily placed until lap six, when he fell heavily at Shaw's hairpin. It was, he growled later, "like riding on ice." Smart, who was developing a healthy dislike for Mallory's hairpin anyway, did the same thing a lap later. Nor were they the only casualties. Jefferies, second at one point, ended the day with his Triumph planted in the earth bank at Gerard's, engine and front forks out of commission after he'd found neutral at the wrong moment, while Castro's engine threw a rod as he rounded the Esses. From a depleted field, Smart – with broken fingers from his first race crash – turned the tables on Pickrell in the second stoush, with Cooper third and Mann fourth.

The walking wounded reassembled for their final encounter around the undulations of Oulton Park, the following day. Tait's bike had been rebuilt overnight, as had Jefferies', and they had at it again with no loss of enthusiasm. Smart, though last away in the opening five-lapper because of his damaged hand, led by the end of the first lap from Pickrell and Cooper. Behind them Tait and Mann resumed their acquaintanceship, with Jefferies also on hand. And that's how it stayed, though Cooper looked threatening until he missed a gear, and Mann consolidated fourth place. The American veteran did better in the second race, leading until Smart passed him on the second lap. Pickrell was there too, vying for the lead until he fell heavily at Knickerbook on the penultimate lap of the whole three-day contest, leaving Smart to win from Mann and Cooper again, with Pickrell's ex-Hailwood BSA being taken back to Meriden to be written-off. UK 183 points, US 137, but America had acquitted itself creditably on unfamiliar circuits in filthy weather. Contrary to popular belief, Americans could indeed ride in the wet.

Mann returned to the USA with his faithful BSA (he later described it as the best-handling bike he ever rode) to do battle with Rayborn and Kel Carruthers for the second of the season's seven AMA road races. Road Atlanta was – and is – a 2.54-mile 'road course' that rewards nimble high-speed handling and good brakes. Carruthers made good use of his Don Vesco-prepped TR2B's 56+bhp and its 60kg weight advantage over the 750s to post his and Yamaha's first national win. Rayborn challenged early, but stopped with transmission failure – his second in as many races. Mann trailed into second place, half a minute adrift of Carruthers, after battling with Suzuki-mounted Jody Nicholas, who himself ran dry after Mann had stopped for fuel.

PROOF

Further changes were being plotted for Britain's now rapidly developing F750 calendar. Chris Lowe of Motor Circuit Developments had been in negotiation again, this time with *Motor Cycle News*. The result of their labours was to be a six-round "Daytona-style Superbike championship," open to 501-750cc motorcycles, with a £2000 prize pool and £500 for the winner – who would not be mounted on a 350 Yamaha.

Meanwhile, Smart had a good day at Cadwell Park, winning the 250 and 350 races on his Yamahas, using the 350 to chase home MV star Giacomo Agostini in the 500 race, and then reverting to his Triumph triple to lead home the rest of the BSA-Triumph wrecking crew, Jefferies and Pickrell leading the way, in the big race. Pickrell then beat his old mate in Britain's first official F750 race, the 200-miler run concurrently with the Thruxton 500-mile Production race. Or almost concurrently. The tiny, ten-bike F750 field pushed off one minute after the Production boys, and put on a stirring exhibition that only went the way of Pickrell's BSA after he'd twice swapped the lead with Smart's Triumph on the final lap. Tait and Dave Croxford, meanwhile, won the 500-miler on a Triumph Trident, but that too was only decided late in the piece, after Peter Williams, leading comfortably on the factory Norton Commando he shared with Charlie Sanby, dropped it, damaging the contact breaker assembly and pushing in. "I've just lost the race," a disconsolate Williams is reported to have said.

Smart's winning streak came to an abrupt end at the North West 200. After winning the 250 race he fell from his 350, breaking a wrist, so he found himself a spectator at the Brands *Evening News* International a week later. There, Percy Tait ran home a clear winner in the opening round of the first *MCN* Superbike Championship, leading at the close of each lap, from Sanby and Martyn Ashwood's Weslake Metisse. And Tait did it again at a wet Mallory Park to bag another win in the British 750 Championship after early leader Sanby slowed with a misfire.

Yamaha, for the moment making fewer headlines than usual, chose the *Evening News* International to launch its TR3, still an air-cooled twin, but now with CDI ignition, a sixth cog in the gearbox and revised engine dimensions (64 x 54mm) that helped to boost power by 2bhp – and a 15mm longer wheelbase. Interesting enough; but the show-stealing news came from Kawasaki, with a tiny whisper blowing in from Japan which suggested the marque was working on a 100bhp three-cylinder racer.

Ray Pickrell had missed the Brands International and Mallory round of the British championships to go to the Isle of Man early, and the extra homework paid off. The Londoner won the Production TT for Triumph after a long scrap with Peter Williams' Yellow Peril; but Williams rolled to a stop on lap three, allowing Tony Jefferies (Triumph) into second spot from Bob Heath (BSA) to make it an all-BSA-Triumph podium. Pickrell's bike, known as Slippery Sam since its engine reacted badly to a change of oil at the 1970 Bol d'Or and ejected its lubricant over rider Percy Tait, was to become the stuff of TT legend.

Jefferies opened his 1971 TT account by winning the Junior race on his Yamsel, and closed it with a win in the inaugural F750 TT, a three-lapper held on the Saturday, on his Triumph. The event was initially a four-way contest, with a Norton factory entry at last taking the fight to Triumph's all-conquering triples in a major event. Even the start had its dramas, with Charlie Sanby frantically changing plugs as the seconds ticked away and Williams push-starting the first of his experimental F750 Nortons, not realising the race was a clutch start. By the end of lap one Jefferies was flying, leading by 6.4 seconds from Sanby, with Pickrell and Williams in hot pursuit. A lap later, 30 seconds covered the leading four, though Sanby soon stopped with ignition trouble, and Jefferies opened a gap on Pickrell. Williams then had to resign himself to third place, his Norton suffering from a slipping clutch as early as the first lap, and a broken exhaust soon after. Nor was its handling all it might be, later diagnosed as having the weight too far forward in the frame, making the back end prone to slide. But the inaugural F750 race was a success for all that, with Jefferies establishing a lap record for the class at 103.21mph.

Percy Tait had a poor F750 TT, stopping at Ballacraine after his triple had gone onto two. He couldn't find the fault, despite a roadside strip of the bike, but got his own back at Mallory Park the following day in the second round of the *MCN* Superbike Championship. He leapt into the lead and cleared off, and though slowing late in the race with broken valve springs, he left Jefferies, Pickrell and Williams to squabble over the lower steps of the podium. Jefferies ran second until his gearbox gave problems, and Pickrell pipped Williams at the flag, critics noting that the Norton was a match for Pickrell's Beesa in speed and handling. Result: Tait led the title chase on 35 points with daylight second.

In America, BSA-Triumph wasn't having it quite so easily. At Loudon in New Hampshire, Mark Brelsford won the third AMA national for Harley-Davidson, squeezing home from Kel Carruthers' Yamaha by a tyre's width. Much of the race had been an enthralling scrap between Carruthers, who'd taken the lead on lap 20 of 60, and BSA-mounted Dick Mann, who'd hounded the Australian all the way. But then up popped Brelsford's XR Harley, working up from seventh, when Carruthers took the lead, passing Mann for second place on lap 49 and Carruthers on lap 53. The Yamaha man came back at him and repassed, but lost the lead for the last time on the final corner of the final lap. Mann, running wide when Brelsford passed him, recovered to consolidate third from Romero's Triumph and Du Hamel's H1R.

Tony Jefferies was first out when cash problems hit Hele's team, but he went out on a high with a win in the Hutch at Brands in August '72.
(Courtesy Elwyn Roberts)

A month later, the circus reconvened at Seattle International Raceway, where Mann and Carruthers staged the scrap of the season. Rayborn made the early running, but after his XR750 holed a piston, Carruthers backed the agility of his Don Vesco Yamaha against Mann's slight speed advantage, and almost made it, the lead changing hands 39 times before he heard an ominous clunk from the gearbox. The Yamaha faltered and Mann nipped past and opened a four-second break at the flag. With Emde (BSA) third and Romero fourth from Walt Fulton's Harley, it had been another successful American weekend for BSA-Triumph.

Back home, things looked less bright. BSA was about to sack 850 of its 2000 staff and cut back on its sports programme as part of a major economy drive. Declining market share in the USA and insufficient resources to manufacture at full capacity left Birmingham Small Arms with debts soaring towards £20 million. Desperate measures were needed.

The climax of the British domestic season contained an added ingredient. Silverstone, then Britain's fastest short circuit, had been lost to motorcycles since 1965 but was now back on the calendar with a major international – and, curiously, a leavening of bicycle races in its first year. Smart was in good form, winning the F750 race despite losing top gear, with a five-second gap back to runner-up Tait's Triumph, Pickrell's BSA and, in fourth place, one Mike Hailwood on a borrowed 350 Yamaha. Smart lifted the lap record to 104.95mph from the 100.74mph, set by Derek Minter and the late John Hartle a decade earlier (the author, perched with his brothers in the Woodcote grandstand for the weekend and, like so many, watching the bicycle races with some bemusement, remembers timing them at about 27mph).

A week later came news of Tony Jefferies' departure from the BSA-Triumph team. "I was told to cut down to three riders," explained a disconsolate Hele. "Tony was the youngest and the last to join." Reduced in numbers or not, in Britain the BSA-Triumph squad continued to be so dominant it wasn't a matter of who'd win, so much as which Trident or Rocket 3 would do the job. At Snetterton on August Bank Holiday weekend Tait and Smart shared the honours for Triumph. Smart walked away with the silverware in the Race of Aces, while Tait won the *MCN* Superbike Championship round to consolidate his position at the top of the table. The event wasn't quite a BSA-Triumph benefit, but was emphatic enough: Tait led early, ran second to Smart for a few laps, then repassed and cleared off to the flag while his team-mate was brought to a halt with a stretched chain and "a nasty noise" from within. Pickrell was on hand to run his BSA into second from Sanby's Kuhn Commando.

A day later at Oulton Park it was Pickrell's turn in the limelight, taking the fourth of the season's six *MCN* Superbike Championship rounds. For the first three laps it looked like Tait's day again until Smart shot past, setting a new lap record for the Cheshire track at 93.24mph. But Smart's newly acquired gremlins struck again and his gearbox expired, leaving

Pickrell to lead home Tait, who nonetheless turned up the following weekend at Castle Combe, this time on a BSA, to secure the inaugural British 750 Championship.

SEEING GREEN

Across the Atlantic, it wasn't quite such plain sailing. Pocono, the part tri-oval, part twisting road circuit in Pennsylvania, proved another happy hunting ground for Dick Mann and his BSA, albeit with Kel Carruthers and his Vesco Yamaha again for company. But the first star of the show was Yvon Du Hamel, the Canadian Kawasaki ace who would, according to later team-mate Paul Smart, "have ridden a bike with square wheels". This weekend Du Hamel and his H1R were on song and, using its demonstrably circular wheels, won his heat and then cleared off from the field as the green flag dropped on the final. The Canadian had an 11-second lead over Mann, Carruthers, and BSA team-mates Aldana and Emde as he streaked into his pit for fuel. He rejoined the race in third spot and stayed there, unable to bridge the gap to Mann and Carruthers as they swapped the lead until the last corner of the last lap – as usual – when Mann again won the drag to the line. Du Hamel was third from Aldana's BSA, with Nicholas running his TR500 Suzuki home fifth, ahead of Emde.

In the Alabama heat a fortnight later, Du Hamel showed that his Pocono ride was but a rehearsal, and led the 50-lap, 200-mile Talladega national from flag to flag, BSA team-mates Mann and Emde in his wake. Carruthers qualified fastest, and, as Du Hamel eased away from the field during the opening laps, he hung on until they began lapping backmarkers, one of whom moved into his path. Down went the Australian in a cloud of dust. Meanwhile, Mann found someone else to contest second place with – Cal Rayborn rode hard and stayed with Mann until the Harley's leaking fuel tank forced him to make an unscheduled stop, ceding third place to Emde. And that's how it stayed, with Du Hamel a winner despite pitting twice for fuel, and collecting some $14,000 for his day's toil – almost $1 for each member of the crowd.

BSA-Triumph next extended its run of victories in the Bol d'Or, Percy Tait teaming up with Ray Pickrell this year to win for BSA at the event's new home, the Bugatti circuit at Le Mans. But the British pair had to work for the privilege, taking the lead only after 8 hours 40 minutes when the leading 850 Moto Guzzi (based on the V7 Sport designed by Lino Tonti and built by Bruno Scola), ridden hard by Vittorio Brambilla and Guido Mandracci, had stopped with a broken rocker arm and lost 25 minutes in the pits, reducing a five-lap lead to a five-lap deficit. By the end of the day's journey the Beesa had seven laps on its nearest rival, the first of Laverda's mouth-watering SFCs ridden by Augusto Brettoni and Sergio Angiolini (who had already won the Barcelona 24-hour). Next came the ill-fated Guzzi, further back still after Mandracci had fallen on spilt oil. But to an international Superbike soundscape dominated by howling triples, rasping two-strokes and, with

Percy Tait won the first MCN Superbike Championship and the British 750 Championship in 1971, but stopped at Ballacraine in the inaugural F750 TT when his triple became a twin. (Courtesy TTracepics.com)

increasing frequency, the bass notes of a Norton Commando, Europe added its own barking twins. Vive la différence.

And more new hardware was on the way. Ducati, having unveiled its GT750 V-twin in October 1970, brought a racing prototype for Mike Hailwood to ride at the August Silverstone meeting. Mike the Bike quietly suggested that it didn't handle well enough, and returned to his 350 Yamaha – but it was a start. Suzuki, meanwhile, had shown a prototype of its own GT750, a 739cc water-cooled three-cylinder two-stroke, at the 1970 Tokyo show, and now had a model ready for sale, the GT750J. Suzuki claimed a power output of 67bhp at a low 6500rpm from its new heavyweight (249kg dry), and though the bike wasn't considered a good handler, it offered 40mpg fuel consumption at touring speeds, setting the Kettle apart from its competitors at Kawasaki – photos of whose new H2 (initially the Tri-Star Mach IV) now began to appear. The new air-cooled triple was said to have electronic ignition, which would help reduce the perennial two-stroke problem of sparkplug fouling, and a power output significantly better than the Suzuki's – a claimed 74bhp at 6800rpm.

Back in the world of the proven, the close of the racing season was largely about two men. Percy Tait, Triumph's development rider, had written much of the story of the British domestic season and, having won the British 750 Championship at the end of August, now threatened to do the same in the first *MCN* Superbike Championship. With two rounds to go, the title was Tait's to lose. Only BSA-mounted Ray Pickrell posed a threat, and to carry off the title he'd have to win both races while Tait stumbled. The BSA man did what he could at Mallory Park in the penultimate round, beating Tait home to win by seven seconds after a titanic scrap that at times saw the two title contenders and Smart three abreast into Mallory's faster corners.

The second man was John Cooper, nearing the end of a highly successful career, and poised to do what even Doug Hele thought impossible. Redeeming BSA-Triumph's promise to supply him with a bike for the Race of the Year, Cooper swapped his 350 Yamsel for a BSA triple, and had the cheek to lead multiple world champion Giacomo Agostini's 500cc MV during the opening lap of the big-money event. They were still together after the second lap, and as the race wore on it became clear Ago wouldn't disappear into the distance. At the halfway mark Cooper led but got into a heartstopping slide at the Esses, and, though Ago took the lead again a lap later, Cooper hung on and got back in front for the last time with eight laps to go. The crowd was on tiptoe when Cooper took the most famous win in British short circuit history. He repeated the dose a fortnight later at Brands Hatch for the Race of the South, this time passing Ago on the second lap and running away to post a new lap record for the Kent circuit at 91.03mph. Perhaps F750 would be a viable alternative to grand prix racing after all.

At the same Brands Hatch meeting Tait made sure of his *MCN* Superbike Championship, thanks in part to Cooper again, who engaged Pickrell in a mighty scrap for the lead. Despite posting the fastest lap the Londoner had to settle for second – and there was Tait in third place, his title lead much reduced but intact.

Cooper had one more port of call: the final AMA national of the year at Ontario in California. BSA-Triumph entered a Triumph for Nixon and Cooper's Ago-licking Beesa with its lighter crankshaft, magnesium-alloy primary chaincase and lightened clutch (its dry weight was said to be around 160kg, down from 168kg). In addition to these were the bikes that had disputed the 1971 Grand National Championship, which had developed into a fight between Mann's BSA and Romero's Trident. It came down to this: with three wins, two seconds and a third in the six AMA road races before Ontario, and plenty of solid performances on dirt, Mann had only to finish 14th if Romero won to secure the number-one plate.

The event comprised two 125-mile legs, and, in the first, Nixon became the man most likely to go home with the big money. Yvon Du Hamel bolted from the start on his new 80bhp H1RA, intent on repeating his Talladega performance. Nixon, however, went with him, and when Du Hamel stopped for fuel he took an 11-second lead, which proved enough. Cooper finished third, and Carruthers fourth from Ron Grant's Suzuki, and while Mann finished an uncharacteristic eighth, Romero was reduced to pushing home after a crash on lap 10.

Nixon was again the early leader in the second leg, this time taking Cooper and Du Hamel with him. Rayborn, who'd run as high as third in the first leg before his Harley fouled a plug, unwittingly rearranged the second leg by dropping oil on turn eight, a fast left-hander, bringing down Nixon, Du Hamel, Mann and Grant's TR500 – seven riders altogether, all of whom restarted, though not in time to trouble Cooper and Carruthers in first and second – or Romero, making a last desperate bid for the championship, coming up fast behind them. Romero took the lead with 26 laps of the 39 to run, and pushed on into an impressive lead until a throttle cable let go. The remainder of the race became another of the BSA-Yamaha duels that had characterised the season, and, again, it came to a drag to the line out of the last corner on the final lap, with the BSA this time coming from behind to win by inches. The one difference was that the BSA to pip Carruthers was ridden by Derby motorcycle dealer John Cooper rather than Dick Mann, who finished 42nd, yet with Romero's retirement was Grand National Champion for a second time. Cooper, on the other hand, went home almost $20,000 richer, and no-one was better pleased than Doug Hele, who remarked later that Cooper had been very easy on the bike – as if it had been his own. Someone who did want the bike for his own posed Hele a final problem before he returned home. Californian motorcycle dealer Bob Bailey invoked the AMA claim rule and said he'd like to buy Cooper's BSA. So negotiations were entered into and Bailey, who said he'd had his eye on Romero's Triumph for some time but hadn't wanted to upset Burritto's championship campaign, was eventually persuaded to hand back the BSA in return for Nixon's second bike and some spares – plus his purchase money back.

The news from home, meanwhile, was less satisfactory. BSA-Triumph's debts for 1971 totalled more than £8 million, and prompted the resignation of group chairman Lionel Jofeh, followed by the closure of BSA's Small Heath plant – and the loss of 2200 jobs.

Two full seasons had now passed since the AMA decided to open its racing to 750cc four-stroke engines of all types. The birth of Formula 750 had followed soon after, and while Giacomo Agostini had made his way majestically to two more pairs of 350 and 500cc world championships against scattered and largely down-at-heel opposition, the opening exchanges in 750cc racing had proven fiercely competitive on both sides of the Atlantic. True, BSA-Triumph had been most dominant in Britain, with scarcely an alternative winner to be seen apart from occasional challenges by Charlie Sanby, Peter Williams and one or two others on an assortment of Norton-powered devices. It even looked for a time as if a Norton factory team might make the journey to Ontario, until tests at Snetterton (with Paul Smart in the saddle, Williams having fractured a hip while trying to vault a wall) revealed ignition problems. But for the moment, BSA-Triumph occupied the box seat.

In the USA, BSA had won four of the seven AMA road races and powered Dick Mann to the Grand National Championship – with Gene

Romero handing over his number one plate, although still finishing second overall for Triumph. But that was surely about to change. Kel Carruthers had performed superbly for Yamaha on his Vesco-tuned TR2B, and now Shigeo Ishibashi of Yamaha NV said the factory would offer wider support for racing in 1972, primarily in grand prix racing, but perhaps others would benefit too. Suzuki's report card for 1971 didn't make quite such happy reading, its bikes being dogged by a miscellany of problems – although Ron Grant was third at Ontario, and its TR500s had finished second (Keith Turner), third (Rob Bron) and fifth (Jack Findlay) in the 500cc world championship. Team Hansen Kawasaki had a better year, overcoming the H1R's problems of width, a high-mounted engine and a thirst that would shame a rugby club, to secure a runaway win at Talladega and third at Pocono. Even Harley-Davidson had reason to smile. Despite Brelsford's win at Loudon, the team's bikes had been dogged by overheating problems, but with the new alloy XR coming (using H-D's first oversquare engine, 79.5 x 75.5mm giving 749.5cc) things might be better in 1972. The races had attracted solid crowds, too: 66,000 at the UK-US Match Races, 25,000 at Ontario; not vast, but something to build on.

Surely now, at another autumn congress, F750 would receive the FIM's blessing and at last become a truly international affair? Yes, said the technical committee. Details to follow from the sporting commission at the spring congress, but international F750 events would receive FIM sanction from January 1972 – though it would be rash, said Geneva, to expect a world championship for the class before 1974 at the earliest. In the meantime, to compete in Formula 750, explained the technical committee, eligible motorcycles must be offered for sale to the public, with a minimum of 200 examples built, and must have an engine capacity of 251-750cc; engine type, number of cylinders, cylinder material, piston stroke, and number of ports in two-strokes were not to be changed; shape and material of crankcases, cylinder heads and gearbox were not to be changed; intake and exhaust systems, primary transmission and number of gears were not to be changed.

Motorcycle racing was striking out on a new course for the coming decade, and the three-cylinder two-stroke roadsters being released by Kawasaki and Suzuki now acquired a new significance. In November 1971, Yamaha chose the Tokyo show to the pull the wraps from the prototype of its four-cylinder two-stroke roadster, the GL750 – to be known by many of those who came later as 'the decoy.' As the year ended, a whisper came that a racing version of the Kawasaki triple was already being tested and breaking speed trap beams at 180mph.

2
GREEN ON BLUE

In January 1972 Paul Smart found himself sitting behind a hedge in the South African sun. He and Ray Pickrell had again been sent south to fly the BSA-Triumph flag at Kyalami and in the South African TT at Roy Hesketh Park; and it was here, after the British pair had taken the lead in the 1000cc race, that it all went wrong: Smart hit a patch of oil in Quarry Curve, collected Pickrell on his way down and both vaulted the trackside hedge, coming to rest on the far side.

"Poor old Ray was hurt," recalls Smart. "He'd broken a collarbone and damaged a vertebra, and would have to be flown home. Anyway, we were sitting there, and seconds later Ago's MV arrived. We heard him change down – roo, roo, roo – then silence, and suddenly Ago was sitting alongside us. Ray was moaning to me about 'throwing your bloody motorbike at me,' so I thought he'd be all right, and Ago got going again – and what was I going to do? I just didn't know. I was going home to no job, really."

Smart's crash was an unwelcome start to what would be a challenging year. In December 1971, BSA-Triumph had confirmed that there would be no racing team for the year ahead, that the group would be "encouraging more private entries." Spares would be available, and support would be offered for Dick Mann (BSA) and Gene Romero (Triumph) in the USA; but in Britain, no-one seemed sure what would happen – though John Cooper had signed again with BSA.

Smart wasn't without options. A raft of wins on his factory Triumph Trident in 1971 had put him firmly in the headlines, and Yamaha wanted him to join Rod Gould and Finnish sensation Jarno Saarinen on its TR3 twins, perhaps with a 354cc version for the 500cc class. Triumph too asked for Smart's signature – Doug Hele said it might be possible to field a reduced team, perhaps along the lines of the tight crew sent to South Africa, with bikes for Cooper and himself, plus Pickrell or Tony Jefferies.

And then there was Kawasaki. More whispers came of the marque's fearsome 750cc racing triple; of 100bhp power outputs and 185mph speeds, but also of crankshaft failures and fuel consumption even greater than the H1R's 12mpg. Bob Hansen, fired by Honda after his successful 1970 Daytona campaign, had found work with Kawasaki and put in a solid 1971 season with Yvon Du Hamel on an H1R. Now Hansen was making headlines with news of a three-rider Kawasaki team for 1972. He'd already signed Gary Nixon to run alongside Du Hamel, and now he wanted Smart.

Big two-strokes were arriving in force. Suzuki had a racing adaptation of its GT750, which, undergoing tests by American team runners Ron Grant and Jody Nicholas, was said to be of comparable weight and size to the TR500 despite its extra cylinder and water cooling – and like the Kawasaki, was said to offer around 100bhp to the stout of heart.

By February, Smart was close to a decision. Hansen had offered him a US Kawasaki ride at Daytona the year before, then called him during the 1972 South Africa junket. "I desperately wanted to stay with Triumph," Smart recalls. "I loved my Trident, and it was probably the best, the most enjoyable time of my racing career – and for a time we were bloody near invincible … and moving to America to race was a big step; Maggie and I had just got married and had no money." But Smart was soon in California, testing prototypes of the H2R alongside new team-mates Nixon and Du Hamel. His initial, cautious assessment was that the bike was "faster than my old Triumph." And these were interim hybrids: still to receive full race engines or chassis, for testing at Willow Springs the Team Hansen bikes comprised tuned H2 street engines in H1R frames with H2 forks, wheels and discs.

BSA-Triumph made an initial adjustment to its cashless future by telling its British riders, Cooper, Pickrell and Jefferies they'd have bikes, but beyond that couldn't expect much. "They did strange deals with the riders," Tony Jefferies remembers. "We looked after our own bikes and they gave us parts. I had a mechanic and used to invoice the factory for expenses – but it wasn't very much and I got a pay deal which worked in conjunction with whatever start money I received." These arrangements didn't include Daytona, where there would be no British factory-backed BSA-Triumph riders. In the USA, team survivors Mann and Romero would be entered on '71 bikes.

Harley-Davidson seemed likely to miss the party altogether, saying it hadn't a chance of making the necessary 200 homologation units in time to field its new alloy XRs for the season opener, and in February disappeared into conference with the AMA to salvage something from a poor outlook – but on 7 March announced it wouldn't be contesting Daytona.

Norton, on the other hand, offered a touch of optimism. After long consideration the Andover firm would send two of its riders to Daytona. Phil Read and Peter Williams would ride its F750 bikes that tipped the

Daytona '72 was about two-stroke triples. Here, early in the race, Art Baumann (TR750) leads Yvon Du Hamel (H2R). Don Emde won on a TR3 Yamaha twin. (Courtesy Ian Falloon)

scales at a trim 150kg and were said to knock out 70bhp at 6000rpm. Modest but enough, perhaps, in the right hands.

Team Hansen Kawasaki's battle to put together a world-beating effort in scant weeks might have been demanding enough, but issues of development and design dogged the bikes. Their engines, when they arrived, had clearly benefited from experience with the fragile H1R, getting stronger crankshafts, sturdier big-end bearings, 14-roller mains and sturdy, ribbed cases. Yet the powerplants were wide and sat high in the frame, and even then cornering clearance was limited. There was more: H2 cylinders used the same spacing as the H1 which, because of the 750's bigger bore, limited transfer port dimensions to two-thirds the width of the 500's – "a kind of built-in half-throttle," according to celebrated engineer Kevin Cameron in his seminal work, *Classic Motorcycle Race Engines*. The 12-plate dry clutch was sound, and the gearbox (apart from the selector return spring) wasn't expected to give problems. Which just left the chassis. Over the years the H2R's frame has largely been acquitted of its alleged crimes, and the responsibility shifted to poorly understood suspension and inadequate tyres. Paul Smart agrees. "I don't think, looking back at the chassis now, that there was anything wrong with it," he recalls. "At Triumph we had very basic suspension: Girling rear shocks, Triumph forks – but we had Doug Hele, the man who made it all work, who understood it. Over there we had wonderful Kayaba forks and stuff, but no-one knew how to change things. And the bike was too rigid – much too rigid." And with a dry weight of just 143kg, every bump and surface irregularity was transmitted to the frame.

At Daytona, Smart fought engine seizures in practice as Nixon and Du Hamel broke chains – and none of the Kawasaki engines had yet developed the celebrated 100bhp of the Japanese tests. The 90bhp or so made by the best of them diminished further in practice on the famous speedbowl. "Mine would have been lucky to make 85 or 86bhp when it got hot," says Smart. Certainly, the three Kawasakis struggled to reach 160mph. Not so across the road at Suzuki, where the heftier (167kg) but lower-revving and water-cooled XR11s, ridden by Jody Nicholas, Ron Grant, and Art Baumann suffered no such decline in performance – which was itself a problem. Baumann qualified fastest at 110.363mph, and blew through the speed trap at a staggering 171.75mph, Nicholas not so far adrift. But tyres quickly became a concern. Regardless of make, it seemed, rear tyres showed signs of breaking up after just five or six laps. Nicholas remembered the horror on Dunlop technician Dave Buck's face as he checked the post-practice temperature of his rear cover.

Goodyear provided a partial solution, with tyres made from temperature-resistant NASCAR rubber; but, in the end, the giants became victims of their own performance as tyres and chains capable of transmitting the Triumph triples' tractable 75-80bhp struggled with the explosive performance of the two-strokes. Not before they'd put on a show, however: Baumann took up from where he'd left off in qualifying, leading for the opening half a dozen laps until Du Hamel, on the best of the Kawasakis, slipped past. Nixon closed up, and then Nicholas and Grant, giving Suzuki three runners in the top five. The third Kawasaki – Smart's – was nowhere to be seen. He was instructed to warm up on soft plugs that couldn't be changed in time for the start. After a memorable exchange of views with his team engineer, Smart took off his helmet and "walked out of the circuit to the hotel up the road in my leathers."

DAVID AND ...

Baumann was out of the running on lap 15 (of 52) with magneto failure, and Du Hamel's Kawasaki stopped with big-end trouble. Nicholas now led, but, entering the infield on lap 29: "I just started to pitch it down," he explained to Ray Battersby in *Team Suzuki*, "and it went sideways, just like Ascot on the cinders." Nicholas got it stopped to find a foot-long chunk of tread missing from the rear tyre.

The last of the factory triples were soon gone: Grant's Suzuki with a fried clutch after a bungled fuel stop, and Nixon's Kawasaki with gearbox failure; all of which left Phil Read an unexpected leader on the remaining Norton after Peter Williams' bike first fouled a plug and then stopped with a broken gearbox (later traced to flex in the mainshaft). Read led for three laps, fighting fading brakes, but then dropped to fourth after a slow fuel stop. Now it was Geoff Perry's turn at the front, coaxing his TR500 Suzuki towards the flag. He almost made it too, his drive chain breaking with little more than a lap to go, and leaving the limelight to settle on Don Emde on his new TR3 Yamaha, who had started the day in hospital after a crash in the 250 race, and ended it by getting the better of veteran Ray Hempstead to win the 31st Daytona 200, collecting a cheque for $13,000.

Yamaha took all three podium placings and provided motive power for seven of the top ten finishers. Only Read's Norton and private BSA-Triumph triples ridden by Eddie Mulder and Michael Ninci broke the pattern on a bad day for four-strokes. The two Krause Hondas, prepared by Pops Yoshimura and ridden by Gary Fisher and Roger Reiman, bowed out with mechanical maladies that included broken oil tanks. BSA-Triumph's threadbare effort ended with a puncture for Romero and ignition problems for Mann.

With the year's opening party over, it was down to work for another season. In the US, that meant the AMA Grand National Championship with its diversity of dirt track races and, in 1972, seven road races. Each of these ran a minimum of 75 miles; some – Daytona, Talladega, Ontario – would be run on speedbowls with a section of infield corners; others – Atlanta, Loudon, Indy, Laguna Seca – on more conventional circuits, known in the US as 'road courses.' Each offered a pot of gold that made most European riders blink – although the concept of start money was foreign to American racing, as would become apparent in the years ahead. Even so, in the USA F750 was a near-perfect fit on the foundations of the series that inspired it. In Europe, organisers began taking speculative forays into F750, while holding to the grand prix-based structure that had given service since 1949. In Britain, the picture was different. Among a raft of national championships that seemed to change in format every year, the MCN Superbike Championship was developing into the prestige series. The six rounds of 1971 became eight in 1972 – including two at non-MCD circuits, Cadwell Park and Scarborough – and the championship attracted backing from John Player and Shell.

The big bangers weren't finished just yet. In the 1971 Transatlantic Trophy the Americans proved they could ride in the wet; and in '72 they brought Cal Rayborn. In the process Britain got its first look at an open F750 field. While the Hansen Kawasaki outfit didn't attend, Suzuki showed up with Baumann, Nicholas and Grant, who were immediately in trouble with their TR750s' flighty handling. Grant hadn't christened the XR11 the 'Flexy Flyer' for nothing. The expatriate Brit said the bike's basic geometry was more or less as needed, but thought its tubing too spindly. Yet for all the strokers' explosive speed and wild handling, a couple of four-stroke riders thrilled the crowd in every race. One of them, Rayborn, had made the trip with mechanic Walt Faulk and his old iron-head XR750, persuading Dick O'Brien that Britain's cooler climate might suit the bike, later described by O'Brien as "a hot son of a gun" – and not only because of its reputation for melting pistons: some said the engine made 80bhp.

The six-man American squad was completed by Mann's BSA and Daytona winner Emde on a borrowed Kuhn Norton. Ranged against them

The '72 Transatlantic Trophy was about Cal Rayborn and Ray Pickrell (pictured at Devil's Elbow, Mallory Park), ending the weekend with three wins and three second places apiece. (Courtesy Elwyn Roberts)

was much of Britain's short-circuit talent: the three Norton boys, Williams, Read and Rutter, plus the triples of Cooper (BSA), Jefferies (Triumph) and Pickrell (Triumph), always the British fan's sentimental favourite, and the man who stood toe to toe with Rayborn for the full weekend.

It was clear from the outset that the XR11s weren't suited to that definition of the scratcher's track, Brands Hatch short circuit. But Rayborn had the time of his life, getting into the groove to lead the first leg until Pickrell, breaking the lap record to get there, caught his man on lap 10 and swept past to open the scoring for the UK, with Read and Williams in third and fourth. Rayborn reversed the result in the second leg, leading from flag to flag with Pickrell snapping at his heels, Read, Williams and Cooper close behind. Pick ended his day with a win in the first round of the *MCN* Superbike Championship, again from Williams and Read – with a promising Dave Potter running fourth on a Kuhn Norton.

Race one at Mallory Park ran to a repeat prescription: Rayborn away from the start, Pick passing with four laps to go and taking the flag with two seconds to spare. But Rayborn made it two-all in the second leg. To begin with, Rayborn had Pickrell and Cooper between himself and leader Nicholas's XR11, but passed them both at the hairpin, and then took the lead through the lumps and bumps of Gerard's to get home six seconds clear of the field, now led by Pickrell, Cooper, Nicholas, Read and Baumann.

The Suzukis looked better at Oulton Park, but by then Rayborn and

Pickrell had stolen the show. In the opening leg, Williams and Cooper made the early running with Pickrell taking the lead on the fourth lap. Rayborn joined the party, passing Pickrell on the last lap to take his third win of the series, and Pickrell his third runner-up spot. British veterans, led by Cooper, again secured the bulk of the points. In the last race of the series Rayborn turned it on from the start, fending off Cooper and Williams with Pickrell squeezing past for his third win as the American's XR began to misfire. Pickrell and Rayborn ended the series all square at 69 points apiece, with the UK taking the series by packing the leaderboard. John Cooper had taken four third places, while the USA's best performer after Rayborn had been Nicholas with fourth places at Mallory Park and Oulton, and a clutch of lesser placings.

Soon after Easter the AMA cavalcade arrived in Atlanta for the second race of the '72 series, for which Paul Smart acquired a new mechanic, Hurley Wilvert – himself no mean rider – as the Hansen outfit began to experiment with, among other things, new frames and cast magnesium wheels (from Elliot Morris). Suzuki, though, looked set for the better day at the office. From the flag, Du Hamel led from team-mates Smart and Nixon, but up came Baumann and Nicholas, Baumann forcing his way into the lead on lap eight while Nicholas moved ahead of Smart. Du Hamel found himself in front again when Baumann's Suzuki broke a crankshaft, but he stopped to tighten a loose plug a couple of laps later, letting Nicholas across the line first for Suzuki. Du Hamel got going again to finish second from Smart, Grant, and Romero's sadly outgunned Triumph.

After Nicholas had overcome badly wearing tyres and a wobbling bike, the fireworks really began. The race had been run under a cloud with Team Hansen concerned about the legality of the XR11's cylinders and heads. A protest was filed, Nicholas and Grant were excluded from the results, and Du Hamel and Smart promoted to first and second. Suzuki decided not to appeal against the exclusion, and the results stood. Ron Grant's mechanic Merv Wright later attributed the whole mess to a single word in the regulations: he thought while the FIM F750 regulations said the casting material of the heads was not to be changed, the AMA regs, based on the FIM's, said the casting *and* material were not to be changed. As the XR11 heads were visibly different from those on the roadgoing GT750, Suzuki grinned, bore it, and withdrew its bikes from competition pending the arrival of new bits.

FLAGFALL

The inaugural Imola 200 in April might have been Europe's introduction to the joys of big-league 750cc racing, but it didn't qualify as an F750 race because of its inclusion of Italian prototypes – and exclusion of 350 Yamahas. Race winner Smart hadn't expected to be there at all, having been refused a bike by Triumph, and was cooling his heels in Atlanta when wife Maggie called to say she'd accepted a £500 offer on his behalf to ride a Ducati

The ride that nearly wasn't: Paul Smart took time off from H2R-taming in the US to win the first Imola 200 on Fabio Taglioni's new 750. (Courtesy Ian Falloon)

at Imola. Bob Hansen had no objection to Smart's riding, so off he went: "They'd obviously asked Vic Camp who should ride the bike. Phil Read had turned it down, and it was totally out of the blue. I didn't even know Ducati had made a V-twin. We were cut off from the outside world.

"So I'm off to Italy. I drive for bloody miles – Philadelphia or Cincinnati or somewhere. I flew to England, hung about at Heathrow, then flew to Milan and went straight to Modena to test the bike. I was like a bloody zombie; I'd been up for the best part of two days. Anyway, I was pretty fit, so it didn't unduly concern me. But when I first saw this thing I thought, oh my God – it was so long … 1420mm was the average wheelbase, this thing had what, 1520? I asked for Dunlop KR83s to replace its TT100s, then went out and did a few laps – and the race tyres transformed it. But I had to take the steering damper off, because it wouldn't go round the hairpin. Then I started to warm to it.

"We put quite a lot of hours in, changed quite a lot – they were a bit like Triumph: everyone wanted to know what it was doing, and they were good at working out what to do, because they were a manufacturer and there was a good relationship between the race shop and the factory. So they could sort out spring rates and damping rates – they were pretty turned on for an old-fashioned company. They got most stuff working very, very well at Imola. Obviously Bruno Spaggiari had tested the bike there, and the bike was really built for that one circuit. That long-wheelbase worked because we had a 150mph corner, or close to it [Tamburello]. You were absolutely flat out there; even in the damp you had to be under the paint."

According to Ian Falloon in his excellent book, *Ducati Racers*, Fabio Taglioni built seven bikes for the event. These had standard frames modified to take big fibreglass fuel tanks and to give a racing seating position. Forks were leading-axle Marzocchi with Ceriani rear units and Lockheed discs. The engines used sandcast cases, lightened cranks and billet conrods. High-compression (10:1) pistons and standard-size (40 and 36mm) valves were used with 40mm Dell'Orto pumpers. Primary drive was higher than standard and the gearbox was a close-ratio five-speeder. Flywheel and alternator were omitted from the racing engines, which were rated at 84bhp at 8800rpm, with a safe redline of 9200rpm. Dry weight was 178kg.

Ducati entered six bikes of the seven, including one for Barry Sheene, who didn't ride because of difficulties over his fee, and because of doubts over whether the bike would be quick enough. Ranged against the Ducatis were factory shaft-drive MVs for Ago and Alberto Pagani, works Moto Guzzis for Jack Findlay and Guido Mandracci, factory-prepped CR750 Hondas for Bill Smith and John Williams, the full John Player Norton team – Williams, Read, Rutter – and a decent showing from BSA-Triumph: Cooper (BSA), Pickrell, Tait and Jefferies (Triumphs) plus Walter Villa on the superb Triumph triple backed by Italian distributor Bepi Koelliker and prepared by Domenico Pettinari.

The race quickly became an all-Italian affair with Ago leading away from fastest qualifiers Smart and Spaggiari. "Ago said to me before the race, don't worry about me, the bike won't last," recalls Smart. "And I knew him that well that I totally trusted him: lovely, lovely man. 'Let me have my moment of glory,' he said. 'I'd like to lead the race.' Well, I wouldn't say I'd totally let him go, because he was going like stink, but the MV was all over the road and had smoke coming out of it; it was surely going to go bang." And so it did, with a shot bearing in the cam drivetrain. By then Smart and Spaggiari had the stage largely to themselves, though Smart's bike had a problem: "It ate first gear about 16 laps into the race, jumping out of first when I put on the power coming out of the hairpin. In your mind you've got broken bits in the gearbox, and that's going to hurt you. So there were five or six laps when I let Bruno go through. But it fuelled so well with those big pumper carbs that I could take a big swing at that hairpin and get through – as long as I didn't get caught in traffic."

So it came down to the pair of them, fuel dwindling, playing cat-and-mouse. Smart: "On that last lap I'm waiting for him to make his move. He came round the outside and I thought, 'there's an answer to this, Bruno; I'm afraid you're going grasstracking.' So I just eased him out a little

Come one, come all. Guido Mandracci at the '72 Imola 200 on Lino Tonti's 750 Moto Guzzi shaftie. (Courtesy Ian Falloon)

bit. He said he ran out of petrol but, well, I think he underestimated the opposition."

Smart, Spaggiari and Ago all shared the fastest lap. Villa was third on the Koelliker Triumph from Read's Norton, Pickrell, who battled clutch troubles, and Jefferies with a curious absence of power. The first two-stroke was Eric Offenstadt's Kawasaki in 16th place.

If the Transatlantic Trophy and the Imola 200 demonstrated anything beyond the capabilities of Pickrell, Rayborn and Smart, it showed that racing without a 350 Yamaha was still possible – just. To underline the point, John Cooper, who'd had his Imola ambitions thwarted by trapped throttle cables, took his BSA home to beat Jefferies and Pickrell in the second round of the *MCN* Superbike Championship at Cadwell Park, then chased Pick home in the third round at Brands after early leader Tait faded with clutch problems. Ominously, perhaps, the John Player Norton boys weren't quite barging into the limelight; Read was best of the bunch at Cadwell with fourth, but pulled out at Brands with a lack of power. Williams bagged third at Brands, but was falling astern of Pick in the title chase.

It was proving to be Pickrell's year. After winning the 750 Production TT aboard Slippery Sam by more than three minutes from Peter Williams' Yellow Peril, he set a blistering pace in the five-lap F750 TT to beat Tony Jefferies by 50 seconds. Jefferies was in trouble early when a loose petrol tank jumped up and hit him in the chest on Bray Hill. Peter Williams went well for a lap and a half, until his Norton's gearbox failed. Jack Findlay's XR11 might have figured more prominently had he not stopped twice for fuel; but it was Triumph's day, with Jefferies pushing hard until Pickrell eased away in the closing stages, to leave the lap record at 105.68mph. Problems were coming for the TT, though, with Ago vowing never to ride there again when Gilberto Parlotti died after crashing his 125 Morbidelli in filthy weather at the Verandah. Rod Gould, too, said he wouldn't be back, and so did Phil Read.

The *MCN* Superbikes reconvened at the Mallory Park Post-TT meeting where the day looked to be Jefferies' until his primary chain broke on the approach to Shaw's on the final lap. Cooper, having shaken off Pickrell, capitalised on Jefferies' misfortune, with Ken Redfern third on his new BSA triple. Jefferies coasted past the flag in ninth place. Williams was best for Norton in sixth, riding the bike Mick Grant was about to take over from Tony Rutter, after the gearbox failed on his own.

Smart, meanwhile, had invested part of his £20,000 Imola winnings on a new Seeley frame for his Team Hansen H2R. Smart had the frame designed and built in "three weeks flat" and got it back to the US to sit alongside frames made by Frank Camilleri and Team Hansen engineer Randy Hall. It helped.

"Oh yeah. The bike now went where you wanted it. It had become something I understood. I wouldn't like to say it was a nice motorcycle because the problem with Colin's stuff – with hindsight – was that it was left over from the old days where you sat too far back. On all Seeleys the seat is low because you wanted the centre of gravity low – whereas in the '70s you wanted weight transference and to sit farther forward. Me and Coops and a couple of other people were starting to realise that you wanted to sit higher and a lot closer to the handlebars."

CAL

Harley-Davidson finished building its 200 alloy XRs in April, and Rayborn turned up with one for the Loudon AMA national. The old Bryar Motorsports Park track packed two hairpins into its 1.6 miles, and three more 180-degree bends besides, so favouring good brakes and mid-range power. Small wonder Rayborn qualified fastest and led the opening laps. However, the XRs had their teething troubles, and after struggling with carburation all weekend, Rayborn's bike dropped 1000rpm and Gary Fisher, riding his new TR3 (he couldn't match the Yamaha's practice lap times on his Krause Honda), led 59 laps of 63 to win well from Mark Brelsford's XR Harley and Romero's Triumph. Smart's was the best of the Kawasakis in fourth. Du Hamel was running second when he retired with a broken gearbox at three-quarter distance, Cliff Carr's Arlington Motor Sports H2R retired with ignition failure. Nixon was 16th.

The Suzukis were absent from Loudon, as they were a week later at the now largely forgotten Indianapolis Raceway Park circuit (not to be confused with IMS) where Rayborn took his fourth straight win at the track after early leader Du Hamel pitted with plug failure. The Canadian got going again and was 40 seconds behind Rayborn at the flag, ahead of Romero and Fisher. Smart finished eighth after the team had planned two stops for fuel. Rayborn made none.

Despite its absence from AMA competition, the Suzuki TR750 made headlines in mid-year when, after his third-place ride in the F750 TT, Jack Findlay publicly wondered why there was such fuss about the bike's supposedly poor handling, declaring that it "handled beautifully" and was "as steady as one of Francis Beart's bikes" – though adding that it was "difficult to get around slow corners." US team rider Jody Nicholas was having none of it: "Jack was not on the gas," he opined in *MCN*. "Any bike will handle if you ride it slow enough."

Grant made his JPN debut at Anderstorp in Sweden, where a one-off F750 race slotted into the grand prix programme. He'd joined the team after being wined and dined by team chief Frank Perris in a pub near Andover: "So we finished up, halfway through the year, with a deal for £1200. I didn't know they'd got that sort of money in the Bank of England." Grant already knew his way around Commando-based Nortons, having ridden one for his first sponsor, Jim Lee: "It's crazy really, but Jim's bike was better. Mick Redfern had done a very good engine, and it was an awful lot lighter because there was nothing of it, just an engine and gearbox suspended in four rubber bobbins, which sounds a bit crude but it worked. The JPN by comparison was very complex. It had a fuel pump finger working underneath the swinging arm to pump fuel from the pannier cans to a header tank. At that time every car in the world, just about, had this system that worked without a problem, and the JPN never ran without a problem. I could never understand that.

"In practice I was going hard down the back straight and fell off," he recalls. "The flat rear tyre that caused the crash happened because the flywheel disintegrated, went through the crankcases and cut the rubber. I found out afterwards that the flywheel was cast iron." Still, there was cause for rejoicing in the Norton camp, with Read coming second from the sole BSA-Triumph rep, Tony Jefferies. The winner was Kent Andersson – on a 350 Yamaha.

Smart's new frame for his H2R acquitted itself well around bumpy Laguna Seca for the AMA national. Rayborn won again after early leader Du Hamel crashed while peering down at a badly misfiring motor. Alas, his bike collected Mann and Cliff Carr as it slid back onto the track and Rayborn slowed in the carnage, letting Fisher's Yamaha and a new kid, a first-year expert named Kenny Roberts, into first and second. Cal was soon back in business, though, outbraking Roberts into turn 2 and then retaking the lead after Fisher ran off. Romero and his Triumph now starred, scorching through the field to get home in second from Roberts and Smart, who'd run as high as second before an expansion chamber broke – and had red, raw hands from Kawasaki-wrestling to attest to his day's exertions.

So four-strokes were still writing headlines: Triumph-mounted Tony Jefferies won the title race at the Hutchinson 100 meeting at Brands in August, fending off Cooper (BSA) and Smart (reunited with his Imola Ducati) in patchy going: "I cleared off and left everybody," he remembers. "The Hutch was run the wrong way round, and as I peeled off into Clearways I was scraping the pegs – which I'd never done anywhere else. My toes were bleeding but I couldn't go wrong. It was just one of those days." At the same meeting Peter Williams won the Evening New Trophy for Norton, and Smart the F750 race on his Ducati by inches after a race-long scrap with Read's Norton. The coming reality reasserted itself soon after, with Jarno Saarinen on his prototype TZ350 Yamaha tidying up the prizes at Silverstone, the fastest track in mainland Britain. Meanwhile, the big Suzukis were coming back for the penultimate meeting on the AMA road racing calendar, at the Talladega Superspeedway, new frames and all.

This time, though – and on a circuit faster than Daytona – Kawasaki did the upstaging. The Hansen bikes had revised fairings to increase airflow over the cylinder bank, and new engines reputedly good for 110bhp. Du Hamel's bike also had Morris mag wheels, with additional help from Dunlop in the guise of a soft-compound 'semi-treadless' KR97 rear. The Suzukis weren't short of speed, but had other problems: Art Baumann had crashed in qualifying at 150mph, cracking ribs and breaking a collarbone, but took his place on the grid and completed the first lap in third, behind Du Hamel and Nicholas. Rayborn's Harley expired soon after with its old bogey, a burnt piston, and Nicholas lasted until half distance before retiring with heat exhaustion. But nothing was going to stop Du Hamel this time, and he won at a blistering 110.441mph, Nixon in second, and Baumann the brave putting Suzuki on the podium by edging out Smart's Kawasaki.

Smart, toting more air miles than anyone else in the business, took a trip down memory lane over August Bank Holiday weekend. Reunited with his old Triumph, he went to Oulton Park to emerge top from a nine-bike dust-up in the best *MCN* Superbike race of the year, after Ray Pickrell had led most of the way. Cooper passed the Londoner on the last lap to take second, with Read fourth on the best of the Nortons. Peter Williams, luckless again, retired with gearbox problems.

The honour of giving the F750 Norton its first win fell to Grant. At a Scarborough meeting dominated by Saarinen and Ago, Grant scored in the *MCN* Superbike race, passing Pickrell at Mere Hairpin to win going away. Williams broke a gearbox mainshaft and Read had a rare fall. Pick now led the *MCN* Superbike Championship with 84 points from Cooper (63) and Jefferies (46). Peter Williams hadn't added to his early-season tally of 27.

Any thoughts that Pickrell and BSA-Triumph might end the year happily were soon dashed. Mallory Park's highlight and season-closer, the Race of the Year meeting, attracted Saarinen and Rayborn, and it was these two who set about giving the crowd its money's worth in the name event. Saarinen disappeared beneath his water-cooled Yamaha's paintwork and bolted, Rayborn chasing to half-distance then fading with a misfire. Second home was Smart, giving his home crowd its first glimpse of his Hansen H2R. He might have done better, he said, with more cornering clearance. Cooper, coming to dominate the second half of the domestic season as Pick had the first, beat the Londoner for third.

The last big race on the programme was the F750 event. The Hansen twins, Smart and Du Hamel, led away, but a brutal three-bike crash at Devil's Elbow robbed the event of its lustre. Pickrell went down, Tony Jefferies tried to avoid the fall but went over Pickrell, and Tait followed them. Long after the incident Triumph discovered that third gear had broken up in Pick's gearbox and locked everything solid. At the time it was said he had a broken leg and internal injuries. Within a week the diagnosis was revised to a broken pelvis, a broken right ankle and damaged vertebrae. He was expected to be in hospital for months.

During the same week BSA-Triumph announced its withdrawal from racing, and this time there'd be nothing partial about it. There would be no factory support for competition in Britain during 1973, because its resources were needed to develop new street bikes. America, apparently, would fend for itself.

The close of the season in Britain brought another pot for Norton's sparsely populated trophy cabinet. Dave Croxford and Mick Grant won the Thruxton 500 – Crockett's second in a row – albeit by pushing his Production Racer over the line with a broken primary chain. There was more good news at the Race of the South, where Read beat off Smart's Hansen Kawasaki to record his first major win for the marque. Cooper collected the *MCN* Superbike Championship, beating Pickrell's tally by winning and setting the fastest lap in the double-points final round. With Jefferies sidelined by a split oil line and Smart by ignition failure, it fell to the Norton boys to pose Coop some problems, and that they did until Williams slowed in pain from a crash during practice. Read chased Coop home in second from Williams. Then, in a gesture typical of the man, Cooper donated £250 of his winnings to top up Pickrell's second place pay out, making him equal champion, at least in cash terms. "He deserves it," said Cooper. "He's been so unlucky this year."

ALL CHANGE

Smart's red letter day came at Ontario, the last road race on the AMA's national calendar. Team Hansen was in the ascendant, but, with Du Hamel starting from the back of the grid after a practice crash, Nixon led away in the opening leg with Carr's H2R for company. While Du Hamel scorched through the field, the race took its toll: Rayborn and Baumann retired after collisions with backmarkers. Romero also crashed, as did Nicholas. Du Hamel passed Carr for second after 14 laps of the 40-lap journey, then

Lancastrian Cliff Carr put in some strong rides on his Kevin Cameron-prepped H2R, running well at Ontario in 1972, and at Daytona the following season. (Courtesy Elwyn Roberts)

found himself in the lead when Nixon retired with gearbox failure. As the remaining 750s stopped for fuel, Kel Carruthers and Yamaha team-mate Kenny Roberts took point. Only Du Hamel seemed likely to interfere – but he too was brought off by a backmarker. Carruthers won from KR (Roberts), Carr and Geoff Perry's Suzuki, with Smart fifth. The second leg was about two Kawasakis after Roberts retired early with a broken crankshaft. Carr led well until his crankshaft failed at half distance. Du Hamel and Baumann both rode with their injuries strapped, and Nixon, after battling through the field, lost touch with the leaders during a long fuel stop. Only Smart continued his metronomic progress to the flag, to win from Perry and Renzo Pasolini's Harley. The Maidstone boatbuilder bought a house with his winnings, and went home to consider his future, as his contract with Team Hansen expired a fortnight after Ontario, and wasn't renewed. The house was, no doubt, more comfortable than the hedge.

While Suzuki and Kawasaki geared up production of their triples for the season ahead (Kawasaki to meet the clamour for bikes from its Italian and French distributors; Suzuki to put four TR750s into the UK – and build one for Geoff Perry), Yamaha made two announcements in the same week: that there would be a new US team comprising KR, Gary Scott and Don Castro and, more important overall, perhaps, that the factory was to sell replicas on Saarinen's water-cooled 350 twin, which was said to make a handy 70bhp.

The FIM made a better fist of F750 at its second attempt, instituting a European Prize for the class from 1973 at its autumn London conference. France, Italy, the Netherlands, Spain, Sweden, the UK, and the USA all declared an interest in running rounds, though dissent arose when the UK and the USA tabled a resolution to restrict homologation to engines and leave frames open. France opposed and so defeated it – for the moment.

Meanwhile, BSA-Triumph contacted Cooper, Jefferies, Tait and Pickrell, asking for the return of its motorcycles. The firm also put Smart's F750 Trident on display at the Cologne show – and refused to give it back. Smart claimed it was his by right, in lieu of prize money, but in any case he had his hands full with other matters, and announced in the opening weeks of 1973 that he'd be joining Team Suzuki in the US alongside Ron Grant and Geoff Perry.

Back came those rumours from Japan: that the new TR750 made 107bhp at the wheel, that it was clocked at 183mph. The reality was less hair-raising, recalls Smart: "Everyone said the bloody thing's awful, you can't ride it. So they gave me one – a Jody Nicholas bike, I think – and I thought, actually, this isn't too bad; this is okay for me. And they said we'll make it better: we'll put some taper-roller bearings in the steering head. And that destroyed it; you couldn't ride the thing. It was awful. I put the ball bearings back and it was fine."

Suzuki's 1973 challenge looked a serious business on two continents. After being restricted to XR05s in 1972, Suzuki GB was to receive XR11s for Stan Woods and Barry Sheene – whose priorities would include the newly instituted European F750 prize and the *MCN* Superbike Championship. On top of that, Guido Mandracci and Jack Findlay would get XR11s through Suzuki Italia, while Smart and Ron Grant would cross the Atlantic to lend a hand when the AMA calendar permitted.

Grant was enthusiastic about his new mount, telling Australian magazine *Revs* his TR had "stock heads, barrels, crank, radiator and cases. Everything else is different – even the cables are tailor-made." He savoured the triple-roller bearings on the primary-drive end of the crank and the "gigantic" double rollers in the rear hub. He even provided the magazine with a standing-quarter time: 11.28 seconds at 128mph.

Meanwhile, Kawasaki had been busy. For the coming season the team's leading riders would be Du Hamel (tuner Steve Whitelock) and Baumann (Chris Young) with Nixon (Erv Kanemoto), Carr (Kevin Cameron) and Hurley Wilvert (preparing his own bikes) in support. The team's bikes now embraced a variety of frames and wheels while different front brakes came and went. But under stricter F750 regulations, the 1973 engines ran cylinders drawn from stock, lacking the bridged ports of their predecessors and running outward-angled exhaust ports. To fit these inside the racing frames' wide-splayed downtubes, the factory trimmed the cooling fins and swapped the outer cylinders, right for left. Finning was also cut down front and back, giving extra power on the factory dyno but also raising cylinder and piston temperatures, with damaging results.

In Andover, meanwhile, Norton's ever lighter, ever smaller F750 bikes received monocoque frames, and would be ridden by Williams, Croxford and Cooper, leaving Read to seek employment in Italy. Ray Pickrell, meanwhile, was facing a far more challenging future. While generally on the mend, he had a locked ankle and, after the first round of surgery, a right leg three inches shorter than his left. It could be fixed, he said, but it would mean having to rebreak the pelvis. "That would mean I'd miss the '73 season," he told *Motor Cycle*, and if that happens, I'll quit."

For Yamaha, Kel Carruthers told the press: "We'll definitely be racing 700cc fours at Daytona next year. The factory is testing the prototype and plans to build 200 so they can be homologated." He added: "Power is about 130bhp, but it'll be de-tuned to broaden the powerband and make the bike more manageable."

For Daytona '73 Saarinen had to make do with his water-cooled Yamaha 350 twin. While there was no such road bike in Yamaha's range, there was indeed a "standard catalogue production model," called the TZ350. It had been manufactured for many months, and there were rather more than 200 examples in existence. It was therefore eligible for F750 competition, though

Jarno Saarinen blew everyone away in 1972 (pictured at Scarborough). He began the following season with wins at Daytona and Imola, and looked set for bigger things. (Courtesy Elwyn Roberts)

whether it had the performance to win at Daytona looked doubtful, at least to begin with. Smart qualified fastest on his new XR11, getting around the revised 3.84-mile circuit, back-straight chicane and all, at 101.87mph. But Kawasaki got the first of the headlines with Du Hamel, Baumann and Nixon breaking from the rest of the field at the start, Ron Grant's Suzuki and Masahiro Wada's factory H2R giving chase. Baumann and Du Hamel swapped the lead as Nixon dropped back a little, and so it stayed until the leading pair entered the infield on lap 10 and found the track strewn with debris from a shunt seconds before. Both went down, both got up again, but the dream was over. Nixon now led from Wada until the Japanese rider's engine seized, leaving Grant and Geoff Perry in second and third for Suzuki. Smart, who'd been rammed early, ran off, stalled and got going again, and was up to third when he retired with ignition failure.

Grant and Perry led after the first stops. By then Nixon was out with a seized motor, then Perry with ignition failure and Grant with a broken chain. Saarinen led the survivors towards the flag from Yamaha team-mate Carruthers, with Carr in third on the last of the H2Rs, apparently forgotten by fate until he was stopped by a puncture with nine laps to go. It was Yamaha's day again, taking all three podium positions and powering six of the top ten finishers. Best four-stroke was Mann's Triumph triple in fourth place, ahead of 1972 winner Don Emde's guest-ride TR750 Suzuki and Morio Sumiya in sixth on the best of the factory-prepared Hondas.

Of the 11 factory Kawasakis and Suzukis starting at Daytona, only Emde's had finished. Interestingly, Carr's – the last to go – had run rich, and he'd told Cameron it wouldn't rev. Down among the four-strokes, Mann's triple was 10mph slower than his 1972 bike for want of spares, and the Nortons, said to be giving 76bhp at 6800rpm, ran a best of 142mph (compared with Wada's H2R at 164mph).

Smart began the 750 two-strokes' long haul back into the limelight. The AMA schedule was relatively crowded for 1973 with no fewer than nine national road races. The second was in Dallas three weeks after Daytona, and here the expat Brit gave the XR11 its first major win after early leader Du Hamel retired with a broken piston. Nixon claimed second for Kawasaki from KR's Yamaha and Perry's XR11.

HOME TRUTH

Daytona had been dismal for Norton. Before the race the factory bikes, ridden by Williams, Cooper, and Dave Aldana, had been suffering fuel-starvation problems attributed to having the header tank feeds just an inch above the float bowls. Even manoeuvring a plug spanner into place was awkward in the cramped monocoque frame. And the race itself had been something to forget: Cooper and Aldana both retired, leaving Williams alone to limp into 23rd place. At home, meanwhile, BSA-Triumph was on the verge of collapse, and after crisis talks in Whitehall founding a new company, Norton Villiers Triumph, was thought to be the answer.

For the opening round of the new F750 FIM Prize at Imola, the organising club, Santerno MC, decided the event would run over two 100-mile legs. That still meant a fuel stop for the big strokers, but, using the maximum permitted 24-litre tank, others could expect to run through non-stop. So the major teams regrouped, mindful that the fast 3.12-mile Italian circuit didn't make quite the same demands on machinery as the sustained flat-out running of Daytona. Mick Grant, having been impressed by Les van Breda's V-twin in South Africa, dropped Ducati a line offering his services for the race. "I got a telegram back saying please come and test at Modena, so I actually rode a factory Ducati at the 1973 Imola 200."

The new Ducati was lighter and more potent than its predecessor. Again using sandcast cases based on that of the 750 GT, the '73 bike used engine dimensions of 86 x 64.5mm, and heads with a narrower (60-degree) included valve angle and higher-compression pistons. In track tests the engine pulled beyond 10,000rpm. Taglioni said it made about 90bhp. A new frame, giving a wheelbase much shorter than that which made Smart's remaining hair stand on end in 1972, made the bike more agile, and early stability problems were cured with centre-axle Marzocchis and shallow offset triple clamps. Weight was given as 155kg.

Its bikes overheating during practice, Norton fitted oil coolers and ducted more air over the carburettors. Fuel starvation was still a problem. Williams qualified, but not Cooper, who'd fallen heavily at a non-championship F750 race in Rouen and was still sore, as was Rayborn, who had crashed at Daytona, breaking a collarbone. Still, the American ace found the Italian circuit appealing. "I like it fine," he told *Motor Cycle*. "But it's way too fast for the Harley – we need more corners."

As sparse as the four-stroke entry might have been (a couple of Hondas, a few private BSA-Triumph triples), the fancied two-strokes had their difficulties. The American Team Kawasakis suffered a spate of burnt pistons due to the low octane rating of the local fuel, and the Suzukis, notably Ron Grant and Smart, had gearbox problems; Barry Sheene, having one of his first rides on the TR750 (for which he'd commissioned a Seeley frame), said he was "sliding about," perhaps because of his small-section rear rim and, like team-mate Stan Woods, was plagued with chain problems.

It wasn't all bad news for Suzuki. Mandracci sliced 1.6 seconds off Ago's outright lap record in qualifying – and then retired on the first lap of the opening leg with a broken piston, along with Tony Jefferies (broken chain) and Mick Grant (burnt-out clutch). Du Hamel led for a couple of laps, when Saarinen's 350 Yamaha swept past and away. Baumann and Smart also passed the Canadian, who soon stopped with a broken rod. Smart then was gone with ignition failure. Saarinen, whose Yamaha could match the 750s on acceleration, pulled a 10-second lead on Baumann, now slowing with oil on his visor after a tumble. Bruno Kneubühler (Ducati) and Rayborn passed Baumann and vied for second until Kneubühler fell, breaking a thumb, and Spaggiari passed Rayborn to begin a forlorn pursuit of Saarinen. When

Carruthers passed Rayborn for third, the final podium spot was decided. Star retirements included Williams (fuel starvation), Ron Grant (gear selector), Carr (seizure) and Sheene, who'd got up to sixth before the chain began jumping its sprockets.

Saarinen did it again in the second leg in a field largely without 750cc two-strokes. Spaggiari and Rayborn kept him in sight for a few laps, but then Rayborn retired with magneto failure, and the Finn headed for the hills. Spaggiari looked good for another second until Walter Villa, this year H2R-mounted, came past. Downfield, Mick Grant and Williams scrapped heartily for seventh place until Williams slid off at the hairpin.

While Saarinen's next port of call was to do battle with Ago in the French GP, the Brits and many of the Americans went to the UK for the Transatlantic Trophy. After the fireworks of 1972, a hefty crowd expected something similar and got its money's worth, if from a new direction. At Brands Hatch, Rayborn began as he had in 1972, now swapping the lead with Peter Williams until the American fell at Paddock, followed by Williams at Druids. With Smart and Sheene already out, Dave Potter's Kuhn Norton led a reduced field across the line. In the second race Sheene, Williams, Smart, and finally Rayborn all had a hand at leading, with Rayborn first from Smart and Williams.

Mallory Park wasn't such a happy hunting ground for Rayborn, his XR's handling badly upset by high winds, but his place in the spotlight was taken by Sheene in the first leg. With tyre trouble on his XR11, Sheene hopped aboard his TR500 and took the lead in the wet, crashed, remounted and got home sixth, then to be disqualified for running an engine smaller than the specified 501cc minimum. Williams won from Nixon, and American fortunes improved still further when Du Hamel won the second leg from Williams and Smart. Britain, however, secured the series when Williams won both races at Oulton Park, leading home Smart in the first race and Du Hamel in the second. UK 416 points, US 398; the margins were narrower every year.

Brands had also seen the opening round of the year's *MCN* Superbike Championship, with visitor Smart taking home the tinware after Williams and Potter had retired. Ray Pickrell, 'joint' champion in 1972, had slipped in to spectate and was heard to say: "It's torture to stand here and watch. I think I'll go."

The British season, acquiring momentum slowly by dint of sullen, uncooperative weather, got going at last. The *MCN* Superbike Championship, visiting Cadwell for its second round a fortnight after Easter, was still a largely four-stroke affair. Williams, hanging onto his Norton's long-stroke (73 x 89mm) engine, showed the field a clean pair of heels at the start, though a pack that included Sheene, Potter (Kuhn Norton), Croxford (JPN), Woods (TR750) and Jefferies (Triumph) closed gradually, losing Crockett (fuel pump) and Potter (crash) along the way. On the last lap Jefferies squeezed past Woods for second, but Williams was still 3.6 seconds clear at the flag. Three weeks later Williams brought a slightly reconfigured Norton to the third round at Brands. The latest monocoque frame also housed the fuel, with an oil tank mounted in front of the engine. Woods and Sheene put their Suzukis in front early from Williams and Croxford on another tank-frame JPN. And that's more or less how it stayed. Sheene retired with collapsed rear wheel bearings, Williams mounted an unsuccessful assault on Woods. Alas, John Cooper crashed at Bottom Bend when his borrowed JPN's primary chain broke – his third heavy fall in a matter of weeks. He broke a leg and announced his retirement, effective forthwith. Eras rarely end to the sound of trumpets.

Beginnings

In Sydney, veteran Australian champion Ron Toombs marked a career change by accepting a contract with the fledging Team Kawasaki Australia to ride its newly delivered H2R. The principal task for Toombs and team chief Neville Doyle was to take on the Australian Road Racing Championship, first blood going to Toombs at the South Australian round. Meanwhile, as Kawasaki went to work in Australia and the USA, Suzuki made hay in the FIM European F750 Prize. Sheene notched his first major win on an XR11 in the second round at Clermont-Ferrand, passing early leader Johnny Dodds. Peter Williams claimed third, his Norton further modified to include

Peter Williams saw Norton's F750 programme through long- and short-stoke Commando engines, monocoque and space frames. Injury stopped him before the Cosworth came on-line. (Courtesy Elwyn Roberts)

an air scoop over the fuel pump. Stan Woods was fourth after a dust-up with Franco Bonera on the Koelliker Triumph, and Jack Findlay didn't start, instead setting off wearily to look for his TR750, which had apparently been sent to Frankfurt while Jack was waiting for it in Turin.

Sheene didn't go to the TT but Peter Williams did, swapping the lead with Tony Jefferies (on Slippery Sam) in the Production three-lapper, easing out to lead by 24 seconds on the third lap, then to hole out at May Hill with a broken gearbox. Jefferies duly gave Sam win number three while Williams' moment came during the F750 race, recording Norton's first TT win for a dozen years, and leading Mick Grant, guest riding for JPN (with oil coating his back tyre from a gearbox leak) to give the marque a 1-2. Findlay, reunited with his TR750 by TT week, ran second for four laps of five, when he too succumbed to gearbox gremlins. Jefferies was an impressive third on his Triumph triple, rebuilt after a major blow-up at Brands.

Triumph made headlines of a different sort at the Mallory Park Post-TT fourth round of the *MCN* Superbike Championship. After getting into an early lead, Percy Tait eased off in pain from grinding his foot through Gerard's. Williams, Sheene and Woods swept past, Williams then retiring with the old Norton bogey, fuel starvation, as Sheene's clutch failed. Woods hammered on to win from Tait and Potter's Kuhn Norton.

Meanwhile, the next stop on the AMA trail was Road Atlanta where Perry won the 75-mile national. While Du Hamel ran off, Smart crashed and Gary Nixon's engine threw not one rod but two, Perry and Kel Carruthers (Yamaha) staged a dice that was decided only in the last bend of the last lap, where the New Zealander came out tighter than the Australian, screwed it on and won by half a wheel. KR was third, and the first four-stroke home was Rayborn's Harley in 10th. Du Hamel did well to climb up to fourth and head home team-mates Carr (sixth) and Wilvert (eighth), giving Kawasaki three finishers from five, their factory engines now running magnesium-body carbs and squish heads. Suzuki managed just one from three after Smart crashed and Grant was given a one-lap penalty for creeping forward on the line. But Suzuki had no mechanical failures at Atlanta – unlike Kawasaki. Early in the season, overheating caused by the trimmed fins of Kawasaki's production-type cylinders had exposed piston weaknesses around the gudgeon pin bosses and the ring lands, resulting in a spate of failures. Heavier pistons came but failures persisted and accurate diagnosis of the problem was difficult. Kevin Cameron, preparing Carr's bikes for the season, later wrote in *Classic Motorcycle Race Engines*, "No one, dumping the pieces out of a hot exhaust pipe, could tell what failed first."

Certainly, Paul Smart had few regrets in swapping his H2R for a TR750. "I rode that first bike at Silverstone in 1973, and no-one could get close to me. We never did anything; we never tuned our engines or ran high compression. That thing was so bloody reliable. Barry ran his in a Seeley frame and blew a head gasket. Franko said, what have you done to yours? I told him we hadn't touched it. He didn't believe me, but we never even had the head off – we ran it for a whole year. Everyone said 'that won't last, you'll put rings in it.' But it was a lorry engine. They were bulletproof and still are."

The Suzukis sometimes had ignition problems and transmission issues; and in longer races they'd struggled with tyre wear, at least until Dunlop came up with something special. Smart: "At Dallas, Tony Mills gave me a new tyre. It's a slick – the first proper slick. He said there was no need for tread, that everyone was working on the technology and Dunlop was first with it. So I did a couple of laps in practice and it's all right. Anyway, the outcome was that we didn't just win, we walked it: and the world changed that day."

Nixon took his first national win for three years at the next AMA race, around the twists and turns of Loudon. The Baltimore rider who'd made the New Hampshire track his own, took the lead after Du Hamel retired early with carburation problems and won from an off-the-pace Roberts and Gary Scott's outgunned Triumph. The best Suzuki was Perry's in fifth behind Steve McLaughlin's Yamaha. The second Kawasaki home was Wilvert's in sixth, after Carr's engine seized and Baumann fell heavily during a heat race.

The second half of the season began with Suzuki on top in the Swedish round of the FIM F750 Prize, the points this time going Jack Findlay's way. Sheene's XR11 blew up in practice, but after a hasty rebuild he led the race until a blown oil seal triggered a misfire. Findlay and Woods passed, but Sheene hung on for third – giving him a five-point lead in the series – from Mandracci on his Suzuki Italia XR11. Indeed, in a surprising reversal of fortune, just two 350 Yamahas made it into the lower reaches of the top ten, among a cluster of unfancied four-strokes.

But the west was still green. New gear for Team Kawasaki at the Laguna Seca national included plasma-coated aluminium discs to reduce unsprung weight for a bumpy track where they'd struggled the year before. That the H2R was an improving motorcycle was underlined by the sight of the five team bikes (plus factory rider Masahiro Wada's), running nose to tail at the head of the pack early in the 75-mile final. It didn't last. Wilvert went first with sparkplug failure, then Wada with a sour engine. Even so, Du Hamel, Nixon, Carr and Baumann tanked along looking secure until, with a handful of laps left to run, Du Hamel went down in the Corkscrew with fuel leaking onto his back tyre and Baumann's ignition failed. Nixon made it two wins from as many starts and Carr took second in spite of brake fluid leaking onto his back tyre. Only two Team Suzuki bikes had made the start: Smart and Grant, and both had retired with gearbox ailments. The third team member, Geoff Perry, had died when the Pan Am flight on which he was travelling from New Zealand back to the US crashed near Tahiti. There were no survivors.

Mick Woollett reflected the anxieties of many in an editorial in *Motor Cycle* about the viability of F750, should TZ350s dominate the class. Yet Suzuki was equal to the task in Sweden, and at the Finnish round, filling the placings – headed by Sheene and Findlay – behind winner Tepi Länsivuori's factory-supported Yamaha, the team doing better again at the Silverstone round of the FIM Prize, with Smart winning both races. In the first leg, Smart had Du Hamel for company at the front, though the Canadian was struggling with gear change problems. He looked likely to fare better in the second leg until, he later said, "I screwed it a little harder and she blew." Peter Williams diced with Smart for a time, but also retired when "the fuel level got too low for the pump." Up came 350 Yamaha-mounted Johnny Dodds, adding a second place to his first race sixth, giving him third overall behind Findlay.

Sheene had his own problems. He finished third in the first race but then his XR11's head gasket blew while warming up for the second. As he had in the Transatlantic Trophy, he hopped onto his TR500 – with similar results. He crossed the line an impressive sixth, giving himself a useful eight points for fourth place overall, and maintaining a break, 45 points to 42, on Findlay at the top of the table. But the FIM deemed his change of bike illegal and stripped him of his points. With two rounds of the FIM Prize remaining, Sheene was second, five points adrift of Findlay.

THREE FOR THE ROAD

Back on his adopted home turf, Du Hamel looked set for good things at Pocono, the AMA's sixth road race national. Kawasaki dominated qualifying, with just Rayborn's Harley breaking the green line on the front row of the grid. Sure enough, Du Hamel led away, but Nixon, enjoying some of the best form of his career, took the lead on the third lap and stayed there while his team-mates fell away: Baumann with a broken gearlever, Carr with a puncture, Du Hamel with an unspecified engine malady, Wilvert with crank failure. By the finish Kenny Roberts was second ahead of team-mate Gary Fisher, Jim Evans' Yamaha, Gary Scott's Triumph and Ron Grant, on the remaining Suzuki after Smart fell on the opening lap.

Confirmation that Kawasaki wasn't quite out of the woods came at the Talladega national a fortnight later. Having claimed pole, Du Hamel scuffled with Nixon and then Smart early, taking advantage of his new Dunlop KR97 Dunlop rear, dubbed the Racing 200. Though still with a tread, the design lacked lateral sipes, minimising the possibility that it would tear itself to shreds on the banking – and Du Hamel gave it every opportunity, building a 40-second lead until a rod let go. To this day people can't agree on the length of the flame that blew from the back of the Canadian's engine, but ten metres seems a popular figure. Du Hamel took to the lifeboats with his burning bike still travelling at 70mph. Smart, promoted into the lead by Du Hamel's misfortune, stopped with a seized engine shortly after, leaving Carruthers to lead home a clutch of Yamahas headed by newcomer Steve Baker. Ron Grant, the one survivor of the 750 triples, was sixth for Suzuki.

Kawasaki's woes looked set to continue at Charlotte with Nixon and Baumann both blowing engines in practice. But Kawasakis ran first to fourth in the national until Baumann and Nixon rolled to a stop and Carr slowed with his transmission misbehaving. Du Hamel ran away and Roberts eased into second from Wilvert with Grant a determined fourth on the remaining Suzuki – Smart having retired with his third puncture of the meeting. And that's how it stayed: Du Hamel celebrated his first national win of the year, and Roberts his first Grand National Championship.

The British season came to its traditional climax at Mallory Park with the Race of the Year. Phil Read, now at MV Agusta and winner of the 500cc World Championship that had changed course so brutally at Monza back in May, gave the 40,000-strong crowd a sample of the sight and sound that had again dominated the grand prix season, though now easing home from early leader Peter Williams' JPN and Dodds' 350 Yamaha.

Sheene, who'd made a poor start and retired with a split exhaust, was going through a bumpy patch in domestic racing, retiring from the Scarborough round of the *MCN* Superbike Championship with a blown oil seal, while Mick Grant, in another successful guest ride for John Player Norton, went on to win after early leader Williams had fallen and remounted to finish third behind Geoff Barry's Norton. Sheene then set the world to rights in the seventh round of the series at the Race of the Year meeting. After another of the poor starts, for which he was becoming infamous, Sheene sliced through the field, passing leader Williams as the race wound down, while Tait got third from Pat Mahoney's Seeley Kawasaki.

Sadly, this was Tony Jefferies' last race. On the second lap, the Yorkshireman tried a move on Dave Croxford's Norton at the hairpin and clipped his read end. Both went down and, recalls Jefferies, "half the field went over me." His injuries resulted in paralysis.

The season closed with perhaps with more battle scars than average, but with heated disputes yet to be settled. With one round of the *MCN* Superbike Championship left, Williams and Woods were vying for the title, with a chance of Sheene or Smart spoiling their party. In the FIM F750 Prize, Suzuki runners Sheene and Findlay were locked together at the top of the table with two rounds to go.

After winning the first leg at the Hockenheim F750 round – a rare example of that unhappy hybrid, the car and bike meeting – Findlay led, but was chased home by Sheene who'd been slowed by another blown head gasket. Then the Australian took a rare fall in the second leg – on rubber left by cars, said some – leaving Sheene in the lead and a prospect to square the meeting – until another head gasket blew, and he limped into fourth behind winner Woods and the 350 Yamahas of Dieter Braun and Dodds.

With just the Spanish round left, the destination of the Prize was still to be decided – and if the competition lasted into a second year, there were clearly problems to be overcome: "Not until the final round," growled John Brown in *MCN*, "did many riders discover that only the best four rounds would count." True; and while some meetings had two races, others ran only one – of differing lengths – which led to difficulties in allocating points. And then there was the car rubber.

The American season closed at Ontario, where the only question

Gregg Hansford brought his mighty talents to Team Kawasaki Australia in 1975, and got to know the world's fastest, most reliable H2Rs. (Courtesy Ian Falloon)

seemed to be which Kawasaki would win. And the team's performance was impressive, with Du Hamel winning both 125-mile heats from team-mates Nixon and Baumann. Carr, dogged by problems, ran 12th in the opening leg and seized in the second, as did guest rider Mick Grant who was fourth in the second leg when his H2R nipped up. In both races, KR finished fourth in front of Smart; the best four-stroke was Romero's Triumph with a pair of ninth places. Unhappily, this million-dollar drama was enacted before just 12,000 spectators.

Sheene completed his season-long march into the headlines with two events. At the first, the final round of the FIM F750 Prize at Montjuich Park in Barcelona, the Londoner took a measured ride to finish second to Dodds, who led from early in the race. Sheene closed, but slowed to hold second. With Mandracci third and Findlay fourth, it was another good result for Suzuki, but it was the Londoner's day – and title.

Sheene's second big event came at the Brands Hatch season-closer, the Race of the South meeting. Before the final round of the *MCN* Superbike Championship, Peter Williams led with 69 points to Stan Woods' 57, Sheene a remote third on 45. But with double points for the final race, Sheene could pick up 30 points for the win and 10 for the fastest lap, and so he did – passing Croxford's Norton for the lead as early as the second lap, with Smart forcing his way into second, fending off Williams (running his long-stroke engine for reliability) in third. At that point the Norton man

With the TZ750 Yamaha banished from F750, the improving triples produced memorable action in 1974. At Silverstone Du Hamel, Mick Grant and Smart went at it, Smart getting the nod for Suzuki. (Courtesy Ian Falloon)

had the championship won, but along came Barry Scully on his home-brewed Triumph, passing Williams to finish third behind the two Suzukis. Sheene logged a 40-point maximum, Williams took 16 points for fourth; all square then at 85 points each, but the title went Sheene's way because he'd won two rounds and Williams one.

"PLENTY EARLY"

The silly season, for once, had substance to it. Ron Grant took his departure from Suzuki, noting that "the TR750 never really lived up to its promise in the US." Suzuki took the opportunity to give its teams an overhaul on both sides of the Atlantic, with Smart as number one and Sheene leading the way in Europe. Then came the news that Cal Rayborn had quit Harley-Davidson: "I've been waiting two years for them to build a winner," he said. "You might say I'm tired of losing."

Yamaha US, meanwhile, had expanded its team, which would now include KR, Don Castro and Gene Romero – saying a sad farewell to Triumph after five years – with Carruthers in a managerial role.

Hovering in the shadows like a pantomime villain was Yamaha's much-posited game-changer, the TZ750. Yamaha had already offered a glimpse of the bike in September at the Sydney show, and surely the good and the great at Iwata were further encouraged when the AMA said it was considering dropping its homologation requirement from 200 complete bikes to 25 in a bid to encourage smaller manufacturers. Not that the FIM was having any of it, insisting on its 200-bike homologation minimum for F750 – although now agreeing to freedom in the choice of frames.

After an early appearance at Ontario, the TZ750 underwent high-profile testing at Daytona by KR, Kel Carruthers, and new recruits Giacomo Agostini and Tepi Länsivuori. Again, figures of 180mph were mentioned, but now seemed to have some plausibility. Enter 19-year-old Kiwi John Boote, who gave the bike a winning debut at Gracefield on 5 January 1974 in the third round of the inaugural Marlboro Series, and won again at Ruapuna a week later.

In the months ahead, dozens of riders in as many languages would try to explain the TZ750's acceleration, but the most vivid picture surely came from Japanese 750 road racing champion, Ken Nemoto, who said: "They go plenty early, too bloody much!"

Dave Croxford became development rider for the Norton Challenge after Peter Williams' career-ending crash at Oulton Park. Thruxton looks as welcoming as ever. (Courtesy Elwyn Roberts Collection)

3
TANGO ZULU

There was more news from New Zealand as 1973 ended. Cal Rayborn, making his first visit down under to race in an F5000 car event, agreed to ride at the Pukekohe round of the Marlboro series on a TR500 Suzuki. The bike was burning methanol, and there were problems in getting it running properly. Rayborn started just the same and, holding fourth place, he'd just begun his second lap when the bike seized, sending him into a timber wall at 120mph and to his death. Rayborn was 33. Coming after the loss of Jarno Saarinen and Renzo Pasolini in May, and Geoff Perry in July, Rayborn's death deepened the pall over the racing community as its preparations for a new season began to peak.

The 1973 oil crisis, triggered by the Yom Kippur War, posed an additional difficulty, as teams conducted their usual dance of arrival and departure under the threat of disrupted fuel supplies. In the US, with major budget cuts looming at Kawasaki, Bob Hansen, Gary Nixon and Erv Kanemoto were all looking for work elsewhere. Yet Kawasaki hadn't lost interest in racing: there were rumours of a new water-cooled 750 triple, and with the establishment of a UK Kawasaki subsidiary, hope of a full British team. For the US, however, development of the H2R came almost to a stop, although for '74 there were new cylinders with reworked port dimensions and timing, sturdier cast pistons and more magnesium covers to shave a little weight.

New faces in US Suzuki's ranks included Carr, stepping in for Ron Grant. He was soon joined by Nixon and Kanemoto. The new XR11s were significantly changed from their predecessors, with a new frame that was lighter, lower and more compact, improving handling during tests on the Daytona banking and in faster corners – though the new trellis wasn't quite as convincing in slow going. Given recent history, the new chain oiler, operated by the back brake, seemed prudent. There was talk of Rob North frames being developed, as there was of 125bhp engine output.

In Andover, Norton was awaiting homologation of the short-stroke (77 x 80.4mm) version of its long-serving Commando engine that was said to make 81bhp. The team, again with Peter Williams and Dave Croxford aboard, expected the new lump in time for the John Player team's campaign in the FIM F750 Prize and, of course, the *MCN* Superbike Championship. There would also be a new and very light steel tube space frame that helped to reduce the bike's total mass by some 25kg on the '73 monocoque-frame version.

The fields of battle had a tentative look about them at the beginning of the year: there would be eight rounds in the *MCN* Superbike Championship, beginning at Brands in April and ending in the same place in October; but in the US just six AMA road races were planned, the result of mediocre spectator numbers in 1973. As for the F750 championship – still an FIM Prize – a show of hands suggested there could be eight rounds, starting at Imola in April and finishing up somewhere on the west coast of the USA six months later.

Anyone talking about dates on this day in the history of motorcycle sport, though, was surely missing the point. Yamaha's new water-cooled, four-cylinder entrant for open-class, AMA and F750 racing, the TZ750, had been arriving since December. In the weeks before Daytona, John Nutting tested Chas Mortimer's example for *Motor Cycle*, and discovered 97bhp at 10,400rpm at the wheel (134 at the crank). In the US, Don Vesco pulled one out of a crate, and ran the quarter mile with an elapsed time of 10.9 seconds at 147mph. Certainly incredible figures – and most incredible of all perhaps, the TZ cost less than £4000 in the UK, and about half that in the US. Contemporary British prices included the 1974 Ducati 750 Sport at £1069, and the BMW R90S at £1800.

'The Beast,' as it became known, had its origins in that fuel-injected, reed-valve, four-cylinder two-stroke seen at the 1971 Tokyo show, the GL750. The powerplant of the GL was Yamaha's best chance of competing in F750 on equal terms with Suzuki and Kawasaki. The Japanese federation approved homologation of the engine in advance, as long as 200 were built. The original plan was to have the bike in competition for the 1973 season, but development of the TZ350 and Saarinen's OW19 GP 500 took priority, and it wasn't until June of '73 that Kel Carruthers was invited to Japan to test the prototype.

Although nominally a doubled-up TZ350, the 694cc (64 x 54mm) TZ750 was significantly different from the twin. While the heads were similar to that of the 350, the 750's reed-valve induction, modified inlet and exhaust port design and timing all helped to boost mid-range power. There were four transfer ports, plus a 'boost' port. Magnesium alloy crankcases housed crankshafts mounted side-by-side with geared primary drive at their inboard ends, running a shaft taking power to the magneto, oil pump and clutch. The 152mm, seven-plate dry clutch fed power to the six-speed gearbox – both of these components, as Colin MacKellar notes

Cantabrian John Boote gave the Yamaha TZ750 a winning debut during the 1973-4 New Zealand Marlboro Series. (Courtesy Elwyn Roberts)

in his book *Yamaha*, were more than equal to the task of transmitting the stated 90bhp of the first TZ750s. Induction was via four VM34SC Mikunis delivering 15:1 premix fired by Hitachi CDI ignition.

The frame was new (adaptations had been tried) – a steel tube double-cradle type with the upper rails angled sharply from the steering head, curving down to the rear engine mounts. Gussets were added around the steering head, and bracing tubes between the frame rails. The steel swinging arm was rectangular in section and sturdy for its time, though suspension components lacked adjustment – the rear spring/damper units offered five spring pre-load settings. Steering geometry of 26 degrees rake and 83mm trail, mated with a 1407mm (55in) wheelbase, made the bike quite agile for its 157kg dry weight. Front discs were 298mm diameter, clamped on early models by twin-piston cast iron callipers, later alloy.

Initial problems included a high-speed weave (cured in part by Carruthers' suggestion of lengthening the swinging arm 50mm); cases that were prone to cracking, and even catching fire, under enthusiastic cornering (they were later changed to aluminium); and cracking of the flat-sided expansion chambers clustered tightly beneath the engine (subject to a variety of fixes but Carruthers' three down, one up-and-over design soon helped to define the look of the TZ).

Carruthers later said he thought the engine was a little 'lazy,' that there was perhaps another 20bhp trying to get out. Even so, when the prototypes went to America for Yamaha US riders Roberts, Romero and Castro to test at Ontario, he could see the challenge the TZ represented to its riders, and how much they would have to adapt to it. In those early sessions he recalled Roberts' lap times were up to eight seconds faster than his team-mates' – while they were fighting the bike because it wouldn't handle as they wanted, KR was looser, more relaxed and much faster because he was "letting it do its thing." Romero remembers the day well: "The acceleration was unbelievable," he recalls, "it was like a grenade going off."

First blood

As in 1971 and 1973, Smart qualified fastest at Daytona, this time hustling his XR11 round the 3.84-mile track at 107.95mph; but the '74 triples struggled to be seen, with as many as 55 of Yamaha's TZ750s on the grid. As well as the Yamaha US team, there were factory bikes for new signing Ago, for Finn Tepi Länsivuori, and for development rider Hideo Kanaya.

At the flag, Ago got away first, was lapping backmarkers within 15 minutes and running faster than Smart's qualifying time. But this was no GP, and as quickly as Ago went, Roberts, Nixon, Castro, Sheene, Du Hamel and Smart weren't about to let him go. By lap 10 of 47 (the race was scheduled to run 180 miles, the 20-mile cut an acknowledgement of the oil crisis) Sheene led, then Roberts; three laps later Nixon, Suzuki's new recruit, put his nose in front and stayed there until Roberts took over again after the first fuel stops. Sheene now slowed with a misfire, Smart with a malfunctioning quick-filler. But Nixon looked strong, regained the

Although nearing the end of his career, Giacomo Agostini adapted well to the TZ750, winning both the Daytona 200 (pictured) and the Imola 200. (Courtesy Mary Grothe)

lead, and held it until lap 37 when he screwed it on too hard coming out of the infield, and slid off. Roberts led again briefly, but by now had become a victim of the TZ's capacity for cracking its flat-sided exhausts, and had a broken cylinder head nut (aluminium), allowing a coolant leak and so an overheating problem.

In the end, Ago got home 40 seconds clear of Roberts, with Hurley Wilvert an unlikely third for Kawasaki. Wilvert's H2R was not only the fastest at the meeting – using the 38mm magnesium-bodied Mikunis suggested by mechanic George Vukmanovich – it was the last of them after Du Hamel retired with gearshift problems and Baumann a broken rod. Yet the Kawasaki effort was compromised from the beginning, when 300 of the new A-type cylinders were destroyed by mistake, and the few that survived were inclined to seize pistons. The H2Rs were rated at a competitive 107bhp at 9500rpm and were at least light, at less than 150kg dry. But it was Yamaha's Daytona for the third year running, powering seven of the top ten finishers. The best Suzuki was Ken Araoka's XR11 in seventh, and the best four-stroke Scott Brelsford's Harley in 31st. There was a flurry of excitement when Patrick Pons slapped down $5000, and took Ago's race winner under the AMA claim rule, but Ago was delighted with a win in his first race for Yamaha, first race in the USA and first ride on a two-stroke "in nearly a decade."

KR, meanwhile, said he hadn't been beaten but had just finished second; perhaps wondering why, as Ago was world champion, he'd never seen him ride at Ascot on a Friday night. But Roberts was used to taking the long view, even at the tender age of 22. To win the 1973 AMA Grand National Championship, he had started work in January at the Houston Astrodome, and finished, after 22 events in between, at the Ascot half-mile in the autumn. Roberts won just three of those 24 races, and none on tarmac. It worked in Roberts' favour that a ferociously competitive season had produced 18 different winners of the two dozen nationals; no-one had won more events than Roberts, though Nixon took three road races for Kawasaki, and Mert Lawwill the Peoria TT and the Indy mile for Harley-Davidson. Roberts got his first number one plate by being there when it mattered, remembering that sixth place in the dust of the Atlanta mile, and fifth at the Terra Haute half-mile, all helped him work clear of Gary Scott in the nine-month chase for the title. Still, Roberts had yet to win a national road race.

At the FIM spring congress everything changed dramatically and quickly. The TZ750 Yamaha had been homologated for F750 on the grounds that it was a standard catalogue model available through the usual outlets, and because Yamaha had rolled up its sleeves and built the required 200 of them – 219, in fact. But misgivings that it wasn't based on a road bike now combined with new concerns about its standard-setting performance. Bottom line, the FIM wanted it excluded from F750, and quickly. The boss of the FIM's technical commission, Helmut Bonsch, was a critic of open 750cc racing, and had said he considered the TZ750 and its ilk "too fast, and therefore too dangerous." So Yamaha would be outmanoeuvred by raising the required homologation total from 200 bikes to 1000.

A howl of protest rose, heightening the reputation of the big TZ from its already stellar heights. Riders, entrants, promoters and racegoers who hadn't yet seen the mythical 750 in action all wanted it reinstated. The first action was taken by Santerno MC, promoter of the Imola 200, saying its headline event would be run as an open race and not subject to F750 regulations. Everybody won, especially Yamaha, whose new bikes took the first four spots in both record-breaking races with local hero Ago the winner, twice seeing off Roberts' challenge when the American's failing tyres slowed him. Once, going through Tamburello at 140mph, where Ago's Dunlops were reported to be sticking noticeably better than Roberts' Goodyears, "the whole thing went sideways," according to KR. Roberts waved Ago through. But he wasn't beaten, he just came second.

Länsivuori took the bottom step of the podium in both outings, with Romero twice fourth after fending of Sheene's Suzuki. And that was as good as it got for the triples: Smart and Carr both stopped with ignition problems, while the Suzuki Europa bikes likewise finished in disarray, Mandracci crashing, and Findlay stopping with a broken crank. As for Kawasaki, Du Hamel and Baumann collided at the start of the opening leg and then seized in the second, with Walter Villa's H2R likewise nipping up.

Roberts at last came out on top in the Transatlantic Trophy, where the TZ750 was made most welcome. He led convincingly in the first race at Brands until a coolant leak dropped water onto his back tyre at the wrong moment, letting Smart through to win for Britain. Du Hamel had likewise been vying for the lead when his H2R's left piston broke up; he fared better second time out, winning from Roberts, now on his spare bike. Smart's third made him the meeting's top British scorer, while Sheene took third and fourth places, closing his day with third place in the opening round of the *MCN* Superbike Championship behind Smart and Woods.

Roberts' moment finally came at Mallory Park on the Sunday. After Du Hamel's Kawasaki had seized early in the first race, the Yamaha number one posted his first win, albeit chased hard by Sheene. He cleared out in the second race too, with Sheene second after a scrap with Nixon. Smart crashed heavily, his Suzuki catching fire while Du Hamel's H2R suffered another seizure. Smart was a non-starter at Oulton Park after his Mallory fall, and Mick Grant had a wrist strapped from a crash at Brands. Sheene did the job, however. Boxed in at the start of the first race, he got free to set off in pursuit of Roberts, passing him and going away to win; but Roberts brought the curtain down in the second race, running away from Sheene and Romero. The UK had won, although just: 415-401.

Man on a mission: no rider is more closely associated with Yamaha's big two-strokes than Kenny Roberts. In 1974 he won three races in the Transatlantic Trophy, and his first AMA road race at Road Atlanta. (Courtesy Elwyn Roberts)

WORK

Roberts got back to the USA around the same time as the AMA decided to withdraw its support for F750. Apparently the FIM's new machinery strictures applied not only to the TZ750, but also to the H-D XR750 which, said the FIM, wasn't based on a road bike either. If that wasn't the last straw, it must have been dangerously adjacent: the AMA decided it would drop its FIM affiliation for the next two road race nationals pending, perhaps, soothing words from Geneva.

While Suzuki's RG500 made its debut at the French GP, in Britain Kawasaki got new impetus with the formation of Boyer Team Kawasaki under the watchful eye of Stan Shenton, for which one H2R had already arrived and another was on its way. Mick Grant signed for the team and made his debut at Cadwell Park, retiring with fouled plugs for his trouble. Barry Sheene carried off most of the prizes, followed home in the *MCN* Superbike Championship race by Stan Woods and Derek Chatterton's Yamaha.

Roberts had little time to reflect on his European achievements. With the Grand National Championship now rolling, the defence of his title took top priority, and that meant dirt. While the Harley-Davidson XR750 had been outclassed in road racing, Dick O'Brien was developing the short-stroke alloy engine into the class act for the mile, half-mile and TT events that typically made up two-thirds the AMA calendar – by the middle '70s the V-twin was making around 80bhp. Roberts' Yamaha, based on the XS1 654cc parallel twin from the late '60s and tweaked by Shell Thuet and his crew to give 70+bhp (stock, 53), was now hampered by the cylinder head's wide (76 degrees) included valve angle and flat, over-sized ports that couldn't "flow enough air."

If Roberts and Romero were struggling on the shale, at least they had the right kit for the road. At Atlanta, the Yamaha US TZ750s had Carruthers' reworked and fracture-free exhausts, while the Suzuki team received new bikes with tweaks that included more new frames, carburettors (38mm, up from 34) and new exhausts. But Carr and Smart struggled with their handling, and Roberts got back onto the top step of the podium just a week after falling at the Denver half-mile. Team-mate Romero was second after a long scrap with Nixon's Suzuki, and Baumann, his H2R now fitted with Kawasaki's new A cylinders, ran fourth, while making the unwelcome discovery that it lacked the top end of both the Yamahas and Suzukis – which, reckoned Cliff Carr, were as fast as the TZs, if lacking acceleration.

Gene Romero partnered KR and Don Castro in the 1974 Yamaha America team, joking that his job was to make sure Roberts wasn't challenged. He won the Daytona 200 in 1975. (Courtesy Mary Grothe)

The shrinking FIM F750 Prize, now without its US round at Ontario as a result of the FIM ban on the TZ750, began its uncertain course with the Spanish round at Jarama at the end of May. Here TZ350-mounted Johnny Dodds led an Australian 1-2 from Findlay's Suzuki XR11, with Victor Palomo third for Ducati in a low-key affair that lacked significant backing from distributors, never mind factories.

In Britain, Yamaha was filling open-class grids through its policy of backing dealers with a history of racing, instead of forming a distributor team. The first TZ750s into the country went to leading champions of the Yamaha cause, Ted Broad, Peter Padgett and Hector Dugdale. By mid-year there were plenty of 694cc Yamahas in evidence, though few were prominent in the results of the Formula 750 Classic TT – as it had become known. Senior TT winner Phil Carpenter, one of the few to opt for the bigger bike in the open race, rather than the tried-and-true TZ350, had a bash at explaining to *Motor Cycle* the challenges posed by riding the TZ750 over the Mountain Circuit: "It's a right bloody handful," he said. "You're on the limit everywhere. You can't just flick it into bends, you have to throw it in with all your strength a long time before you get there. You've got to watch what you're doing, though. When I come out of Quarry I can keep it flat out all the way to Sulby, but [the road] seems about six inches wide."

In the end, the 350s carried the day for Yamaha, led by Chas Mortimer. Carpenter's TZ750 led for much of the first lap, then into the rain of the second – and stopped at Sulby, ironically, with a water leak. Of the Suzukis, Findlay parked his '73 TR750 at Windy Corner with ignition failure, and Smart ran dry coming off the mountain during the second lap. Charlie Williams and Tony Rutter filled the podium for Yamaha, with Percy Tait's Triumph the first 750 home in fourth place. The race proved a shocker for Norton, especially after Peter Williams practised fastest, matching his own 750 lap record at 107.27mph. His and Croxford's machinery looked as purposeful as ever, their short-stroke engines now equipped with one-piece crankshafts and giving 3-4bhp more than the '73 bikes. Both stopped at Ballaugh with cracked pistons, however: Williams on the opening lap and Crockett a lap later.

Barry Sheene, who didn't ride at the Island, kept Suzuki on top in the mainland by winning the third round of the *MCN* Superbike championship at the Mallory Post-TT meeting. After an epic scrap between the poor-handling Suzukis of Sheene, and Smart and Williams' Norton, Sheene took the points from his brother-in-law, with Pat Mahoney putting his TZ750 into third after a late pass on Williams.

During the two-month gap between the first two events of the three-round FIM F750 Prize, the ACU held a meeting to discuss the future of class. The AMA's reduction of its homologation requirement for pro racing to 25 motorcycles and 25 engine/gearbox units, was gaining international support, and the ACU wanted to make the measure central to its push for getting F750 world championship status.

After Suzuki's patchy results at Atlanta, Erv Kanemoto took matters into his own hands, and worked with C&J Frames to provide a new frame for Nixon at Loudon, the third stop on the AMA's six-event road race schedule. The factory took a dim view of such private enterprise but Nixon used the new frame – complete with adjustable rake and trail, recalled Ray Battersby in *Team Suzuki* – and Nixon was remorseless in his own back yard, passing Romero and early leader Roberts to take his fourth national win at the track. Smart, still struggling with the new XR11, and Carr, who didn't make the final after a big crash in his heat, were soon petitioning Kanemoto for similar frames by the next race at Laguna Seca. Kawasaki, still struggling to set up its new cylinders, was championed by Du Hamel in fifth, his bike, according to Ian Falloon in his book, *Kawasaki Racers*, "barely faster than Gary Scott's Harley." Nixon now went to Japan to test the new RG500 at Ryuyo, where he broke both arms and an ankle when the bike seized. Suzuki soon announced that in 1975 it would concentrate on grand prix racing, and leave the 750s to its distributors.

Suzuki's decision was, perhaps, just as well, considering the problems befalling F750. Like Imola and Ontario, Anderstorp opted out of the championship, preferring to have 700 Yamahas at its meeting than championship (or Prize) status. Unfortunately, it seemed neither the organisers nor the FIM told the competitors of the change, angering Suzuki Europa and John Player Norton. "We've travelled a thousand miles, and spent a small fortune to compete in an open event that carries no championship points," growled JPN Team Manager Frank Perris. Sure enough, big Yamahas finished 1-2-3, Chas Mortimer again claiming the big tin of biscuits, and to JPN the modest consolation of seeing Peter Williams give chase early, before being swept up by the Yamaha wave. A week later the championship proper resumed at Hameenlinna in Finland, with local hero Pentti Korhonen winning from Patrick Pons, and Johnny Dodds doing enough with fifth place to keep his title bid alive. The top ten finishers rode TZ350 Yamahas.

BREAKING WAVE

If Loudon was Nixon's adopted back yard, Roberts' home turf was Laguna Seca, venue for the fourth AMA road race. The champion was in competitive mood: he won his heat and eased out from the start of the final from Du Hamel, who was riding with a broken hand following a heavy practice fall. Romero and Smart followed, the Yamaha man repeatedly fending off Smart's Suzuki with its Kanemoto-modified frame. Gregg Hansford, making his first appearance in the USA, finished seventh on Hurley Wilvert's spare Kawasaki; and Warren Willing made it a good day for Australia by putting his TZ750 into ninth, behind Scott's Harley.

At a wet *MCN* Superbike Championship round at the Hutch meeting in August, Peter Williams made up for the costly trip to Sweden by disputing the lead with Grant's Kawasaki and Sheene, holding his own until the track began to dry when Sheene got away. Still, he held second from Grant and looked an outside bet for the title. But then it all went disastrously wrong at Oulton Park in the next *MCN* round – the fifth – where leader Sheene was stopped on the last lap by an oil leak. While Woods won from Smart and Kork Ballington, Williams crashed heavily at Old Hall when the JPN's one-piece tank/seat unit came loose. Williams was taken to the intensive care unit at Chester Royal Infirmary. His injuries included a broken left arm and wrist and, most seriously, a punctured lung.

Smart fared better at the British final round of the FIM F750 Prize, run as part of a feature-laden Silverstone meeting. While Sheene ran away with the John Player Grand Prix, he retired from the lead of the F750 race with ignition failure to let Grant, Du Hamel and Smart stage the scrap of the meeting around the wide open spaces of the 2.927-mile airfield circuit. For 11 laps the three triples swapped the lead every few yards until Grant's Team Boyer H2R went out: "We were having a cracking dice, and then, three laps from the end, the crank broke and the rotor fell off," recalled Grant. "That race was the highlight of the H2R, I think." Smart and Du Hamel began the last lap neck and neck, but the Suzuki proved to have a little extra wind, and Smart led across the line. Dodds, meanwhile, put his TZ350 into fifth place to take the championship with 27 points to Patrick Pons' 22.

Du Hamel re-crossed the Atlantic to meet Roberts on the Talladega banking, and in irresistible form. Gary Scott ran him close on the dirt in mid-season, but KR was now back in the box seat. Sheene, deputising for the injured Nixon, qualified fastest, but Roberts led from the first lap and pulled away at a second per lap, taking team-mate Castro with him. Jim Evans was third after a long dice with Carr, who was passed by Sheene on the last lap. Kawasaki had a mediocre day, their air-cooled engines gasping for top-end. Du Hamel crashed at an estimated 130mph, leaving Wilvert to wave the green flag with sixth place.

Smart retired with front tyre problems, and fared little better across the water at Scarborough a fortnight later. The '73 XR11 he'd been riding in Britain was ailing, he said. "The bike is made out of old, secondhand parts – and now I've run out of spares for it. It's a waste of time." With his brother-in-law struggling and Williams fighting bigger battles, Sheene had some breathing space at the top of the *MCN* Superbike table, and won the sixth round comfortably from Tait's Triumph. With two rounds to go, he led Smart 90 points to 49, with Woods third on 47.

Sheene carried on plundering at the Race of the Year, fighting off Phil Read's MV while Roberts, having his first ride in the wet, led briefly but faded with a chunking back tyre. In the penultimate round of the *MCN* Superbike title, Sheene led again while Smart came through the field to challenge at the hairpin as the race wound down. He fell badly, breaking both legs, while Sheene won from team-mate Woods and Ditchburn on Ted Broad's TZ750.

There were two more major events before the administrators resumed centre stage. In California, Gene Romero stole his Yamaha US team-mate's thunder by becoming the first American (and member of Team Mexico) to win the big-money Ontario season-closer. Romero won the opening leg after an early scrap with Sheene – whose gearing was way out – while Roberts, who struggled with the wrong tyres, limped into third behind Jim Evans' private Yamaha. Roberts got it right in the second leg, leading from start to finish, but Romero, planted in second place, took the cash. Sheene's was the best Suzuki, finishing fifth in the opening leg and fourth in the second, while Kawasaki had a day to forget. Du Hamel ran sixth in the opening leg, only to seize in the second. Wilvert finished ninth overall despite riding with a hand damaged in a practice crash at Talladega, and

Baumann didn't make the Ontario grid. He'd crashed in practice and, suffering concussion for the third time of the season, went home to San Francisco and a career as a motorcycle mechanic.

At Brands Hatch, Sheene won both the Race of the South and the final round of the *MCN* Superbike Championship, bringing down the curtain on his rampant domestic season. He and Grant provided a suitable climax to the series, with Sheene passing the Yorkshireman to win, fittingly, at Clearways on the last lap. Sheene logged 135 points for the series, far ahead of Woods with 78 and Smart (54).

Within a week of Sheene's popping the season's final champagne cork, the FIM had at last decided on the substance of F750 racing for the seasons ahead: (1): F750 races would be 200 miles in length, two legs each of 100 miles if desired; (2): the number of complete bikes required for homologation would be reduced to 25; (3): F750 races would be separate from existing world championships; and (4): the TZ750 Yamaha would be eligible to compete from 1975. As for the title itself – yes, still a prize – there would be nine rounds (points from the best five to count) with Daytona the first cab off the rank – though the US season looked thinner than ever.

The oil crisis of 1973 was among the earliest causes; add to that the stock market crash, a steel crisis and the partial failure of common monetary policy among western countries, and a depression was the inescapable result. Soaring inflation on both sides of the Atlantic resulted in belt-tightening everywhere, and motorcycle racing suffered its share of pain. With more people turning up for a Saturday night dirt track meeting than at most road race nationals, it wasn't surprising that the AMA's road racing calendar was cut to four meetings in 1975. After Daytona the circus would go to Atlanta, then the Californian dates, Laguna Seca and Ontario; and that would be that.

By the end of November Paul Smart was out of hospital and putting the new pins in his legs to the test. He'd heard nothing from Suzuki US, he said, but still hoped for a contract to race in America. Meanwhile, brother-in-law Barry Sheene had signed not one contract but three: with Suzuki Japan to ride the RG500 in the world championship; with Suzuki US to ride the new XR11 in the four AMA races, and with Suzuki GB to ride in the F750 Prize – and, of course, the *MCN* Superbike Championship. There would be two new XR11s each for Sheene and team-mate Woods, with John Newbold riding in UK races on a '74-spec XR11. Also new to Suzuki International was Tepi Länsivuori; but Smart was dropped from Suzuki's plans, and Suzuki Europa withdrew from racing, putting Mandracci and Findlay on private Yamahas.

Back in the UK, Boyer Team Kawasaki signed Barry Ditchburn while Dave Potter slipped neatly into the newly vacated seat of Ted Broad's TZ750, where he'd ultimately make his name. Meanwhile Norton was now struggling with John Player cutting its sponsorship, blaming the "economic climate." But the new collaboration with Cosworth would continue, said Andover, never mind the declining fortunes of the government-brokered creation, NVT.

B IS FOR BETTER

Banned in F750 or not, the Yamaha TZ750 was surely the success story of 1974. It had won at Daytona and Imola, and had largely brushed aside its opposition in the US. During its first season plenty of those odd, flat-sided expansion chambers had fractured through resonance flexing, along with the odd seized main bearing, broken head nut, and fracture of undersized gears in the transmission – but nothing systemic, nothing fundamental.

Ted Broad's first year with one yielded few problems you wouldn't expect from a high-performance two-stroke. He pointed out to *Motor Cycle* that the four grand he'd spent on the bike included a spares kit worth £1200, and that most of the work he'd done was in servicing. That said, he reckoned the shaft running the oil and water pumps was too short, and so fitted a new one. At Imola the engine began overheating; he'd also had two-cylinder studs fail, one barrel cracked at a transfer port and a case of 'moth-eaten' pistons resulting from pre-ignition. He changed the crank every 600 miles, and rods on alternate changes.

Following the initial 219 bikes, production of the TZ750 resumed in October 1974, with another 46 made to the original specification. These would become the first of the B models with the original 219 known retrospectively as the TZ750A. The changes came with the bikes made early in 1975: these had a 2.4mm increase in bore diameter, bringing capacity up to 748cc. There was also an uprated water pump and a sturdier second gear pinion. As for the expansion chambers, they'd been reshaped, and were now supported with steel straps – but it still wasn't the answer.

The 1975 works bikes were that bit different again, with chrome-lined barrels and a new look for three of them as a result of having their engines slotted into cantilever chassis from the 1974 0W20 500 grand prix bike – and these three were expected at Daytona for Roberts, Ago and that skinny kid with glasses, Steve Baker. The production TZ750B in 748cc trim was rated at 110bhp, the factory specials at closer to 130. And Roberts would be using Bill Edmonston's new jetless, flat-slide Lectron carburettors.

Ranged against them in Florida were new TR750 Suzukis, sporting yet another new, lower frame, this one with a rectangular-section swinging arm and lay-forward Kayaba shocks. They were leaner at 148kg, and, for the first time, thanks to more liberated homologation rules, came with six-speed 'boxes. Power output was up to 116bhp at 8250rpm. But the real unknown quantity was the new water-cooled 750 Kawasaki, as provided for the British pair, Grant and Ditchburn, for Du Hamel and new team-mate Jim Evans, with a fifth bike for Japanese rider Takao Abe.

Barry Sheene recovered in record time from his shattering crash at Daytona in 1975 to put together a good season, culminating in a win at the Mallory Park Race of the Year. (Courtesy Elwyn Roberts)

Work on Kawasaki's new water-cooled KR750 – factory designation 602 – began in the autumn of 1974. Like its predecessor, the engine was a piston-ported triple, though with the aluminium cylinder bank in one piece. Unlike the oversquare H2R engine, the KR had near-square dimensions at 68 x 68.6mm, giving a capacity of 747cc. Although narrower than the air-cooled H2 engine (the crankshaft was 19mm shorter), the cylinders were rotated to give more transfer port capacity, if less than hoped because of the water jackets. Induction was via the same 35mm Mikuni carbs as the H2R. The crank ran on six ball mains, and the big-end bearings and conrods were the same as the H2R's. Straight-cut primary drive took power via a 12-plate dry clutch to a six-speed 'box. Like the TZ, the frame tubes were 28mm diameter steel – with rubber mountings for the engine – and a rectangular-section swinging arm. Steering head angle was 27 degrees, rear units were Konis, and the wheels Morris mags. Dry weight was below 145kg. Serious urge came in at 6500rpm, and peak power – 120bhp – at 9500rpm. For the lucky few who'd ride the bike, a beautiful friendship was about to begin – just not at Daytona.

By the final day of Speedweek, Kenny Roberts had lapped Daytona a full five seconds inside the lap record on his new TZ750. Meanwhile, the new KR750s were suffering a gearbox malady traced to defective circlips that were supposed to retain second and third gears, but which could pop out. Over at Suzuki, the new TR750s had a reworked exhaust system that ran one pipe up under the seat. New rear suspension brackets allowed the angle of the rear units to be altered, and the team had experimented with a new crankshaft – lighter, less flywheel than earlier types – that wasn't used at Daytona but was thought might be just the job for squirting around European short circuits. And there was Barry, head down, winding up for a fast qualifying run:

"All of a sudden the back wheel just locked solid. I pulled the clutch in because I thought the engine had seized, but it didn't free the thing … I was up on the banking, and it just kind of went sideways …" If Sheene became sure the cause of his 170mph crash in the Florida sun lay in his rear Dunlop, others were less so: the tyre had not deflated – the following day it was still holding 30psi – but it had lost part of its tread. Mechanic George Vukmanovich was adamant nothing was amiss with the XR11, internally, no trace of an engine or gearbox seizure; but he did suggest that a faulty chain tensioner might have torn the tyre. Suzuki team boss Merv Wright told Ray Battersby in *Team Suzuki*: "we did find marks on the swinging arm … chunks of tyre came off, but whether they made the mark, or whether the tyre grew to such a degree that it was dragging there, has never really been established."

Sheene was taken to nearby Halifax hospital and diagnosed with a broken left thigh, right arm, wrist and collarbone, two crushed vertebrae and skin torn from his back, elbows and knees. So began one of the greatest comebacks in the story of the sport.

A subdued effort from Suzuki, and a spate of gearbox and crankshaft problems among the new Kawasakis (and a broken collarbone and concussion for Jim Evans in a practice fall), meant Yamaha had Daytona largely to itself, taking the first 16 places in the 200. Again, the favourites fell by the wayside. Gary Nixon withdrew after practice with pain from his left forearm. An X-ray revealed that the bones were parting again, dashing his grand prix plans for a while. Kenny Roberts took the lead after Länsivuori slowed with his chain jumping its sprockets, but then stopped at his first fuel stop with clutch failure. While Steve McLaughlin took over at the front, Johnny Cecotto on a stock TZ worked through the field. Ago ran consistently in the top four on a bike that wouldn't rev cleanly, and when McLaughlin crashed after ten laps at point, Baker and Romero led, leapfrogging one another at fuel stops. Baker then slowed with an overheating motor, and the race was Romero's from Baker, Ago, Cecotto, Warren Willing, and McLaughlin. "I've been three times bridesmaid here," said the genial Mexican-American while collecting his cheque for $17,485. "At last I've made it."

In a shrinking four-stroke realm, Norton's enduring Commando engine was revived for the '75 season in yet another new frame ultimately intended for the new Cosworth motor. In the meantime, the new chassis took a short-stroke F750 engine – of 830cc for the new, 1000cc upper-limit *MCN* Superbike Championship – and used it as a stressed member, with the steering head, swinging arm, and rear subframe all bolted to the power unit. Weight continued to be cut with the new bike apparently tipping the scales at 147kg, and the isolastic suspension of earlier bikes axed in anticipation of the Cosworth's counter-balancers. The chassis of the new bike – designated P86 – would be ridden by Dave Croxford, perhaps at the Transatlantic Trophy.

4-1

Sheene's enforced absence might have been the difference between the two teams in the Transatlantic Trophy but Roberts was supreme, taking three of the four races left after Brands, carpeted with unseasonable snow, was cancelled. Bitter cold underscored the whole weekend, but Roberts took control of the first race at Mallory from the third lap until Mother Nature weighed in with a snowfall, and he won from Pat Mahoney (Yamaha) and Dave Aldana's XR11. With more snow, sleet and rain falling between the outings, the Americans tried hand-cut Goodyear slicks, and Roberts brought a dismal meeting to a close with a win from Aldana and Castro. "I could have gone faster," said Roberts. "I never got the bike sideways, not even once."

Woods was on his spare bike after crashing at Mallory, so couldn't help Newbold when he crashed at Oulton, breaking his XR11's forks. Then, on the opening lap of the first race, Croxford's Norton died from ignition failure. Small wonder, perhaps, that early leader Aldana was able to get home third, behind Roberts and Romero, with his Suzuki running on two. Roberts looked like making it four in the second race, but lost the front wheel at Old Hall, and Woods got a consolation win for the UK, leading home Mahoney, Pat Hennen and Castro. So ended the UK's weakest Transatlantic Trophy performance to date, the biggest surprise perhaps that the winning margin was so slender – 278-243.

Roberts was still in pain from his Oulton Park injuries a week later at the Imola 200, the second round of the F750 prize, and for once he played little part in proceedings. Even so, engaging racing made the point that a near-monopoly by Yamaha had no adverse effect on the quality of the event. In the first leg Länsivuori led well from Ago and Cecotto, until he fell (and hastily remounted) after his fuel stop; Ago inherited the lead but toured in with a broken cylinder stud and a badly overheating engine. Cecotto then led, and after a slick pit stop (Kel Carruthers was part of the Venezuelan's team) won well from Länsivuori, Patrick Pons and Steve Baker. In the second leg John Newbold took the fight to Yamaha, sticking his '74-build XR11 into a scrap for second with Baker and Pons. Cecotto, meanwhile, had cleared off into the lead, and that's how it stayed, with Cecotto getting home two seconds clear of the American, and Pons third as Noddy faded with front brake problems.

The pleasant surprise of the meeting went to Dave Potter, putting in steady rides on Ted Broad's TZ750 for sixth and fourth, hoisting him into fourth place overall. Paul Smart, though, having his first ride back since his heavy Mallory Park fall in September, had been struggling for speed on his semi-factory Ducati, and was circulating in 16th when the bike began vibrating heavily. He pitted to have it checked but then pushed on to finish the race. Accelerating out of a slow left-hander the bike locked up and threw him off. It was thought at first that Smart had cracked the left thigh he'd just had pinned. His wife Maggie collected him from Luton Airport. "You can tell your readers Paul has ridden his last race," she growled at waiting reporters.

As one branch of the family went back to hospital, the other returned to racing. Just eight weeks after his Daytona crash, a convalescent Barry Sheene was at the Cadwell Park opening round of the *MCN* Superbike Championship. He did just ten laps, but won the start and was still handily placed when he decided he'd had enough and retired. By the flag the Boyer Team Kawasaki pair had stolen the show, with Mick Grant passing everyone in the final laps, while Ditchburn tangled with a backmarker and fell at Barn Corner. Stan Woods took second for Suzuki from Pat Mahoney's Yamaha.

Elsewhere, Kawasaki was struggling. Yvon Du Hamel damaged an elbow after being hit by a backmarker at Imola, and Team Kawasaki Australia was down to one fit rider – Murray Sayle – after Ron Toombs broke an arm so badly in an Amaroo Park crash that it needed surgery, and new signing Gregg Hansford had broken both wrists in a Bathurst crash. Yet the Australian team's problems were no more than a temporary halt on its march to near-invincibility. Ian Falloon notes in *Kawasaki Racers* that the team took a dozen wins from 14 starts in 1973, its maiden season, and team boss Neville Doyle was quietly building the fastest H2Rs in the world – and the most reliable, recording few of the problems that had plagued American runners.

Doyle's approach to engine building was to ensure fastidious preparation and assembly, and to be generous with two-stroke oil: "I know we ran richer oil mixtures than most," he explains, "and that was based on experience with other engines. But I could count on one hand, in the whole time we were involved with Kawasaki, where we had engine failures due to bearings or pistons or that sort of thing: very few cases. High mix-ratio oils were then in development and people were trying to run 50:1 and 60:1, and I'm fairly sure that's why a lot of them had trouble. We would use the 50:1-mix oil, but would use it at 20:1. I think that was probably an important factor." That, and Doyle's impressive porting, carburation and exhaust development.

A match made in heaven: Mick Grant won the 1975 MCN Superbike Championship on Kawasaki's KR750. The 1976 bike (pictured) had a revised crank, bigger carbs and a new fairing. (Courtesy Elwyn Roberts)

Now with its best bikes to date, the American branch of Team Kawasaki was running out of places to race them. The AMA's national road racing programme continued to slump with the cancellation of the Road Atlanta meeting, scheduled for the end of May. A poor crowd in 1974 meant the organisers were reluctant to post up the required $27,000 prize fund, and attempts at compromise ended in stalemate. That left just three road races on the AMA Grand National circuit – Daytona, Laguna Seca and Ontario. Perhaps, mused the AMA's Competition Director Bill Boyce, it was time to introduce a dedicated US road racing championship, offering more races with reduced prize money.

Barry Sheene's return to form continued at the Brands Hatch short-circuit international. He won the 500 and 1000cc races, and while he broke a chain while scrapping for the lead in the *MCN* Superbike Championship round, none of his rivals were under any doubts about his fitness. Mahoney picked up the running, leading for nine laps before sliding off at Paddock. That left Grant and Ditchburn cantering home from Croxford and Dave Degens' 1000cc Dresda Honda.

Kawasaki was still on top at the Isle of Man a fortnight later. Mick Grant broke Mike Hailwood's eight-year-old outright lap record (108.77mph, set on the infamous RC181 Honda during his duel with Ago in the '67 Senior) during the newly renamed Classic TT, leaving the mark at 109.82mph before the KR750's drive chain broke, to let John Williams' TZ350 Yamaha in for the win.

Too big to fail

Gradually, the TT was slipping into a kind of no-man's land. From 1970, when there had been six deaths in practice or racing, discussion of the TT's status and safety standards had grown a little louder and more impassioned each year. Although the event was still accorded world championship status, the stars' boycott since Gilberto Parlotti's death in 1972 added a new impetus to the anti-TT lobby, and the FIM was under constant pressure to review the TT's place in the scheme of things.

To underline the point, while Croxford gave Sam its fifth Production TT win, Ago led home Du Hamel in the Moto Journal 200 at Paul Ricard. And those British stars who missed the TT gathered for Mallory Park's Post-TT meeting, where MV Agusta-mounted Phil Read made off with most of the pots. Barry Sheene joined the leading bunch in the third round of the *MCN* Superbike title – though neither he nor anyone else could hold Barry Ditchburn, who put in one of those class-of-his-own rides, clearing off and setting a new lap record while Sheene, Newbold, Potter and Grant (hampered by fuel spraying from a breather) argued in his wake.

The FIM F750 Prize, which at last seemed to have a little substance, reconvened for rounds on successive weekends at Mettet and Magny-Cours. In Belgium, XR11-equipped Barry Sheene was finally able to stand toe to toe with the strengthening TZ750 lobby. He did well, coming through the field to hold a good second astern of Yamaha-mounted Patrick Pons in the opening leg, as well as posting a new lap record. Grant was well placed for a time until his KR seized in a fast left-hander and team-mate Ditchburn fell. Ago retired with handling problems and Sheene slowed with a broken exhaust, but held second from Findlay, Mortimer and Dave Potter. In the second leg Sheene looked even better, clearing off into the wet on hand-cut Michelin slicks, to lead by 28 seconds when he stopped for juice. Three laps later he was in front again but stopped with another fractured exhaust, this one robbing him of all power. Potter emerged from a scrap with the Yamahas of Kork Ballington and Findlay to win, with John Newbold claiming second for Suzuki and round winner Pons third. As points were awarded on aggregate performances, Sheene got nothing for his first-leg second place.

There were more breakages for Sheene at Magny-Cours – a total of five cracks in three pipes – despite an exhaust system "extensively strengthened" during the intervening week. Yet he won both races over the "bumpy little track" that blistered his hands, and against opposition that included Cecotto and Du Hamel. Indeed, the Kawasaki man led the first leg from Pons, who slowed and then stopped with a binding back brake. Sheene then slipped into the lead, leaving Du Hamel and Cecotto to scrap until the Yamaha man too went out with brake problems and the Canadian slowed with a tightening motor, that seized as the race closed to let Christian Estrosi into third from Christian Bourgeois and Findlay. Sheene had his pipes welded again, and was last onto the grid for race two. He made up for it, passing early leader Estrosi, but then slowing to let Du Hamel and Cecotto set the pace. Cecotto again pulled out with a binding rear brake, leaving Du Hamel to head for the hills until Sheene caught the Kawasaki that was by then slowing with its drive chain jumping sprockets. Sheene won from Estrosi, Findlay, Bourgeois and Noddy.

Sheene's crew got more exhaust-swapping practice in Sweden a month later. Here, the Londoner won his second round of the series, passing Länsivuori to pull away in the opener, and winning comfortably from the Finn and Ditchburn's Kawasaki. Ditch turned the tables in the second leg, holding off Sheene in the closing laps to win a tight race (and making the most of the new Dunlop front slick), but after Pons' Yamaha expired with a broken crank and Findlay's engine seized, the round win put Sheene at the head of the championship, leading Pons 30-27.

The last embers of the old British motorcycle industry smouldered fitfully, but smouldered still. In July, NVT chairman Dennis Poore said NVT could expect to close its remaining factories by October "unless the government injects massive funds." In the same week Andover said that the first Cosworth engines had been delivered. A test run had, however, broken a drivebelt at around 4000rpm.

Across the water, KR's 0W72 struggled against Harley on the dirt, even with legendary tuner Tim Witham in his corner – but was still on top in road racing. At Laguna Seca a crowd of some 40,000 saw California's favourite son do battle in his own back yard, with a classic scrap between KR and Du Hamel. The pair swapped the lead until the Canadian fell on oil from his own engine in turn 6 and Roberts cleared off for an emphatic win. Kiwi visitor John Boote wrested second place from Baker and Ron Pierce while Pat Hennen got his ill-handling Suzuki into fifth, the only non-Yamaha in the top ten – although Aldana (Nixon still wasn't fit) had hustled his XR11 up to third before a sparkplug failed. Daytona winner Romero had also been handily placed until the engine of his Yamaha US bike nipped up – the team's first engine malady in 18 months of campaigning the TZ750. Perhaps that was why KR's next ride was on a TZ750 in a Doug Schwerma frame at the Indy Mile, beating Corky Keener in the ride of his life. "They don't pay me enough to ride that thing," he reported afterwards.

RISE AND FALL

Back in Britain, a resurgent Barry Sheene was the star. He skipped the Finnish F750 round, a risk that paid off when local ace Tapio Virtanen took both races while both Sheene's main rivals recorded DNFs, Pons with a split fuel tank, and Findlay with a leg injury after being rammed. Sheene went to Brands instead, hoovering up the tinware at the Hutchinson 100 meeting. Experimentation with the XR11's exhaust system (cutting the tailpipes by 90mm) had released another 4bhp, and he cleaned up all four feature races, including the fourth round of the *MCN* Superbike Championship, getting the better of Ditchburn, who struggled with the misery of a migraine while trying to maintain contact with the flying Suzuki (Sheene's orange, yellow, white and blue colour scheme can't have helped). Grant fought clear of the pack in third, while Potter took Newbold for fourth. With half the series done, Grant led on 55 points from Ditch (44), Sheene (32) and Noddy (22).

Cecotto retired at Brands with a fouled plug but fared better at Silverstone, winning the first race of the F750 Prize round. Sheene lost the battle for second to Pons, his XR11 handling poorly (later traced to low-pressure tyres), and its drive chain jumping the sprockets under acceleration. Finally, his TR750 began misfiring as fuel ran low and Länsivuori slipped past for third. The UK Kawasakis suffered too: Grant with a broken chain adjuster and Ditchburn with an overheating engine, though it got him home fifth.

Cecotto's problems began before the second race. His gearbox failed and Ago agreed to lend the Venezuelan his spare engine subject to Japanese approval. It didn't happen: Sheene stepped in and got Johnny a ride on Länsivuori's spare TR750, which lasted just five laps, after which he retired to receive an angry message from Japan demanding the return of all his factory Yamaha kit. Out on the track, Grant led early but retired with more chain problems. Ditch then took over until Sheene swept past to win by 1.8 seconds. Pons had retired with a seized engine, and Findlay finished sixth overall, so Sheene found himself 17 points clear at the top of the table.

The British action continued at Oulton Park on August Bank Holiday Monday, where Sheene did it again, winning the 500 race and lapping the field up to third place in the *MCN* Superbike outing. Everything now seemed to be going Sheene's way, and there was more good news with the cancellation of the Spanish F750 round. With luck, Sheene could wrap up the title at Assen.

The Sheene effort faltered, however. He qualified fastest in the Netherlands despite blowing an engine in practice, and he, Ditchburn and Cecotto were warm favourites, though that reckoned without Du Hamel's hard-headed determination. The Canadian won both legs, taking the opener after Cecotto crashed, and early leader Sheene stopped with a split fuel line. As the race wound down Ditch had a clear lead over Du Hamel, but ran dry a mile short of the finish. John Boote came in second from Findlay and John Williams.

Sheene looked good in the second leg, hustling through the field until more carburettor problems brought him to a halt. Now Wil Hartog led

Pictured at the Ulster GP with his TZ750's expansion chambers taped to reduce cracking, Jack Findlay won the 1975 F750 Prize – without winning a round. (Courtesy Elwyn Roberts)

from Du Hamel and Newbold, with Findlay 11th. As Hartog dropped back with gearbox problems, Du Hamel, Newbold and American visitor Hurley Wilvert closed up for a strong finish, swapping the lead as the laps ticked away. But Du Hamel crossed the line first. Findlay was fourth, behind Noddy and Wilvert – enough to get him second overall, and 12 valuable points closer to Sheene.

The Londoner was coming under pressure at home, too. At the Scarborough round of the *MCN* Superbike series, on the same weekend as the Assen F750 round, Grant led from start to finish, well clear of the Potter and Tait Yamahas; but at the Mallory Park Race of the Year meeting Sheene overcame a strong field to win three races: the 500, the name event, and the penultimate *MCN* Superbike run. He found Grant in determined form, despite crashing three times over the weekend – on a new front tyre at Devil's Elbow, after being rammed, and, lastly, running into a rope stretched across the paddock entrance. Ditchburn too fell hard, damaging a shoulder in a 100mph get-off in the wet at Gerard's, so when the flag fell to start the *MCN* Superbike race, Sheene was in the unusual company of Dave Aldana (on Sheene's spare XR11). Grant then passed Du Hamel and Aldana to wrest the lead from Sheene at the Esses on the last lap. Sheene repassed at Shaw's, but with one race to go Grant led the points tally 92-72.

By the following weekend Ditch was diagnosed with a chipped bone in his right shoulder and would miss Ontario. Sheene, meanwhile, had broken his right leg at Cadwell Park while pulling a wheelie on stuntman Dave Taylor's Bultaco. He was whisked into hospital to have his breaks screwed. Medics said the trouble might have started with cracks caused by enthusiastic cornering in the Race of the Year – and he was likely to be out for the rest of the season. So Jack Findlay took the F750 Prize with third overall at Hockenheim, while Pons won both legs, and John Williams, deputising for Sheene, took second in each. When *Motor Cycle Weekly* asked the elder of the Cheshire Williamses for his views on riding the XR11 he paid tribute to Sheene: "Pons' Yamaha was definitely faster," he said, "though the Suzuki has bags of gutsy power in the mid-range so I could catch him on acceleration – but there's no doubt Barry makes the Suzuki look better than it is."

Roberts brought the curtain down on his season with another win on the tar, this time at Ontario. It was a virtuoso performance: he passed early leaders Hennen and Baker in the first leg and pulled away to win comfortably from Nixon, who was at last back in harness after his 1974 Ryuyo testing crash. Hennen was third. Du Hamel was subdued in the opening race due to oil on his back tyre from a leaking gearbox seal but got going in the second. It wasn't enough to stop Roberts, though, who cleared off again, leading home the Kawasaki man, Takazumi Katayama and Warren Willing. The event was Roberts' sixth win of the 1975 Grand National Championship, and that in a season in which no-one else scored more than two. But it hadn't been enough: Gary Scott, with two wins to his name, was the new AMA Grand National Champion.

Mick Grant, who'd had a high-speed fall on the Ontario banking similar to Sheene's Daytona crash, dusted himself off and went home for the Brands Hatch final round of the *MCN* Superbike Championship. No-one could catch Grant for the title, and, after the Yorkshireman's Kawasaki seized, Ditchburn cleared off to take his second win of the series on a restart from Newbold, who'd had a race-long dice with Pons. The scheduled event lasted only yards before a catastrophic opening-lap crash at Paddock left Pat Mahoney in a coma, and took out a total of eight bikes, ending guest rides by Tait and Read on Team Suzuki TR750s.

Dave Croxford was also among the fallers, ruining the long-awaited race debut of the Norton-Cosworth Challenge. Although Alex George took over for a sore Crockett, a leak in the cooling system caused a major overheating problem, stopping the bike "with a bang after all the coolant had boiled away."

END GAME

Across the Atlantic, the 1976 season began to assume shape. While the AMA restored Loudon to the calendar, there would still be just four road races among the 28 rounds of the Grand National Championship, beginning at Daytona and ending again in California with Laguna Seca and Ontario. And there would be fewer factory bikes to contest them. Suzuki and Kawasaki both withdrew from US racing, though leaving Du Hamel to ride the last year of his contract for Kawasaki. Yamaha too was tightening its belt, providing bikes for just KR in 1976.

For all the changes in the US and rumoured manoeuvrings in Japan, 1976 began as 1975 had ended for Team Boyer Kawasaki, with Grant and Ditchburn once again at the controls – but with new 750s. At Suzuki, Merv Wright returned from the US to run the team, while Sheene, Newbold and Tait all signed, and talk continued with Williams and Woods. At least there would be spares – Suzuki GB bought the contents of the former Suzuki US race shop, lock, stock and barrel.

Meanwhile, NVT pressed on with the Challenge, building 25 bikes for homologation and offering them for sale at £5000 apiece. The liquid-cooled parallel twin was largely a twin-cylinder 746cc slice of the 3-litre Cosworth DFV engine that won 155 F1 races between 1967 and 1983. The bike engine used the 85.67 x 64.9mm bore and stroke, the same pistons

Croxford rode the Norton Challenge in its debut at Brands, but was involved in a pile-up at Paddock. Alex George (pictured) took over, but the bike stopped with a major coolant leak. (Courtesy Elwyn Roberts)

and the same rods. With four valves per head set at a 32-degree included angle, shallow combustion chambers and double overhead cam valve actuation, much high-rev deep breathing was expected from the new motor – 75bhp in street trim, 100 for racing. There were changes from the car engine – toothed-belt cam drive instead of gears, for one. Norton also wanted a 360-degree crankshaft for ease of emissions tuning; and to negate the resulting vibration, counter-balancers weighing 9kg were added. On top of that, a hefty flywheel went between the crankpins, so there was no central main bearing. Problems with vibration and carburation persisted, and the engine weighed 88kg; so at the start of 1976 there was still a lot to do on the Challenge.

As the year began, Kawasaki reconsidered its racing position in the US, and provided KR750s and some support for Gary Nixon (with Erv Kanemoto) and Ron Pierce (Kevin Cameron). Down under, Gregg Hansford got a KR for the first time and opened his year with a win in the Australian TT from Pat Hennen's XR11. The new bikes (for the UK as well) had new crankshafts, sturdier big ends, and 38mm carbs replacing the 35s; there was also a new radiator, and a new, flat-sided fairing that would serve the model for the rest of its life.

In January, all seemed to be quiet at Yamaha: some 40 C-model TZ750s were being made: these were, for all practical purposes, identical to the 1975 B-model. Modest enough, perhaps, but there were rumours – as ever – of something better in the wings.

And there it was, at Daytona. In outline, Yamaha's new factory bike was nothing new: a revised TZ750 engine in an 0W23 grand prix cantilever frame, but the four at Daytona, provided for Roberts, Cecotto, Baker, and factory rider Hideo Kanaya, redefined the TZ750's performance (there was a fifth bike for Ago, who decided not to make the journey to Florida, annoyed at the absence of start money and the AMA claim rule that might again see him lose his motorcycle). The factory engine differed principally from the stocker in having six transfer ports rather than four, and the bikes were dotted with titanium (axles, fairing brackets, mudguard stays, brake pistons, fasteners and chain adjusters) and magnesium (lower triple clamp, engine casings and covers). The bottom line was a 140bhp motorcycle that weighed 130kg (a drop of 18kg on its predecessors). This was the fabled 0W31, and Kenny Roberts used his to good effect, clocking 182mph through the speed trap and qualifying fastest at 111.456mph. Roberts thought it all a bit much, however. "We don't need this," he told *Cycle* magazine, "all it's going to do is piss people off."

The opposition was in some disarray, even without the Yamaha. Du Hamel was sitting it out with a broken leg from a snowmobile accident. Gary Nixon's KR was melting pistons and suffering from fork flex, while the Kawasaki UK bikes missed the event altogether, citing a lack of spares. Suzuki's major presence came from the new British Texaco Heron Team Suzuki, using its 1975-spec bikes (as was Pat Hennen, whose mount

Sheene was back at Daytona in 1976, sparring with mate Gary Nixon. He retired with his drive chain jumping its sprockets. Nixon was second, but nothing could live with Yamaha's 0W31s. (Courtesy Ian Falloon)

was rated at 124bhp). Team number one Barry Sheene was beset with problems that included a blown head gasket, failed water pump drive, and gear-selection difficulties. "In three days of practice," growled Sheene, "I did just 21 laps." Sheene was himself struggling: the leg he'd broken at Cadwell was giving him trouble, and fluid on the knee had to be drained by syringe.

So the story of Daytona 1976 was the story of the 0W31: Cecotto was first into the lead, then Roberts, then Cecotto again. Baker moved up, and the three pulled clear of Kanaya's 0W31 and the KR750s of Hansford and Nixon. Baker retired with ignition failure on lap 10, Hansford on lap 22 with a broken chain; Sheene, using an aerolastic to help movement of his injured leg, held sixth, his XR11 appreciably slower than the leading Yamahas, until he too went out with a broken chain (as did team-mate Newbold). From half distance Cecotto pulled away despite seizing his best engine in practice, and now holing an exhaust in cornering and so losing power – which, said some, might have saved his tyre. Roberts, still second but losing ground, was battling a badly worn rear cover that punctured on lap 43 as he entered the chicane at around 155mph. He stayed on, limped back to the pits and lost two laps while Carruthers and his crew changed the wheel. As the laps ticked away Nixon secured second and Hennen – fresh from winning the Marlboro Series in New Zealand – third. Cecotto won on a tyre that was down to the cords. It was Yamaha's fifth Daytona in a row, this time with eight TZ750s in the top ten.

COUNTBACK

Two weeks later the cavalcade regrouped at the San Carlos circuit in Venezuela for the second round of the F750 Prize (of 11). This was the first major meeting in South America since the '64 Argentinian GP and the organisers offered a £10,000 first prize. Roberts, however, had apparently mislaid his passport. Despite the significant drawbacks of poor organisation and near 40°C heat, Cecotto eased away to win the first leg comfortably, while early leader Hansford stopped with a seized engine, Sheene with a broken conrod, and Pons after crashing and breaking his left leg. Baker was second from Nixon (running an engine borrowed from Neville Doyle after his crank had failed) – though whether second place was indeed Baker's was a matter of dispute: the Yamaha Canada man had pitted after four laps to clear a flooded carb, and although his team said he was stopped for just 10 seconds, others thought he'd been in the pits for a full lap.

None of which was of great concern to Cecotto, who got away at the start of the second leg to put a minute on Baker in second place. Sheene scrapped for third with Michel Rougerie, Nixon and John Newbold, but then pulled out saying he had no hope of winning. Baker then fell at the hairpin, but remounted to win after Cecotto retired with something like heat stroke. Nixon was second from Newbold's XR11 and declared overall winner, the official timekeepers believing Baker's first leg stop had put him a lap down. Before the day was out, though, they'd given the points to Baker from Nixon and Newbold. Protests were lodged, angry words spoken. The issue was referred to Geneva and the FIM, where a decision would be made later in the year.

Baker won both legs of the third F750 round at Imola from a field that included Roberts, albeit briefly. Cecotto was quickly gone, crashing on the opening lap of the first race with a broken clip-on; he was unharmed but his engine shipped sand. Roberts led for that first lap, then Baker passed him and got away. KR's engine then tightened, chucking him off and giving him a bang on the head that was serious enough to end his day. Ago too was out, slowing as his engine lost its edge to join a list of retirees that included Ditchburn and Grant with crank failure. Michel

Rougerie moved into second, and stayed there despite being hustled by Sheene, who later said: "I couldn't even stay in his slipstream."

Baker had a moment of excitement late in the opening leg when his engine nipped up and then freed itself. His crew chief, Bob Work, rebuilt it using bits from Ago's bike. The Italian then took to the PA to explain why he wouldn't be riding in the second leg. The crowd responded with the Bolognese equivalent of a raspberry. Baker led from start to finish, again from Rougerie and Sheene. Cecotto lasted just a lap, discovering that his engine was still choked with sand. Still, he'd done better than Nixon, whose KR750 had disappeared in transit, and was thought to be heading to Australia. Erv Kanemoto had two engines with him, so Nixon asked to borrow a Kawasaki UK chassis – but Stan Shenton couldn't get Japan on the line to ask permission. If that wasn't enough, Kanemoto had his briefcase stolen, losing ten years' worth of records.

Croxford rode the Challenge briefly at Imola but failed to qualify, clocking 69th fastest before a recurrence of the gearbox problem. At the opening round of the Transatlantic Trophy the gearbox played up again, and Croxford promptly announced his retirement. "I feel someone else would do far better," he explained. NVT chairman Dennis Poore stepped in to say the Challenge would be withdrawn from competition until further notice.

With Barry Sheene back in the fold, the UK team wasn't quite so easy to knock over in the Transatlantic Trophy; but at cold, blustery Brands Hatch Baker took both races, Roberts and Sheene bagging a second and a third apiece. Nixon, reunited with his KR750, was fourth in the first race, and scores were close going into the second round at Mallory Park where Sheene and Roberts had one win each; but with the UK packing the midfield, the home side led going into the final round.

Baker collected two more wins at Oulton Park, but the series belonged once again to the UK. In the first race Roberts got the better of Sheene for second, but the Brits again packed the middle placings, led by Ron Haslam's Yamaha and John Williams on a Texaco Heron Suzuki XR11 reduced to second and third gears. Even so, with Roberts and Baker leading the last race of the six, the USA led the series by a single point – until Roberts crashed, looping his 0W31 on Clay Hill at 110mph. Jim Evans, too, went down and then Ron Pierce stopped with gear selector problems; so with Haslam up to second and Williams third, the flag came down on Baker with the final margin a more respectable, if still slender, 412-384 in favour of the UK.

Sheene had had a good weekend, as second individual scorer with 77 points to Baker's 92. He also started his *MCN* Superbike campaign with a win at the Brands Hatch opening round, getting home from Grant after the Yorkshireman had been forced wide by a backmarker on the ninth lap of ten. With Ditch a solitary third from Williams, Dave Potter brought the first Yamaha home in an uncharacteristic fifth place.

Precocious talent: John Newbold ran well for Suzuki GB in 1976, finding himself in contention for the FIM F750 Prize as the season wound down.
(Courtesy Elwyn Roberts)

For the meantime, 50,000 British fans could attest to the good health of F750 racing. The FIM was worried, however, and set about its spring conference determined to tackle its misgivings about the class and its rampant machinery. Led by the technical commission, the FIM proposed a series of performance-cutting measures for F750 that intended to reduce the possibility of catastrophic tyre failure. These could include a reduction in engine capacity, a reduction in carburettor intake size and/or silencing the engines further from the 115dB levels introduced at Daytona. Sentence was deferred, however, until the autumn congress.

The FIM made one firm decision, however. The Isle of Man TT would lose its world championship status from 1977, and would instead become the focus of a new world series for 'pure road' circuits. "To eliminate the TT straightforward from the calendar of classic events would harm the TT in itself and motorcycle sport in general," asserted the governing body, which asked the ACU to prepare regulations for the new series. ACU chairman Norman Dixon cast the move in its best possible light: "The TT series will now be recognised as the supreme prize of the FIM," he explained.

Beyond the glitter of the big-money season-openers, F750 still struggled. Ago and Cecotto took their 0W31s to a cashed-up non-title meeting in Belgium, while the Spanish round of the title went ahead at Jarama. It attracted just six riders from beyond Spain's borders and both races were won by one of them, Parisian Michel Rougerie.

Barry Sheene was, likewise, elsewhere, staying at home to notch a win in the second round of the *MCN* Superbike Championship at Cadwell Park. In a classic piece of melodrama, Sheene's crew worked feverishly to replace a radiator hose clip and broken tacho cable on his XR11 as the grid formed up. Sure enough, Sheene made a poor start, even by his mediocre standards, and wheelied away in pursuit of leader Grant. By half distance he was just three seconds adrift; on the last lap he and Grant went up the mountain side by side, and concluded their scrap through the woodlands with Sheene in front by a wheel. Geoff Barry put his Yamaha into a distant third after Barry Ditchburn had stopped with oil pouring from his gearbox.

In distant and sunnier climes, Australia's racing community spent Easter at Bathurst and its picturesque Mount Panorama circuit, 130 miles west of Sydney. Motorcycles had been racing there since 1938, and the crowds that lined much of the track's 3.8-mile length had seen stirring dices: Bill Horsman and Ginger Molloy in 1972, Hansford and Willing in 1974 – but this year they'd seen something different: Yamaha development rider Ike Takai took the big race, using the 0W31 Kanaya had ridden at Daytona. He was clocked at 186.3mph on Conrod Straight, while Warren Willing's private Yamaha logged 181mph and took eight seconds off the lap record while chasing the Japanese; most surprising of all was that Masahiro Wada's factory KR750 Kawasaki was 10mph slower than Hansford's Neville Doyle-fettled H2R. Kawasaki asked Mr Doyle if he would kindly stop racing the air-cooled triple so it might examine the bike, and try to establish what made it so fast. It was the beginning of a beautiful friendship.

LAST MAN STANDING

F750 stuttered along. As Sweden cancelled its round of the title, due to run alongside the Anderstorp GP, the field regrouped at Nivelles in Belgium where Nixon took the points after more fancied runners retired: Sheene led early in the opening race, but stopped with a broken water pump, Grant lost a lap fixing a loose plug, and then battled with a chain hopping its sprockets, Ditchburn blew up, and van Dulmen crashed at the hairpin. Noddy Newbold then looked good, but lost a lap fixing a broken zip on his leathers. At the end of the journey, Nixon won from Dave Potter with Noddy a game third. Grant upheld Kawasaki's honour in the second leg, pushing through the field to pass Nixon and Potter on the penultimate lap and lead a 1-2 for Team Green. Noddy was fourth this time, battling with a broken clutch cable.

At Nogaro the following weekend for the sixth round, local boy Christian Estrosi went at it with Swiss sparring partner Philippe Coulon, finishing 1-2 in both races. Again, a number of the more fancied runners stopped, including Sheene with a broken gearbox in the opening leg, Grant (ditto),

Cecotto with tyre and handling problems. Ditch, who finished third in the opening leg, was thrown off by a broken crank in the second. Ago led for a time in the first leg but didn't really trouble the leading pair, and Nixon doggedly battled into sixth and fourth to take a seven-point lead at the top of the table.

Sheene fared better back at a sodden Brands for the third round of the *MCN* Superbike title, where, as at Cadwell Park, he came from behind, but this time only getting up to fourth behind the Kawasaki twins, led by Grant, with Potter third – whose day's racing (including a win in the 350 race) made him King of Brands.

Williams' good form continued at the Isle of Man, where he won the Open Classic TT by more than a minute on an XR11 that was so "hopelessly overgeared" that he didn't once get into top. Favourite Grant went out after one lap with clutch failure and Alex George finished second on his Nico Bakker-framed TZ750 after choosing the wrong tyres – intermediates instead of slicks – and Tony Rutter put his TZ350 into third.

Sheene rejoined the action at the Mallory Post-TT meeting to win the fourth round of the *MCN* Superbike series, passing Ditch after early leader Grant had jumped off over the bumps at Gerard's. There seemed little doubt that open-class racing was proving awkward for the stars in 1976. Even Sheene, who was doing much as he liked in the 500cc World Championship, found it difficult to coax winning performances out of his increasingly stale XR11 at international level. Kenny Roberts, too, still battling in the dirt, was having perhaps the one mediocre season of his professional career, colliding with a backmarker at Loudon, the second of the AMA's four road races, and handing the race to Baker.

Preliminary sketches from the ACU of 'Formula TT' were released in July, and Neville Goss, a member of the FIM technical committee, pushed them around the press. The formula looked familiar, at least in part: catalogue bikes, four-strokes only, 300 to 1000cc; standard barrel and gearbox castings, standard cases; slicks prohibited in favour of 'all-weather' tyres; race duration between 250 and 500km. Before the end of the month, the detailed formula had been submitted to the FIM – and rejected. Exactly why the plan failed no-one seemed quite to know, though some suggested the ACU hadn't done enough preparation, and *Motor Cycle News* thought it might have been because the ACU plan contained no provision for two-strokes. Whatever the reason, Geneva wasn't saying: "I cannot give any information on Bureau Centrale directives," said FIM Secretary Jean-Francois Chevalley.

Back in the real world, Barry Sheene claimed the Brands Hatch fifth round of the *MCN* Superbike series, while most points went to Mick Grant, who finished second but helped himself to five bonus points for setting the fastest lap. In the US, Steve Baker took his second AMA win of the year in KR's back yard, at Laguna Seca. As at Loudon, he was in a class of his own; and, as at Loudon, Nixon fell, though not before he'd taken his Kanemoto-prepped KR750 (equipped with a new, sturdier C&J frame that moved the engine forward) to a good second in the opening leg. Which just left Roberts, who again struggled, this time with tyres: in the first leg he ran Goodyears, and was sliding badly enough to let Nixon (Michelin) and Baker (Dunlop) disappear. He switched to a Dunlop rear in the second leg, and held second despite gearshift problems. Nixon, meanwhile, unloaded at half-distance: "Erv and I lose again."

Recrossing the Atlantic didn't look like stopping Baker either. He cleaned up in the first race of the Silverstone F750 round before a crowd of 60,000. In the wide open spaces of Northamptonshire Baker pulled away from Grant's KR, while Sheene struggled to make the top three, scrapping with Ron Haslam and Pons. Nixon worked into the top ten until stopped by a failed big-end bearing. Grant's KR broke a chain and Haslam's Yamaha seized, so after the stops Sheene plugged away in a respectable second from Pons, Read and Palomo. Grant got his revenge in the second leg, taking the lead from Sheene – for once making a decent start – then sitting behind Baker for five laps, until the American pitted twice with a deflating front tyre and then retired at Stowe. Sheene stopped with a suspected broken crank on lap 22 but Grant was away, leading home Palomo, Ditch, Jack Findlay, and the rapidly improving Potter. Palomo got the points as overall winner and began his climb up the table. Nixon, still leading on points, hadn't started the second leg because of a row over start money.

Sheene was soon notching up another win in the *MCN* Superbike series, this time at Oulton Park. He sampled a new 837cc version of the XR11 in practice, but stuck with the proven – and as it turned out, faster – 750 for the race. Still, he struggled to match the Kawasakis for pace, with Grant jumping into a clear lead, and Ditch passing Sheene for second before the flag, Roger Marshall hustling past Potter for fourth. Four rounds to go, Sheene 93 points, Grant 76, Ditchburn 71.

Grant won again in the next round at Scarborough, albeit in a race marred by mechanical problems. Sheene fielded a new bike for the occasion, a 54 x 54mm RG500 to which Frank had fitted 56mm pistons, giving a capacity of 532cc. It wouldn't meet the homologation requirements of F750 but was fine for the more liberal terrain of the Superbike series, and Sheene led for three laps when a crankcase breather burst. He stopped and spent 40 seconds cutting and refitting the hose while Grant (riding alone for Kawasaki with Ditch at Assen) swept past and held on to win, despite struggling with a chain jumping its sprockets. Geoff Barry was second from Steve Manship, with Sheene fourth. Sheene 101 points, Grant 96, Ditch 71.

The penultimate round of the F750 Prize, at Assen, went ahead in mixed weather. Read won the first leg after Ago had problems with oil on his visor and Cecotto fell after losing the back end in the chicane, then watching in horror as his 0W31 caught fire. Read led home local hero van

Dulmen and Victor Palomo, while more fancied riders fell away: Ditch with a misfire, Nixon after being caught in the rain with a slick on the rear. Ago fared better in the second leg, breaking clear of a six-way dice to win from Ballington and Newbold. Palomo, on a Sonauto Yamaha, added a fourth place to his third in the opener, giving him the overall win from van Dulmen. Nixon failed to finish with a broken gear selector shaft, and with one round to go Nixon led Palomo by a single point at the top of the table, 47-46.

Baker completed his European season with a win in the Race of the Year while early challenger Phil Read's Yamaha stopped with a seized engine, and Sheene hustled his 532cc square four into second place with an out of balance flywheel. But Sheene had no problem in the *MCN* Superbike outing, passing Grant for the lead early, and then fending off Baker, who'd pushed Grant back to third. Two rounds to go: Sheene 116, Grant 106, Ditch 79. At Cadwell, both Grant and Sheene got poor starts while visitor Gary Nixon made a break from Read. Sheene pushed through the pack; Marshall still led into the last lap, but then got it wrong at Park Corner and ran wide, letting Sheene through from Ditch and Grant, with Marshall fourth. Sheene 136, Grant 121, Ditch 96.

Then, at Brands Hatch, Sheene won the *MCN* Superbike title going away, passing John Williams and Grant, then fighting off the Kawasaki man's last-ditch challenge to secure a third *MCN* Superbike title: Sheene 176, Grant 155, Ditch 96. For Ditch came the consolation of a win in the Gauloises Powerbike International, revving his KR750 to an unheard of 10,500 to beat Read and Grant.

At Riverside, whence the final AMA road race of the year had been moved, Kenny Roberts at last came out on top – though without facing Baker, who'd crashed and hurt himself in the 250 race. KR led from start to finish, with Yamaha-mounted Takazumi Katayama and Pat Evans following him home. Kawasaki had a poor weekend, Ron Pierce leading the broken green wave in fifth, with Nixon recovering from carb problems to finish eighth and Du Hamel ninth. Kawasaki was again on the point of withdrawing from US racing, now admitting that the team's bikes were "no match for the factory 0W31 Yamahas."

Finally, at Hockenheim, John Newbold gave himself a chance of taking the FIM F750 Prize after winning a hard-fought opening leg, passing Guy Coulon at the Sachskurve on the last lap to lead him home from Grant and Palomo. Nixon was seventh in the opener, slowed by a loose filler cap, but made amends by winning the second race from Palomo and Kneubühler. Newbold led from the start but collided with a crashed bike and fell, while Grant retired with a wheel out of balance. Palomo had done enough to win the round, and led the overall points score with 61 points to Nixon's 59, a decision on Venezuela still to come.

The racing was over. Now it was up to the FIM.

4

PUSHING ON AN OPEN DOOR

The FIM autumn congress, held in Bruges for 1976, had plenty to discuss; among other things, the future of the TT, the future of F750 and the identity of the 1976 FIM F750 Prize holder.

The last item: after the final round of the 1976 F750 series at Hockenheim, Victor Palomo led Gary Nixon in the final tally 61 points to 59. The count was predicated on the belief that Steve Baker had been runner-up to Cecotto in the first race in Venezuela (placing Nixon third) after stopping for seconds to clear a flooded carb. The Nixon camp thought that Baker had lost a full lap in the pits, and that Nixon had therefore finished second and so won the round – which would give him 62 points to Palomo's 61. They lobbied accordingly, but the Venezuelan organisers were unable to produce the time sheets from the meeting, and so the matter could not be unequivocally put to bed. The FIM therefore struck the Venezuelan round and its dramas from the record, and subtracted its points from the final tally. Without Venezuela, Palomo was still the 1976 F750 Prize holder from Nixon, but by 61 points to 47.

F750 itself continued to prove contentious. The FIM technical committee restated its view that the class bikes were too potent and outperforming their tyres and suspension. Again, constraining measures were considered: limiting bike capacity, limiting the carburettor intake area, but few decisions concerning F750 were made. Of those that were, the most important was that, "despite opposition from the Bureau Centrale," congress voted overwhelmingly to give the class its world championship, starting in 1977 – a year earlier than expected. Congress further voted to raise the minimum capacity for the class to 501cc and to reduce the minimum racing distance from 200 miles per round to 200 kilometres, with everywhere except Spain running two 100km legs to avoid fuel stops. Lastly, the noise limits imposed in 1976 were to stay at 115dB.

Altogether, 11 rounds were sanctioned for the world championship, with additions in Austria and Canada, and two – Daytona and Laguna Seca – in the USA. The French round would be moved to Dijon, and the British meeting to Brands Hatch (moved from Silverstone to make way for the inaugural British GP). There were still problems. In the pages of *Motor Cycle*, scribe Chris Carter criticised the disparity between F750 prize funds, comparing the thousands of dollars offered at Daytona with the meagre sums posted at the lesser European meetings. Moreover, he said, even the existing scales of start and prize money had not kept pace with those paid at grand prix meetings.

Yamaha's preparations for the season began with a major overhaul of the instrument that dominated the era, the TZ750. The coming year would be the year of the TZ750D, a replica, in outline at least, of the 0W31 the factory campaigned in 1976. In fact, the production bike's engine wasn't much changed from the C that preceded it. Top end mods were limited to pistons with shorter skirts, and cutaways rather than slots, and a couple of changes to the ports – the inlet booster was widened 2mm, and the exhaust port raised 1.5mm and widened 3.5mm. Down below there were minor changes to main and small-end bearings to improve durability. Bigger news was the use of the Carruthers-designed over and under exhaust system that released more of the engine's power; and the biggest news was of a production version of the 0W31's monoshock chassis, which lowered the bike's centre of gravity and trimmed 6kg from its mass, even with the frame's extra bracing tubes. Steering was sharpened with 24.5 degrees of rake, and rear wheel travel dramatically increased. There was also a fatter rear wheel rim at 3½in, up from the C's 3in. The TZ-D might have lacked much of the exotic material packed into the 0W31, but it could still make careers. The new bike was priced at £6500 and $5195 in the US.

Development of the TZ750 stopped with the D, although the bike would be sold with minuscule changes during 1978 (E) and '79 (F). Greg Bennett, in his epic work *Yamaha Production Two-Stroke Road Racing Motorcycles*, notes that 609 TZ750s of all types were sold during its six years in production, 30 of which were Ds, and a further 162 Es and Fs.

The factory bikes sent to Daytona for Baker, Cecotto, and Roberts, now dubbed the YZR750, were in largely the same as they'd been in '76 but for strikingly revised streamlining. Kawasaki, on the other hand, had reworked its KR750 and produced a lightweight version, dubbed the 602L. Modifications included magnesium cases, a bigger radiator, and improved porting. The 38mm carbs were mounted to the chassis to reduce vibration, and rubber-mounted to the inlet ports. There was also a reworked exhaust system and revisions to the swinging arm. Dry weight of the newcomer was a trim 136kg; new bikes went to Gregg Hansford and Murray Sayle in Australia, and Mick Grant and Barry Ditchburn in the UK.

Suzuki, on the other hand, had nothing to campaign. The TR750 was pensioned off, and a bigger version of the RG500, the 652cc XR23, was in

The final refinement of the KR750, the 602L, came in 1977. Mick Grant used it to take back-to-back Classic TT wins. (Courtesy Ian Falloon)

development for the 1978 season – when Suzuki had expected the F750 world championship to begin. The newcomer was the forerunner of the XR22 500 grand prix bike and the first of the stepped-cylinder disc-valve square fours, the modified layout being adopted to drop the centre of gravity and improve airflow around the engine. The principal differences between the big banger and the 54 x 54mm GP bike were a 62mm bore and 36mm Mikuni carbs, rather than 34s; as delivered, the XR23 made around 135bhp, de-tuned from earlier specifications but still enough to meet the factory 750 Yamahas toe to toe – should it happen.

A handful of XR23s were readied for 1977, well short of the 25 needed to meet F750 homologation requirements. "These aren't just overbored 500s," said Suzuki team boss Rex White. "The engines have the same layout, but all the components have been beefed up to handle the extra power." The only other possibility, Sheene's home-brewed 532cc RG500, simply wasn't eligible for F750. In any case, Texaco Heron Team Suzuki had some rebuilding to do, after tensions between Sheene and John Williams divided the team in '76. Perhaps new recruit Pat Hennen was thankful to be in New Zealand contesting the Marlboro Series, with the first of the XR23s coming his way.

Hennen won the series – his third in a row – ceding overall points to Stu Avant in the first round at Pukekohe, but then taking both wins around the cemetery at Wanganui and at Timaru after being harried by John Woodley in the first race, and Warren Willing in the second. Hennen clinched the series at Ruapuna, taking a tight win from Willing's TZ750 in the first race and then finishing runner-up to the Australian in the second: Hennen 192 points, Willing 163, Chas Mortimer 137.

While Hennen's achievement fleetingly made Suzuki the dominant force in international 750cc competition, Yamaha suffered a setback: in February the TZ750Ds so far sold were recalled for rectification of a crankshaft problem (the 35 that had gone to the US for Daytona getting priority treatment), traced to the engines being assembled with their outer main bearings the wrong way round. Meanwhile Helmut Bonsch, the president of the FIM's technical commission, had an exchange of views on F750 with *Motor Cycle*'s veteran technical scribe, Vic Willoughby. Bonsch restated the commission's concerns that the modern racing 750 (ie, the TZ) could overpower its tyres at speeds up to 125mph, and again recommended a reduction in carburettor intake area to reduce power. He also highlighted the thirst of the modern racing two-stroke, and pointed to the discrepancy in fuel consumption between two-strokes and four-strokes. Willoughby let rip: it was "no part of the FIM's brief to attempt the task of protecting riders," he said. "Any rider worth his salt will regard these mollycoddling proposals as an insult to his intelligence."

Such salt as there might have been was used to pay for new TZ750Ds, grumbles about price and allocation notwithstanding. In Britain Ds had been ordered for, among others, Ron Haslam, Dave Potter, Roger Marshall, and John Newbold. In Australia, Warren Willing had sold his '76 Bathurst-lap-record-setting bike, with its 0W29 engine and Peter Campbell/Chris Dowde chassis, to Greg Johnson, and had acquired a new D model in time for Daytona. Bob Rosenthal, spending the season in domestic campaigns, rode a D for Victoria's Yamaha distributor, Milledge Motorcycles. The Europeans were headed by Patrick Pons and Christian Sarron; the phalanx of American D-runners included Skip Aksland, Gary Nixon, Phil McDonald and Randy Cleek.

Tyres again made news at Daytona. With Michelin and Dunlop both pulling out, saying they couldn't guarantee their covers would last the distance, Goodyear was left to go it alone, and despite Kenny Roberts' assertion that the American outfit's new tyres had a 30-lap safety margin in them, the FIM intervened and after a three-hour meeting it was announced that the 1977 Daytona 200 would be run as two 100-mile legs separated by a 55-minute break.

Baker won the first leg by 28 seconds from Roberts, who was using his spare engine after Carruthers had pulled the better one with a problem diagnosed as gearbox oil getting into cylinders one and two. Cecotto parked his factory Yamaha with a gearbox oil leak while Katayama claimed third place from Aussies Hansford and Willing. During the break the rain came, stayed for the afternoon and forced the cancellation of the second leg. No one was happy, but least distressed was Baker, who picked up $19,000 for the afternoon and had given himself a handy lead in the newly instituted 'World Cup,' which included the Imola 200 and the *Moto Journal* 200. The three-event series was backed by AGV, and anyone winning all three events would collect $60,000.

KR

So the factory Yamahas aimed for Europe, but not until Kenny Roberts had won the Charlotte national in a resurgent AMA programme that scheduled six road races. Roberts was still on top when the caravan got to Imola. In a meeting punctuated with crashes by at least 40 riders, and many of those more than once, Roberts was reunited with the good Daytona engine Carruthers had reckoned was 5-6mph faster than the competition, easing away to win the first leg by 13 seconds from Baker. He repeated the dose in the second leg, again leading Baker home with Ago third. After two rounds of the inaugural F750 World Championship, Baker and Roberts had 27 points each, Katayama 15.

Sheene and Hennen were at last able to join the party with their new, and largely untried, XR23s for the Transatlantic Trophy, but with Roberts again in imperious form, they made limited impression. After a second at

By right and by conquest: he'd been favourite every year since '74. Kenny Roberts at last got a Daytona 200 win in 1978, leading home Johnny Cecotto. (Courtesy Mary Grothe)

Brands and a third and fourth at Mallory, Sheene got a win on the board in the first race at Oulton Park; but by then the horse had bolted – KR took four wins and Baker closed the weekend with a win in the second race at Oulton: USA 410, UK 379, Roberts in unstoppable mood.

An unhappy footnote came at Oulton Park when Paul Smart crashed at Cascades in the final race of the series, and so said goodbye to racing as a participant. He got up and dusted himself off in time to see his recently acquired TZ750 catch light, standing by helplessly as it burnt itself out. "A lot of people said I shouldn't have been in the British team," he told reporters later. "And the fire was the last straw."

The *MCN* Superbike Championship, now co-sponsored by Brut cosmetics, made its customary start at the Brands Transatlantic Trophy meeting, but the event was run under a national permit and so subject to the ACU's new ban on slicks. The big names pulled out after qualifying, leaving Potter's Ted Broad TZ alone on the front row; after he went out with a seized engine, Marshall was on his own, winning from Haslam and Woods.

Sheene next went to the *Moto Journal* 200 at Paul Ricard, but pulled out in disgust after twice pitting for misleading signals shown on the electronic scoreboard. He was in good company. Gregg Hansford, after making his first visit to Imola and stopping with a misfire, took his bow in the south of France, and had to pit repeatedly for 'fuel adjustment.' He also rode with a broken bone in his foot from a practice crash. So the Americans and their YZR750s were out front again, with Baker this time beating Roberts – who said he had no power coming off turns – and Guy Coulon.

Now, with the early spectaculars over, the long haul of the season got under way. For Roberts, that meant returning home to dispute the grand national championship under its new name, the Camel Pro Series, while Sheene's primary task was to defend his 500cc world championship. Baker and Cecotto were likewise bound for the 500c world title, with their 0W35s. Baker also had the F750 world championship on his list of priorities and so, with a total of nine other international riders, made the journey to Spain for the third meeting on schedule, already criticised by *Motor Cycle*'s Chris Carter for its "miserable" start money. Just 16 riders came under starter's orders at Jarama and Baker won comfortably, easing away from Boet van Dulmen at three-quarter distance. Van Dulmen then fell, braking too hard for a double right-hander, and letting Sarron into second from Hubert Rigal. While Sarron and Rigal each received prize money, van Dulmen began his 1200-mile journey to Salzburg and the Austrian Grand Prix with a damaged TZ750 and his £40 start money. Baker 42, KR 27, Sarron 24.

Baker faltered at Nogaro, where Christian Estrosi again cleaned up, winning both races from Philippe Coulon and the subdued American; but he was back on top at Brands Hatch, and, although harried by the locals, won both races. In the first leg Potter gave chase but fell at Westfield. Ditchburn took up the pursuit, and then Grant after Ditch stopped with brake problems. Grant was less than three seconds adrift at the flag,

High tide: Gregg Hansford (leading) and Yvon Du Hamel ran 1-2 for Kawasaki in the 1977 Canadian F750 World Championship round at Mosport Park. (Courtesy Mary Grothe)

but Baker, as so often, controlled the pace – yet Grant at least hoisted something other than a Yamaha onto the podium for the first time in the championship. Baker was back in control for the second race, albeit with a different supporting cast, after Grant fell at Dingle Dell. This time Haslam was second despite a swollen wrist from a practice crash, with Ditchburn third. Five rounds done: Baker 67, Roberts 27, Sarron and Coulon 24 apiece.

After a false start at Brands, the Brut-*MCN* Superbike Championship got going at Cadwell Park where, with the Kawasakis of Grant and Ditchburn away at the Spanish F750 round, the Texaco Heron Suzuki outfit ran 1-2-3, Sheene leading the way from Steve Parrish and Hennen – all on their new XR23s. Sheene did it again in the numbing cold of Brands; Grant was out on the first lap with a leaking fuel tank, and Potter gained the lead and disappeared, but not fast enough for the Londoner, who recovered from his customary poor start to chip away at Potter's 54-second lead, getting in front with four laps to run.

Grant's turn to top the podium came at the Classic TT, where he led home Charlie Williams' Maxton TZ350 and had his '77-spec KR750 clocked at 190mph into the bargain (though the moped that tripped the lights at 50mph took a little explaining). Back on the mainland for the Post-TT meeting at Mallory Park, Sheene again did his burn from the stern thing in the *MCN* Superbike race, squeezing past early leaders Marshall and Haslam. Four rounds gone: Sheene 60, Marshall 40, Haslam 29 and Parrish 27.

Meanwhile, Kenny Roberts' last domestic season was producing results commensurate with his talent. Life was still difficult on the dirt: at the San Jose mile he'd been sidelined by a rod through the cases, had scored a modest fifth in the Oklahoma half-mile, then a ninth at the Louisville half-mile, there saying he had trouble getting power to the ground, but on the tar he was in a class of his own. After another frustrating second at Daytona, and his win at Charlotte, he won again at Loudon, overcoming a hand hurt in a short-track crash a fortnight earlier, an exhaust holed by enthusiastic cornering and a late charge by local hero Nixon, to win by ten seconds. A month later at Sears Point he made it three in a row, starting from a lowly grid position caused by a broken chain adjuster in his heat. It made no difference. By the end of the first lap Roberts was on leader Skip Aksland's back wheel and three laps later was out front carving a clinical loop through the California track's 2.5 miles of undulating twists and turns, pulling away from Aksland and Dale Singleton, who'd fought clear of Romero and a fading Nixon. At the halfway point of the Camel Pro Series, KR led Harley man Ted Boody 135 points to 134.

King Kenny, though still a long way from negotiating with Yamaha about racing in Europe, was, nonetheless, recalibrating himself on new opposition. On the subject of Steve Baker he told *Cycle News*: "He keeps the bike heeled over until he's past the apex, so he's getting the power back on before he's straightened up – that's what causes his wobbles." Considered judgement from the leading edge.

Sheene, by now in rather better control of the 500cc world championship than of the *MCN* Superbike chase, was caught on the hop at Snetterton. Making a bad start in the damp going, he got into second but was still 20 seconds down on Frenchman Bernard Fau's TZ-D at the flag. In a poor meeting by Sheene's standards, he managed just fourth in the Race of Aces, well down on winner Hennen, making his first visit to Snetterton. A wet Oulton Park ran to a similar formula: Sheene started badly and pushed into second, but couldn't catch Hennen. He fared better than Grant, however, who added a DNF to his third at Snetterton when he fell while scrapping with Hennen. While the Yorkshireman regained momentum at soggy Scarborough for round seven, Sheene stumbled, retiring his 532cc RG from the 1000cc event with a collapsed wheel bearing, and from the *MCN* Superbike scrap with gearbox failure. Grant won both, and Hennen took second in the Superbike race from Potter's TZ-D. Seven rounds gone, Sheene 84, Hennen 56, Marshall 44.

There was less drama at the top of the table when the F750 World Championship resumed in August. Baker carried on where he'd left off, winning the first race in Austria from Ago and Sarron. As at Daytona, the second race was washed out, but Baker hadn't long to wait before he became the USA's first world road race champion. At Zolder he was again unbeatable, clearing out in both races from Marco Lucchinelli and Katayama, both on Yamaha TZ-Ds. With just seven of the 11 rounds done, Baker couldn't be caught on points, and joined Sheene in becoming world champion at a canter. Not that he let up: a week later at Assen, Baker and Lucchinelli again went head to head, Baker winning the first race, Lucky the second, the Italian claiming the overall win by 0.6 seconds on aggregate time – and Christian Sarron getting a good view of the action with third in both. Eight rounds gone, Baker 109, Sarron 44, Lucchinelli 40.

CLOSING TIME

The culmination to KR's season didn't have quite the same ring of triumph. In the four dirt track events following the Sears Point road race, Roberts recorded two DNFs and a fourth place, with the Santa Fe short track rained off. The Pocono road race was very different, of course, with KR again powering away, again from Aksland, at two seconds a lap. Nixon and Singleton went at it for third after Romero faded, but the man at the front had notched his 24th national win, and his fourth of the year. In spite of everything he was still in front of the Camel Pro Series: Roberts 176, Jay Springsteen 159.

American and European interests coincided at Laguna Seca for the second US bite at the F750 world title. With Roberts absent (the event paid no Camel Pro points) Aksland took on newly minted champion Baker and came out on top – with a little help from Gregg Hansford, who dived underneath Baker in the last laps of the opener, pushing him back to third while Aksland got away to win. Baker won the second race, but with Aksland on his tail and Hansford this time third, the day belonged to the privateer. Hansford went even better a week later at a wet Mosport Park for the Canadian round, beating local hero Yvon Du Hamel, out of retirement for the occasion, in a 1-2 for Kawasaki. The Queenslander pipped Baker in the first race and then got the best of a four-way dice on a drying track second time out. Hansford, Baker, Du Hamel and Mike Baldwin (TZ-D) went at it for the full distance in "one of the most exciting races seen at Mosport," reported *Motor Cycle*. Hansford crossed the line to collect his first overall win of the championship.

Baker sat out the Hockenheim final round, leaving Ago to take up the running on his YZR750 and post a valedictory double win from Katayama. Sarron secured runner-up spot after Lucchinelli stopped with ignition failure. Final points: Baker 131, Sarron 47, Ago 45, Hansford the first non-Yamaha in seventh overall with 33 points. In the manufacturers' championship the gulf was even wider, with Yamaha notching 160 points to Kawasaki's 33.

Two YZR750s finished in the top three of the F750 world title. A third, Roberts', completed the final AMA road race of the year – at Riverside – in first place, KR passing early leader Aldana to lead the bulk of the race with the future Mr Superbike, Steve McLaughlin, third at the front of an all-Yamaha top 20. Of the usual suspects, Aksland fell in practice, Nixon pulled in with clutch trouble, and Singleton suffered a misfire. Warren Willing was the best visitor in sixth. Springsteen 235, Roberts 203. Roberts had barely troubled the scorer in the dirt races before Riverside, and certainly didn't in the two after, dropping to fourth in the final Camel Pro Series rankings.

Which just left Barry Sheene's run through the closing rounds of the *MCN* Superbike Championship. The series resumed at Cadwell Park where the now twice 500cc world champion notched three wins, the Superbike 20-lapper among them. In a virtuoso performance Sheene threaded his way past Potter, then Grant, then Haslam; Grant got past Haslam for

Privateer, US: engineer Kevin Cameron (right) formed a winning partnership with rider Mike Baldwin in '78, taking AMA nationals at Pocono and Sears Point. (Courtesy Mary Grothe)

second, but there was no stopping Sheene, taking 20 points and cutting a second off his own lap record. He didn't fare as well at Mallory Park for the Race of the Year, pulling out of practice with acute leg pain from a trapped tendon and then slowing while leading the feature race, first with a loose exhaust and then with a cooked intermediate on a drying track. Enter Pat Hennen, taking a hat-trick that included the *MCN* Superbike race, getting home from Grant and Potter while Sheene limped into fourth. The fourth of Yamaha's '77 factory bikes, the YZR750 of Johnny Cecotto, was expected to stiffen the opposition, but when his bikes didn't turn up Cecotto went home. "Never again," growled promoter Chris Lowe. Sheene 112, Hennen 79, Grant 67.

Hennen had a slim chance of taking the title at the double-points Brands final round, but this time the Kawasaki UK boys stole the show, Ditch again winning the Gauloises Powerbike international and breaking the short circuit lap record in the *MCN* Superbike final, only to run off and hand the win to team-mate Grant who'd had a wheel-to-wheel scrap with Potter. Sheene was eighth on a badly misfiring bike but had kept his title. Sheene 118, Grant 97, Hennen 95.

So the pattern for 750cc racing, largely set in 1976, was firmly underlined: as ever, factory bikes won internationals everywhere, and nationals when and where they entered. In Britain, that meant Suzuki XR14s and 23s with a little variety from the Team Boyer KR750s, and occasionally TZ-Ds – Haslam, Marshall, Potter; in F750 it meant YZR750s, and, rarely, Kawasaki KR750s, and the occasional TZ-D; and in AMA racing it meant Yamahas: KR with help from Aksland, Nixon, Singleton and Romero. The FIM, however, seemed to like F750 racing no more at its 1977 Caracas autumn congress than it had at Bruges in 1976. While some delegates wanted the class incorporated into grand prix meetings, others wanted rid of it altogether, suggesting that the class had failed by not attracting broad factory support, or even a decent crowd at many of its meetings – the Brands Hatch round had attracted 20,000, low by British standards and an indication of just how much Barry Sheene could add to a gate.

The FIM closed the year with a reminder that F750 continued to live a precarious existence. There were plans, in outline only, to streamline the whole world championship structure, by separating the classes into two groups: 500cc plus two more classes to replace the current grand prix series; and a formidable-looking amalgamation that included F750, the existing endurance championship and the new TT-F1 class. Each group would run 15 rounds.

But not yet. The F750 World Championship got a second year in 1978 with the same 11 rounds, though with one key difference at Daytona where carburettor restrictors would be used – drilled plates to be fitted between carburettor and inlet port, with circular apertures of different diameters for engines with different cylinder counts – 23mm for fours, 27mm for triples, and 35mm for twins. The aim was to reduce power outputs to below tyre-shredding threshold, and AMA tests at Riverside and Daytona suggested the plan would work. After Riverside, Roberts said the restrictors reduced the power of his YZR to about that of a TZ750A – some 12 per cent. After the Daytona tests Roberts, Nixon and Singleton all said their bikes were more controllable out of corners, and technicians reported a 20-degree drop in tyre temperature.

One more thing: Daytona (the France family) and the FIM were at loggerheads on the matter of start money. The issue bounced across the Atlantic for much of the close-season, but came down to this: the FIM insisted all entrants be paid FIM minimum start money; Bill France said he hadn't paid start money before, and wasn't about to start now; but he would, he said, ensure all 80 qualifiers got paid at least the FIM minimum. And that's where it stayed: the Daytona 200 lost its status as an F750 World Championship round, and went ahead just as it always had – except for those restrictors.

After keen negotiations, KR agreed to go chasing world championships and put his signature on a Yamaha Motor USA contract. He, Kel Carruthers and veteran mechanic Nobby Clark would initially pursue 250, 500 and 750 world titles. "We've got enough money to go," said Roberts. For a tight schedule that allowed few appearances outside world title rounds the team budget was said to be around $350,000. Roberts wouldn't say what he was getting, but did say it was "enough not to race dirt or even think about it."

Johnny Cecotto, meanwhile, would be backed by the factory and ride alongside Roberts in 500 GPs and F750 – but F750 World Champion Steve Baker wasn't offered factory bikes: he looked set to race in Canada and the US on production models supplied by Yamaha Canada until he acquired backing from the Italian Nava Olio Fiat team after Sheene put in a word for him. From elsewhere too came the sound of belts being tightened: Suzuki trimmed its operation by rehiring just Sheene and Hennen to ride its 495cc XR22s for grand prix and 652cc XR23As in major internationals – and still the factory declared no interest in pursuing the F750 title. Modification of the bigger bike was kept to a minimum, the changes including cylinders lined with Nikasil – a hard nickel/silicon carbide coating – to cut weight, and a tweak to the Mikuni carburettors to combat fuel surge.

With most of Kawasaki's resources going into the 250 and 350 world championships, TKA's Gregg Hansford and Neville Doyle would be going it alone on the 602L on a part-time basis in the F750 world championship while new recruit Rick Perry minded the shop at home; and the Kawasaki UK team was cut to one rider, Mick Grant, who'd been wooed by Honda Britain to ride its four-strokes but opted to stay green and divide his time between 250 GPs and his 602L at home. Barry Ditchburn left and went private, riding Yamahas for Sid Griffiths.

GIANT

Come the southern summer, Hansford and Jeff Sayle put in some useful track time during New Zealand's final Marlboro series. Beating off international opposition from Lucchinelli's TZ and Kanaya's YZR750, the Aussies each took a win in the opening round at Pukekohe and did the same at Gracefield. In each meeting Hansford's KR750 had stopped in the second leg, at Pukekohe with ignition failure and Gracefield with a broken crank. At Wanganui Rick Perry crashed the 750 in a support race, leaving Hansford just his KR250 for the two feature races. Even so, he finished second to Jeff Sayle in the opener and nipped past the Sydney man's misfiring TZ750 on the final lap of the second race to win. Timaru came next, where Hansford retired in pain from a shoulder blade broken in a 250 race crash; Sayle took the series by winning both legs, the first from Warren Willing, and the second from American visitor Wes Cooley. The series wound up at Ruapuna with Sayle again on top in the first race, but then retiring from the second with an engine seizure and letting Ray Quincey through to win. Sayle was champion, getting home with 27 points to spare from brother Murray's KR750 in second (riding his last series for Kawasaki) and Willing third.

As Jeff Sayle and Quincey packed up their bags to head for Europe, the headlines in Britain carried news of Barry Sheene's MBE in the New Year's Honours List "for services to motorcycle racing" and then, in still bigger print, of Mike Hailwood's return to active service on Martini-backed factory Yamahas for the TT. If Britain was readying itself for the second coming,

Hansford fitted in F750 races where he could during 1978, more often than not thrilling the crowd despite a lack of horsepower. He was fourth overall at Imola (pictured). (Courtesy Ian Falloon)

there were changes too in the USA. Just five national road races appeared on the AMA calendar for 1978 and Daytona, affected by a partial European boycott that resulted from the barney over start money, proposed a new formula for American racing that capitalised on the growing success of the new Superbike Production formula (see Chapter 6). From 1979, said Daytona, it would open the 200 to restricted 750cc two-strokes, unrestricted 500cc two-strokes – and 1000cc four-strokes, putting Superbikes and GP hardware on the one grid, so planning to avoid the one-make, one-model dominance of F750 – the entry for the '78 Daytona 200 listed only one non-Yamaha: Gregg Hansford's KR750.

Leading the way for Yamaha at Daytona was, of course, Kenny Roberts, whose new YZR750 boasted more changes to its chassis than to its engine: along with a new frame and suspension components (including a rectangular-section swinging arm) the bike also had quick-detach wheels. And, naturally, KR used it as well as anyone could, qualifying fastest and coolly taking his first Daytona win, setting a new race record of 108.39mph, 23mm restrictors and all. Indeed, Roberts lapped the field, including Cecotto in second and Aksland in third. Hansford was fifth behind Ron Pierce's Yamaha, lapping some six seconds a lap slower than his '77 times – Neville Doyle blamed the KR's 27mm restrictors, pointing out that while the new regulations had the KR and TZ 750s flowing the same volume of gas at 9000rpm, the TZ revved to 10,500rpm where most KRs signed off at 9500.

As in '77, Barry Sheene and Pat Hennen joined the party at the Transatlantic Trophy, now doing rather better with their XR23As. Hennen took three wins from the six races, with Roberts getting two, and Sheene the first race at Brands. Again, a strong British midfield performance won the tournament for the home side. Sheene hustled his way up from seventh in the opening Brands race to pass Roberts, then scrap with Hennen for the lead. When the American ran onto the grass, Sheene took the win from Roberts, Hennen and Ditchburn. Second time out Sheene made another sluggish start, again passing Roberts who was battling a sticking throttle; but this time Hennen made a tough move on Sheene to make it one-all with Ditchburn and Grant coming in third and fourth. Hennen did it again in the opening scrap of the *MCN* Superbike series, winning while easing off from Potter and Ditchburn; Sheene, battling an oiled plug, finished seventh.

At Mallory Park Sheene came from behind while Roberts and Hennen scrapped for the lead, the win going to KR after Hennen slowed with brake problems on the last lap. Hennen got it right in the second race and ran away from Roberts to win by eight seconds while Sheene stopped with a broken disc valve, this time with Potter third from Ditchburn and Romero. The UK had its nose in front going to Oulton Park but the balance of power shifted a little when, in the opening leg, Sheene had his first crash in almost two years, leaving KR to win from Hennen and Potter. The final race was typical of the whole contest: Roberts and Hennen away, Sheene bustling through the pack after a bad start; but Roberts' ignition then failed and Hennen won from Sheene, Aldana and Potter. UK 435, USA 379: the champion team beat the team of champions.

The F750 World Championship began in earnest a week later at Imola where Roberts and Cecotto again looked set to dominate, along with Baker's private Yamaha – "there was no way I could match Cecotto's acceleration" – and Hansford's lone KR750. Roberts, though, wasn't quite able to reproduce his Daytona success. In the opening laps of the first race he came from third behind Baker and Cecotto to take the lead briefly before his engine began to tighten. Sarron closed, coming from fifth to second and colliding with Baker, which resulted in power-sapping exhaust damage for the American. Cecotto and Sarron then scrapped, the Frenchman putting his head down for a determined win. Baker was third from Graziano Rossi and Franco Uncini, with Hansford sixth. In the second leg Cecotto again got away, pursued by Baker and this time Sarron and Hansford, who survived a collision with Roberts in the chicane; Roberts fell while Cecotto went on to win from Baker, Sarron and Hansford's Kawasaki.

Cecotto became winner of the AGV World Cup the following weekend by cleaning up in the *Moto Journal* 200 at Paul Ricard. While both Roberts and Baker suffered tyre problems, Cecotto took the lead on the seventh of the 55 laps and was never headed. Hansford led early but fell, and neither of the pursuing Yamahas looked as quick as Cecotto's. Roberts ultimately took second from Baker at the second round of fuel stops,

Suzuki never committed its 652cc XR23 to a full F750 campaign, but it could be seen at non-title internationals. This is Baz during the 1978 Transatlantic Trophy. (Courtesy Elwyn Roberts)

with Ike Takai's YZR fourth, plugging on after Virginio Ferrari stopped with brake problems. Jeff Sayle and Warren Willing went out with seized engines, and Aksland dropped out of sixth with ignition failure. Already, this began to look like Cecotto's year. "The bike is so good," he said, "and I feel so fresh I could do another 200 miles." Two rounds down: Cecotto 30, Baker 22, Roberts 12.

His name isn't in the overall results: the winner of the Brands Hatch third round of the F750 World Championship was Kenny Roberts, winning the first leg from Baker and Cecotto, the second from Potter and Cecotto. Gregg Hansford is credited simply with a fourth place in the first leg, but he gave so much more than that. In the opening leg the Australian got alongside early leader Steve Baker at Clearways but fell at Druids on the second lap, and while Roberts cleared off, Hansford remounted and tore through the field giving a braking masterclass, getting up to third before stopping for fuel. Roberts lost the lead to Baker while refuelling, but set a new lap record to catch and pass his man, and Hansford got in fourth at the flag. In the second leg Hansford took the lead and pulled away. Roberts used the speed of his Yamaha to catch him, and the pair looked set for a memorable dice until Hansford was forced wide by a lapped man on the approach to Westfield and fell. There was no way back now but Dave Potter filled the role of hero admirably, getting home in second place from Cecotto and Pons after Baker had stopped with a blown oil seal.

Roberts, in indomitable form, took another double at the Zeltweg Austrian round of the title chase, passing early leader Hansford in the opening race to win by 30 seconds from Cecotto and Franco Bonera, while Hansford crashed trying to pass Pons for fourth. Second time out KR led home Cecotto and Baker, with Hansford fifth behind fellow Australian Greg Johnson. Four rounds done, Cecotto 54, Roberts 42, Pons 29.

RETURN OF THE KING
In the UK, Sheene and Hennen swapped their XR22 grand prix bikes for XR23As in more *MCN* Superbike Championship rounds. First stop was Cadwell Park, where Sheene won well from his American rival and Grant, who led home a grand dice with Yamaha-mounted Ditchburn, Potter and Roger Marshall. The Mallory Post-TT was likewise Sheene's, and in the absence of Hennen following his catastrophic crash in the Senior TT, Potter provided the opposition, beating Ditch for second. Three rounds done, Sheene 36, Potter 30, Hennen 29.

Meanwhile, Mike Hailwood went back to his island in the Irish Sea to make history again. In the Classic TT, his appearance was brief, holding his own against Kawasaki-mounted Grant until his Martini-backed Yamaha seized, breaking a piston at Ballacraine. Grant forged on to win, despite a rear master cylinder working loose. He crossed the line with 50 seconds to spare from John Williams' RG500, posting a scorching race record at 112.40mph and a new lap record at 114.33mph. Hailwood's performance in the F1 TT, remorselessly hunting down life-long rival Phil Read's 810 Honda, is covered in Chapter 5 …

The F750 World Championship resumed at Jarama with a single, 60-lap race that Roberts won by half a minute from Cecotto, and, 48 seconds further adrift, Sarron. Roberts took the lead on lap 10, setting a new lap record, but finding an hour and a half round the twists and turns of Jarama hard on his hands. Baker was seventh, suffering brake fade and then a misfire. At a wet Hockenheim it was Sarron's turn to shine. With rain stopping just before the first race, tyre choice became tricky, but the Sonauto man got it right and led by 16 seconds at the end of the second lap. While Cecotto retired with a sticking throttle and Roberts battled a misting visor, Hansford worked his way up to second and that's how it stayed, with Franco Bonera third. Cecotto fared no better in the second leg, retiring after being judged to have jumped the start. Roberts made amends, however, winning from Sarron and Bonera on a drying track, with Hansford fourth; it was enough to get Roberts fourth overall and eight valuable points.

The Australian missed the next round at Nivelles in Belgium to race at the Czech GP, and Roberts might have done likewise, but now threw in the towel on the 250cc title to concentrate on the bigger classes. Not that it helped him in Belgium: KR lasted just three laps of the opener before his drive chain tensioner broke, snapping the chain and damaging the YZR's cases. He didn't start the second leg. Cecotto, meanwhile, won both races from Herve Moineau's TZ; Steve Parrish (Yamaha) got third in the first race, Bonera in the second. Steve Baker was also among the casualties, running a main bearing in the opening race and sitting out the second. Seven rounds down: Cecotto 81, KR 65, Sarron 55.

With KR away, American privateers had the AMA's handful of pro road races to themselves. Where the UK had been allocated just six TZ750Es (for Ditchburn, Marshall, Potter, Stan Woods, Steve Wright, and Derek Chatterton), the US got 40, for Nixon, Aldana and Romero, among others. Roberts' sparring partner, Skip Aksland, drew first blood after a stirring dice with Richard Schlachter at Loudon. Schlachter slowed late on, and Mike Baldwin caught and passed him for second. Schlachter had still done better than Nixon, who retired for no immediately clear reason. "I was just going slow," he later explained. Aksland then crashed at Sears Point, bottoming his suspension in the Carousel. Aldana went down with him, leaving Schlachter in the lead from Nixon and Romero until Baldwin passed, winning from Romero and Singleton after Nixon crashed and Schlachter went out with a jammed throttle. None of which had much effect on the dirt-dominated AMA Camel Pro Series, where Harley dirt aces Steve Eklund and Jay Springsteen comfortably topped the table.

Back in Britain, Sheene had a new rival at the head of the *MCN* Superbike Championship. The action resumed with the first international meeting to be held at the newly reopened Donington Park circuit, dramatically shortened from its prewar 3.125-mile configuration to 1.96 miles, but with the chicane at Park Corner providing a fine argument-settler. The first Superbike scrap at the new track began in familiar style, with Sheene making a poor start while Potter shot away at the lead and stayed there. Sheene fought past Noddy, Ditch and John Williams, but then slowed with ignition problems while Potter took the win from Grant, posting a new lap record. Sheene was back on top at Snetterton, but Potter ran in a dogged second (on his spare bike after his better engine had blown, damaging its cases) from Grant. The title leaders finally got together at Oulton Park and staged a memorable dice. Sheene passed early leader Ditchburn and took Potter with him, the Yamaha man pouncing when Sheene missed a gear at half distance. Sheene repassed, but Potter hung on and was less than a second adrift at the flag, with Ditch third. Six rounds done: Sheene 74, Potter 73, Ditchburn 51.

Baldwin made it two wins in as many starts in the fourth of the AMA's five road races, at Pocono in Philadelphia. With Aksland (shoulder injury) and Nixon (lacking cash to rebuild his E) both out as a result of falls at Sears Point, Baldwin won after passing befreckled newcomer Randy Mamola at the end of the opening lap, while Romero and Singleton haggled over second after Schlachter fell. Two weeks later the domestic season came to a close back at Loudon, where Baldwin looked like making it three in a row until Singleton caught and passed him on the last lap. Baldwin proved better through traffic, but Singleton was faster out of corners and the pass stuck.

Meanwhile, America's most famous road racer had become 500cc world champion, but by the time Roberts left a sodden Dutch round he could perhaps see the F750 title slipping from his grasp. The weather might have upset the form book anyhow; Assen was never among KR's favourite tracks. He retired from the first race with a broken steering damper mount, and from the second with clutch failure and a chunking back tyre. Cecotto wasn't at his best either, falling in practice and hurting the hand he'd damaged at the Swedish GP. Hansford, however, was in fine form, and used the torque of the KR750 to win the first race from Bonera and Katayama. He was on track to make it a double until his front end washed out on the last lap of the second race, removing him from the points, giving the race win to Katayama and the round win to second place finisher Bonera.

Roberts was back on top with a double at Laguna Seca, while Cecotto failed to score, retiring in the first leg with a broken gearlever and so eliminated from the points. Aksland looked likely to take his place, finishing second to Roberts in the first race but then retiring from the second with ignition problems. Back came Steve Baker with his private Yamaha for second overall, cracking the 100mph lap in practice, finishing third in the first race and chasing Roberts home in the second. Third overall was Mike Baldwin, who wore away part of his toes on both feet while cornering, so earning himself the nickname 'bloody boots.' Perhaps Roberts was feeling

Privateer, UK: entrant Ted Broad and rider Dave Potter (pictured) formed one of Britain's most successful alliances, bagging the MCN Superbike Championship in 1979 and 1980. (Courtesy Elwyn Roberts)

Baldwin's pain when he said of the meeting, "That's the hardest I've had to ride all year."

Going into the final round at Mosport Park, Roberts was 11 points behind Cecotto, and it was more than enough. Baldwin ran away with both legs, sliding his intermediate front where necessary to keep a handy gap between himself and Roberts. Du Hamel, again out of retirement for the occasion, took third in the opening race by getting the better of champion-presumptive Cecotto, and came in fifth second time out. Hansford, Kawasaki's double winner in '77, was concentrating on his 250 and 350 GP campaigns and missed Mosport, as he had Laguna Seca. Cecotto added sixth place in the second race to his fourth in the first – enough for fifth overall, adding six points to his total and so taking the championship with five points to spare over Roberts: Cecotto 97, Roberts 92, Sarron 57.

For all Mosport's uncertain weather, it's doubtful it attained the unpleasantness of Scarborough and the seventh round of the *MCN* Superbike Championship. Leaves, mud, and branches covered the Oliver's Mount track. The race was cut from 15 laps to 10 because of the conditions, but the weather didn't seem to faze Sheene, who cut past early leader Grant to win comfortably. Potter, dogged by a persistent misfire, limped home in sixth. Back at Cadwell for round eight, the old firm – Sheene and Grant – went at it, though Grant seemed content with second, saying he'd have lost the drag from Barn Corner to Sheene's XR23A anyway. Potter, meanwhile, posted another sixth place. Eight rounds done: Sheene 110, Potter 85, Grant 72.

Sheene was still on top at the Race of the Year, taking the name event from Hartog and Roberts. The Dutchman had to ride his XR22, new cases for his XR23A not having turned up in time. "It just wasn't quick enough in the fourth gear places, like down Devil's Elbow and out of Gerard's," he said. KR was just as candid: "I just wasn't riding good today," he explained. "I had a couple of problems that didn't help, but it was me, really." Sheene didn't fare as well in the *MCN* Superbike race: while Potter took the lead, Sheene made a trademark poor start, got up to fourth on a poor-handling XR23A – and that was the best he could manage; he was passed by Ditch and took the flag in fifth. Potter, meanwhile, got a solid win from Roger Marshall and Tom Herron, which was high tide for Potter in 1978. At the Brands final round he high-sided, while Hartog won the race from Grant and Sheene ran in third to claim the championship. At least Potter was series runner-up in his best season yet; although tied on points with Grant he got second place by winning more races than the Kawasaki man.

EXIT

As autumn took hold in the northern hemisphere the good and the great headed for Poznan in central Poland for the FIM congress. There the unwanted child of the AMA and the ACU was at last laid to rest: the 1979 F750 World Championship would be the last. For the final season of the

Steve Parrish rode for Suzuki GB in 1977 and 1979, pictured here during the '79 North West 200. (Courtesy Elwyn Roberts)

class all homologation requirements were to be dropped, prompting fresh speculation that the XR23 Suzuki – in its further modified B model – and the yet-unseen trapezoidal four from Kawasaki, the 602S, might be entered. In his book, *Kawasaki Racers*, Ian Falloon explains that two prototype engines for the 602S were built. The reed-valve power plant was said to make around 143bhp at 10,500rpm, and was offered to teams in Britain, the US, and Australia, "as they stood," with limited development and an uncertain spares supply. Only Team Kawasaki Australia took up the offer and work began on a chassis in January 1979 with Neville Doyle steering the project. Early tests were encouraging, but severe vibration proved a problem in practice at the Italian opening round of the F750 world title. Hansford resorted to his old KR750 for the two Mugello races, while the 602S went to Japan and was never returned. As for Suzuki's XR23B, it differed slightly from its immediate predecessor in its modified porting, exhaust system, and reworked rear suspension, but again the bike was largely confined to international non-championship duties.

The little factory support there was for F750 gradually melted away. Yamaha pushed on, offering factory support for the French Sonauto team: Sarron in the 500 and F750 championships, Pons in the 350 and F750. Roberts and Cecotto, however, vowed only to ride in those F750 events that offered credible start money; and in any case, Roberts had enough to do in defending his 500cc world title, while Cecotto was moving with gathering certainty towards a career in saloon car racing.

Come season's end, Pons took the third and final F750 World

Championship – becoming France's first world champion – after a season-long battle with Swiss Michel Frutschi's private Yamaha. Johnny Cecotto enlivened the series in winning more races than either of the title contenders, but at the last round at Rijeka in Yugoslavia, Pons needed a single point from either race (finally, points were awarded in every race of the '79 season) to take the crown. That he did with two third places while Frutschi and Cecotto took a win and a runner-up spot apiece. Their efforts were watched by a crowd of just 3000. Small wonder the meeting merited just eight paragraphs (plus results) in Britain's *Motor Cycle News*.

In its closing year the F750 world championship format arguably reached its zenith, providing the basis at each meeting for the most exciting competition yet between the world's most potent motorcycles. In an overcrowded calendar, and with lukewarm support at best from the FIM, the class had never become sufficiently established to attract full-scale factory backing, much less the strength and support to challenge the existing grand prix structure. In its history of F750, the FIM website suggests the lack of a clear identity lay at the root of its failure: "was it supposed to be a grand prix, a 'true' road racing competition for prototypes, or a competition based on the large-production street motorcycle?" Had the question received a clear answer at the beginning of 1974, when Yamaha outflanked the class homologation regulations and made the first 200 TZ750s, its history might have been different. As it was, Formula 750 died as it had lived, with most of the people who mattered looking the other way.

The 'villain' of the piece, Yamaha's great leveller, the TZ750, would continue to win races for another half a decade; but there would, after

Graeme Crosby began sampling open-class two-strokes in 1978, when he signed to ride Team Kawasaki Australia's KR750. (Courtesy Ian Falloon)

Patrick Pons during his winning ride at Daytona in 1980 – the seventh straight win for Yamaha's 750s, and the ninth for the marque. (Courtesy Mary Grothe)

1979, be no place for it in championships above national level. In Britain, Dave Potter did well to claim Duckhams-*MCN* Superbike Championships for Yamaha and Ted Broad in 1979 and 1980, the last before four-strokes regained control. He won the 1979 title by just three points from Haslam, and the 1980 contest by a more comfortable margin from Marshall – who were, likewise, powered by TZs. In the US, the TZ would win, among a raft of AMA nationals, another four Daytona 200s: Dale Singleton in 1979 and 1981, Graeme Crosby in 1982 and, most memorably, Patrick Pons in 1980 after Freddie Spencer's blistering effort on his Kanemoto-built Yamaha had ended in a broken crank; and then back came KR on the last and mightiest of all the big two-strokes, Yamaha's 695cc 0W69 square four, to win again in Florida and California. Down under, Murray Sayle and Bob Rosenthal used their Milledge TZ750s to clean up in the Australian Road Racing Championship, then ceding the stage to Jeff Sayle, who won the inaugural Swann International Series in 1978-79 on his Donny Pask TZ750. Most impressive of all, perhaps, were Patrick Pons and Sadao Asami, doggedly bringing their Sonauto TZ750 into second place at the 1979 Bol d'Or behind the superb, built-for-purpose RCB Honda ridden by Jean-Claude Chemarin and Christian Leon.

If Yamaha's TR/TZ twins had coaxed racing out of its cash-strapped postwar era dominated by British four-stroke singles and into the jet age of the '70s, then the TZ750 was surely rocket propulsion for the common man: a missile for the working day that won the respect of all and affection of many; a bike that offered perhaps the first glimpse of life at 180mph for rider and spectator alike, and so changed racing forever. Most of its admirers would never get to ride one, of course, but among the thousands who did were a number of articulate punters able to convey something of how the biggest TZ felt to ride. Greg Bennett penned this passage about the TZ750C for his encyclopaedic *Yamaha Production Two-Stroke Road Racing Motorcycles*: "When accelerating out of a corner the bike would come on the pipe at around 8000rpm, howl in approval and rocket forward like nothing before, causing the front end to get very light. It was necessary to negotiate most corners with the engine slightly off the boil or the rider was in danger of lighting up the rear tyre ... but such a power slide was relatively easy to control, with the bike's heavy flywheels helping [here]. It was essential to load the front end by tucking in over the fuel tank under hard acceleration in first and second because sitting up would make the bike try to flip over backwards ..." Australian Bob Rosenthal, a committed and enthusiastic TZ rider recalls: "When you fired the TZ down a straight it was like a starburst coming at you – something only the lucky few who rode them would understand." Awesome in its impact, unsurpassed in its accomplishments, the Yamaha TZ750 was as impressive in reality as it is in legend; and if for that alone, it is unique.

Yamaha down under: Andrew Johnson dives through Skyline on his way to winning the Bathurst 1980 Australian Unlimited GP on Pitmans' TZ750. (Courtesy Phil Aynsley)

5

FORMULA ONE

While the future of F750 proved intractable at the 1976 FIM autumn congress, the new TT Formula couldn't wait: after being bounced back and forth between FIM and ACU, the plan for the TT had a life on paper but lacked substance. Under the FIM ruling, the TT Formula would be open to two principal classes: F1, for 1000cc four-strokes and 500cc two-strokes, and F2 for 600cc/350cc. There were smaller classes, but the major talking point was the big bangers, with some FIM delegates concerned that they'd be too potent for the Mountain Circuit. The technical committee thought a 200-bike homologation minimum would weed out the most egregious of home-brewed rockets, and suggested leaving things at that. And so the TT Formula became reality by FIM vote, 42-31.

The broad provisions: racing motorcycles – Yamaha TZs, the Suzuki RG500 – specifically barred. "Sports motorcycles are the basis of the new formula," emphasised Neville Goss, Southampton club man and member of the FIM's technical committee. To be eligible for F1 competition, each of these sports motorcycles had to be offered to the public, with proof available that at least 200 had been sold, and sold moreover with full electrical equipment. "Racing frames, forks, wheels and tanks may be used," said Goss. "Only the roadster engine must be retained, and it may be extensively modified." Although not too extensively: the stroke, materials and castings of cylinders, heads, cases, and gearbox had to be retained, along with stock types of exhaust and induction systems – the number, type and size of carburettors had to be as stock.

TT-F1 was "the formula of the future," according to the chairman of the FIM's technical committee, Helmut Bonsch. Not everyone agreed. Another chairman, Clifford Irving of the Isle of Man Tourist Board, denounced the new formula as "nothing more than glorified Production races – the Senior, Classic and sidecar TTs are sacrosanct," he warned. The ACU had big plans for the revised TT, though, wanting the 1977 TT to be a £150,000 affair with eight races, five for racing bikes – including of course the Senior – and three for the bigger TT Formula classes.

Among the foot soldiers the new series didn't make much immediate impact. In south London, a couple of likely lads named Richard Peckett and Peter McNab had recently left the employ of sage veteran Dave Degens at Dresda Autos to set up on their own. They'd each sold their Triumph Tridents to help finance the new business – P&M Motorcycles – and were determined to stick to the straight and narrow, doing road bike repairs and servicing to keep the till ringing. Still, Peckett was keen to carry on racing: "I had a fast Dresda Honda I'd built but which didn't handle as well as my Trident, so I designed and built my own frame for it using the Trident's geometry," he recalls. "First time out, it broke the primary chain, wrecking the crank. We were helping Dennis MacMillan with his production CB750 at the time, and he lent me a crank for the rest of the year. Next season – 1976 – Dennis raced a BMW R90S for Ongar Motorcycles at the Barcelona 24-hour. He told me it didn't handle well and lacked ground clearance, so I stupidly said we could make a frame for it …"

Months later, when the first details of TT-F1 were announced: "We set about making jigs for swinging arms and fork yokes, and finalised the basic P&M frame design, starting with one for the CB750 Honda and another for the Z1 Kawasaki."

P&M's frames used Reynolds 531 or T45 in 17-18swg. Fork yokes were steel bronze, and could be supplied with different offsets for changing trail. Steering-head bearings were tapered rollers, as were bearings in the rectangular section – and standard length – reinforced swinging arms. Steering-head angle settled at 28 degrees.

TT-F1 began to interest the mighty. Seven-time world champion Phil Read was wooed back into competition to ride for the new Honda Britain team at the '77 TT. His bike arrived in May: its heart was an 810cc version of the CB750F2 engine, overbored from 61mm to 64 – as much as the standard liners could take. It came with a close-ratio five-speed 'box, increased oil capacity at 4.5 litres, an oil cooler, CDI ignition, and the 31mm CR Keihin carburettors that were homologated in Japan when Honda built a batch of engines using them. Other important details included specially made steel rods, and a heavy-duty camchain. The engine was said to be good for more than 90bhp at 9500rpm. The frame came from an early RCB endurance racer, which made sense because the RCB used CB750 cases. Team boss Gerald Davison guessed all-up weight at about 175kg, comparable to the four CR750s taken to Daytona in 1970 and well below the road bike's 225kg.

Read had his first race on the Island since declaring his support for the 1972 boycott, and won the F1 TT by 38.4 seconds from Roger Nicholls' Sports Motorcycles Ducati, collecting his eighth world title in the process. The event ran in filthy weather and was shortened from five laps to four in mid-race. When he stopped for fuel at the end of lap two Read was 46

After long discussions at ACU and FIM level, F1 got going during the 1977 TT, with Phil Read bagging the race (and title) from Roger Nicholls' Sports MCs Ducati and Ian Richards' Honda. (Courtesy TTracepics.com)

seconds in front. Helped by Read's long stop, Nicholls led by 22 seconds at the end of the third lap; but he lost that and more when he stopped for fuel. Before Read made his second stop, Davison learnt that the event was to be shortened by a lap because of the weather. He waved his man through, knowing he'd have enough fuel to finish, and so Read won – with just a pint of oil left in the motor.

Ian Richards and Stan Woods brought two more 810 Hondas into third and fourth, Woods after a long push in with a dead engine and a lengthy stop to remedy waterlogged electrics; but many thought Nicholls and his modified NCR endurance racer – with narrow, sandcast cases and a dry clutch – were the heroes, with Nicholls riding injured after a heavy fall in practice, and then losing the lead when the duration of the race was changed.

Honda did it again in the TT-F1 race at the Silverstone British GP. Ron Haslam, embarking on a long relationship with the marque, led from start to finish on Read's TT bike, while behind him a ding-dong scrap developed between Nicholls' Ducati, Peckett on P&M's 984 Kawasaki, Peter Davies' Laverda, Malcolm Lucas (840 BSA triple), Alex George (Ducati), and Bill Smith's 810 Honda. But Davies fell from his Laverda at Woodcote, Smith retired, and then Nicholls and Peckett went into Beckett's together and neither came out. Asa Moyce saw the action and said a backmarker had pushed the two together, leaving them nowhere to go but down. Haslam, oblivious to it all, won by 11 seconds from Lucas, Moyce's Kawasaki, and George.

Both Honda Britain and Peckett & McNab made a major effort for Brands Hatch at the last major meeting of the year, where racegoers and competitors got another sample of short-circuit TT-F1. While Honda fielded Haslam and Woods on 810s, P&M had a hand in no fewer than four potential winners. "We ran Asa Moyce and me on Kawasakis," recalls Peckett, "John Cowie on our second Honda-powered bike, and Mocheck borrowed our first Honda chassis for their runner, Tony Rutter."

For a time it seemed P&M might take its maiden win. The Honda Britain pair bolted at the start, but, after Haslam's clutch started giving trouble, Cowie moved up to challenge for the lead, and although Woods took the flag first, the P&M boys packed the places: Cowie, Peckett, Rutter and Moyce crammed in behind Woods, relegating Haslam to sixth. "The rise of P&M had started," remembers a smiling Peckett.

K IS FOR ...

For now, P&M's motor of choice was the the Kawasaki Z1's, as it had been since Asa Moyce rode the first P&M Kawasaki in the '77 F1 TT and largely because it came with 28mm carbs rather than the Z900's 26mm units.

The first tweak was to lift capacity from 903 closer to F1's 1000cc ceiling. "When we started, the only piston kit from Yoshimura was 69.5mm," says Peckett, "and that made the engine slightly oversize – about 1002. Anyway, Paul Dunstall was doing the 69.4mm pistons we'd used in the Hondas (giving 953cc), so we used them in Kawasaki motors, making them 998cc.

"But they didn't work as well. In 1977 John and Bernie Toleman borrowed my Kawasaki for the Mettet 1000km race, and it went onto three while they chased the works Hondas. When it came back, one of the pistons had disappeared: there was nothing left of it. But Gus Kuhn was then involved with Suzuki, and Omega had made them a set of pistons. They were no good in the Suzuki so Jim Phillips, known as Jim the Fish because he delivered prawns to Chinese restaurants, got them for us. I fitted them to my bike and they worked, so Omega said they'd make us pistons: 69mm, giving 984cc. Later, when Graeme Crosby came over, Moriwaki started doing stuff, and we used some of that – pistons, cams, buckets.

"In the early days we'd run Yoshimura Bonneville cams, have our own valves made by GNS at Godalming, and I'd do the heads. We fitted bigger valves – to start with we'd go 1mm oversize on the inlet and keep the exhaust standard. Later we went 1mm oversize on the exhaust, but we had to be a bit careful with overlap – we'd set the cams in the head with some light springs and turn them over to see how close the valves came to one another, and then cut them back or radius them, so if they touched they'd glance off rather than dig in; but if people missed gears they would bend valves. Early on, compression wasn't very high – I doubt whether it was even 11:1."

The bottom end was very sturdy, Peckett recalls. "We used the standard crank. We welded it to stop twisting and then it was perfectly okay. We had a crank snap once at a crankpin; it sort of wedged the thing apart and destroyed the crankcases. Later, when we went to 1100cc cranks would break, but then Kawasaki had the Mk II, with bigger crankpins and that solved that."

In moderate tune, the Zed motor would make 95bhp in F1 trim and about 100 for endurance, revving to 9000rpm (F1) and 9500rpm. There wasn't much difference in specification: "For endurance we ran a 630 O-ring chain which absorbed power and was heavier, but it meant the chain would last the race without adjustment. For short circuits we went to a 530 non-O-ring chain." The only other changes were to swap the carburettors (endurance regs were then more generous). "It was the early days of cast wheels and disc brakes. I would imagine weight was about 400lb [180kg] – but we only had spindly little 35mm forks and 10in discs."

News of a revised Honda F1 bike for 1978, running to 888cc (67mm Mahle pistons in CB350 liners), and making 95bhp, came as menswear house Mr Topps announced it was to back a nine-round British ACU TT-F1 championship, with a race at most major mainland tracks and the Ulster GP. While persistent rumours of a new GP bike took the lion's share of Honda's headlines, other news had it that Phil Read would defend his new world title, and contest the ACU-Mr Topps F1 Championship.

As ACU Chairman Vernon Cooper said he expected TT-F1 to become the world's premier class in the decade ahead, the domestic ACU series opened on May Bank Holiday weekend at Oulton Park, where Haslam led early but then fell at Esso. Read took over on the other 888 Honda Britain bike and won going away from Tony Rutter's Mocheck 810 Honda and the P&M trio, led by Cowie's misfiring 984 Kawasaki. First blood to Honda.

Three weeks later the class reconvened at Cadwell Park where Stan Woods ran away for most of the race on a Mocheck Honda of larger but unconfirmed displacement, falling on the penultimate lap and handing a comfortable win to Haslam from Rutter, with Read third from Cowie. Brands Hatch was the last stop before the TT, where Woods finally got his win, taking the lead with three laps to go in a classic short-circuit scratch. The Honda Britain boys were a touch below par, Haslam finishing third after getting it wrong at Paddock while Read retired with 'valve trouble.' Woods ran his Mocheck Honda – now pegged at 942cc – home from team-mate Rutter, Haslam, Cowie and Moyce. Three rounds gone: Rutter 36, Cowie 26, Haslam and Read 25.

The domestic series came to a halt while the single-race F1 world championship was decided on the Island. Honda was well prepared with Read and John Williams (in for Stan Woods, who'd injured a shoulder in

Stanley Michael Bailey Hailwood: they gave him number 1 at Silverstone in 1978, where he was third to the faster bikes of John Cowie and Tom Herron. (Courtesy Elwyn Roberts)

the Spa 24-hour) campaigning the Honda Britain bikes, and Tom Herron leading the way for Mocheck after Rutter had broken a leg in practice. Ducati meanwhile had recruited Mike Hailwood and built, according to Ian Falloon in *Ducati Racers*, a batch of 18 F1 bikes and 20 spare engines for 1978. The engines, housed in 12kg frames, boasted sandcast cases with spin-on oil filters, lightened crankshafts and big-port heads with an 80-degree included valve angle. Valves were 44mm inlet and 38mm exhaust, pistons 10:1 Borgo, and carburettors 40mm Dell'Ortos. Capacity was a very stock 864cc (the engines ran 900SS engine numbers) but power output, rated at 92bhp at 8500rpm, was not. Delivery was via a dry clutch to a close-ratio six-speed 'box. All-up weight was given as 160kg.

Hailwood qualified fastest at 111.04mph and started with Ian Richards' 984 P&M Kawasaki, 50 seconds down on Read. He took the lead from Herron by Ramsey on the first lap, getting back to Douglas six seconds up on the Irishman – who by now had received warning from the rear end of his Mocheck Honda that all was not well – and 20 seconds in front of Read on corrected time. Hailwood set a new lap record at 110.62mph on the second lap, passing Read on the road a lap later. Herron, meanwhile, had skidded to a stop, and found both rear suspension units had broken off at their top mounts, jamming the wheel under the seat unit.

Read regained the lead on the road after the fuel stops, but by now the Honda was making smoke and Hailwood was soon past again, though easing off to conserve the engine. Read retired on lap five after major slides on his own oil, and Hailwood cruised home with two minutes to spare from John Williams' Honda Britain 888 and, another 50 seconds back, Ian Richards, who'd been slowed by two fuel stops and by oil leaking onto his back tyre.

Hailwood repeated his success at Mallory Park in the Post-TT bash. Here, in the fourth round of the ACU series, he and Read resumed their scrap, this time with Cowie's P&M Kawasaki for company. Moyce led for the first three laps, then Read, then Cowie; finally Hailwood made his move, passing the P&M man at the Esses and easing home to another rapturous welcome.

Not everyone was happy, however. Read had been less than delighted with the performance of his bike in the F1 TT. Gerald Davison attributed its catastrophic oil loss to a fractured oil line dumping its load onto the exhaust. Whatever the cause, there had been words between Read and Honda UK manager Eric Sulley. Meanwhile, others grumbled about Hailwood's bike, notably its specially cast cases with the spin-on oil filter, neither of which were features of the catalogue 900SS. According to Ducati expert Ian Falloon, however, Ducati identified the Hailwood bike as a catalogue model in its own right.

Honda Britain had manpower problems: Woods was convalescing, and Haslam had jumped off in practice at Mallory Park and knocked himself about. Add to that Mocheck man Tony Rutter's leg broken at the TT and Honda's representation began to look threadbare, even with John Williams waving the flag for Honda Britain and Barry Ditchburn filling the breach at Mocheck. It looked thinner still after Read pulled out of the Donington Park round of the ACU title with bronchitis and Williams retired from the race with a loose clip-on. Hailwood, enjoying his third ride on the Sports Ducati at the front of the field, tried too hard at Coppice with three laps to go and lost the front end, giving the win to Mocheck's new recruit, double British champion Roger Marshall, from a convalescent Haslam and P&M Honda-mounted Steve Manship.

COMETH THE HOUR

A week later at Snetterton, Cowie blasted clear of a four-way scrap to post his first win in the ACU series. Read, back to fitness, led early with Williams, Manship and Haslam snapping at his heels. Cowie then pulled through while Read and Williams vied for second, which Williams consolidated with three laps to go. Six rounds down: Cowie 53, Haslam 45, Read 43.

Tom Herron (940 Mocheck Honda) was well placed early in the 1978 F1 TT, but broken shock mounts ended his race. (Courtesy TTracepics.com)

Cowie cleared out again at the non-title Silverstone race, getting away from Moyce and Haslam (without team-mate Read, who hadn't arrived at the meeting). Herron, meanwhile, was putting in the ride of the day, passing Haslam, moving into third when Moyce crashed at Copse and then clocking a 110mph lap to close on Cowie. Hailwood rode the wheels off his visibly slower Ducati and almost caught Herron, but Cowie won by a wheel from the Irishman after a last-ditch effort through Woodcote – and then found himself excluded on a suspected carburettor irregularity. The ensuing episode, described by Peter McNab at the time as "a farce," Richard Peckett now recalls with weary amusement: "I went to race control and was told we'd been disqualified for running big carbs. I told them the carbs were stock, that they'd come with a scrap engine we'd bought. But no, the scrutineers said we'd bored them out 0.5mm." The Peckett smile appears. "Do you think I'd bore them out half a mill? Makes a lot of difference, that." The authorities re-measured the carbs – at the wrong point to begin with, but eventually correctly, when it was discovered they were indeed of homologated size. Cowie was restored to the results and the circus moved to the Ulster GP.

In an Ulster that will always be blackened by the death of John Williams following his crash in the 1000cc race, Herron won the F1 event after a scrap with Rutter's Mocheck Honda. Cowie was third with Williams fourth (on Read's Honda Britain ride) from team-mate Haslam. Read and Haslam were each allocated a new 980cc Honda for the meeting, but Read's went to Williams when the eight-time world champion arrived late for practice after a problem with his flight from France. "I hope to be back next year," Read told the crowd, "perhaps on more competitive machinery." Within the week, Read had been "released from his contract" with Honda Britain. The team announced its withdrawal from the TT-F1 series, but thought again after testing one of its bikes at Brands with a P&M frame. "It gave us two or three seconds a lap," said racing manager Barry Symmons. "It was fantastic."

At a wet Scarborough, Steve Manship, nursing damaged ribs, slipped and slithered into fourth place on one of the old Honda Britain mounts. Title leader Cowie was out with a broken collarbone from a practice fall, and Steve Tonkin won on a Sports Motorcycles Ducati from Read on a Mocheck Honda – "very competitive," he said – and George Fogarty, also on a Sports Duck.

Rocket Ron, a non-starter at Scarborough since the death of his brother

Read (3, 888 Honda) rounds Gerard's from future British TT-F1 champion John Cowie (984 P&M Kawasaki), and Hailwood's Sports MCs Ducati, at the '78 Mallory Post-TT F1 race. Positions were reversed at the flag. (Courtesy Bauer Media)

Phil there in 1974, finally got a start on the P&M-framed Honda Britain bike at the Brands Hatch ACU TT-F1 finale and cleared off, passing Cowie for a handsome win and a new lap record. But with second place on the day, Cowie took the title with nine points to spare from Haslam, who finished a point in front of Read.

Just a day later a high-speed fall from his TZ350 Yamaha brought Cowie's career to an abrupt close. He struck a concrete post on Paddock Hill Bend and broke an elbow so badly it took six hours on the operating table to fix. After being wired and plated, he was discharged and told he might, in time, expect to regain up to 90 per cent movement. But his racing days were over.

Britain's first national TT-F1 title had done well enough to attract more cash: the Forward Trust finance house would back the 11-round championship in the '79 season with £500 for each round winner. Mick Grant, meanwhile, announced he was joining Honda Britain. Kawasaki had been good to him, he said, but with Ditch rejoining Team Green to ride its KR750 triples, Honda would supply his firepower in the bigger classes. He would also be helping with the development of the marque's new 500cc GP runner. Big four-strokes might be the way forward, he reckoned: F750 was dead and F1 "the natural successor."

Long before Honda Britain's new bikes, based on the new CB900FZ, reached the UK, Honda said a TT-F1 kit for the new sportster was to be offered through UK Honda dealers – who immediately told team boss Gerald Davison that it was too expensive at £3142 (plus VAT). Cheshire dealer Bill Smith led the way, slamming "ridiculously expensive factory parts." Some reckoned a competitive CB900FZ-powered TT-F1 bike could cost up to £8000 – more than a new Yamaha TZ750F. The kit gave its buyer pistons, liners, cams, rods, crank, ignition and exhaust systems, sprockets, tacho and a dry-sump conversion, to which had to be added a donor bike and a chassis – Harris, Mocheck, P&M – along with spare wheels and tyres.

Gerald Davison made the best of it. "In which other form of racing," he asked in *MCN*, "can you buy all the tuning gear for that price and have a bike the same as a works machine?" Looking back, former team co-ordinator Barry Symmons recalls how Honda Britain responded to the emerging problem: "We were very disappointed when the prices for the kit parts were announced, so we set about getting UK companies to produce less costly parts: Quaife did gearboxes, Kent made cams; we found companies to produce exhausts and clutches."

From Ducati, news came that Hailwood might campaign two bikes in the season ahead – an 860 (making about 100bhp at the wheel) for the TT and something bigger (developing 110-115) for short circuits, and that Sports Motorcycles was putting £40,000 into the project. There was, however, a difficulty. "The rules allow for engines to be bored out to 1000cc," Sports Motorcycles' Pat Slinn told *Motor Cycle Weekly*, "which presents a problem, because to do that it's necessary to increase the thickness of

John Williams bolstered Honda's ranks in mid '78, putting his 888 into second in the F1 TT and collecting useful placings at Snetterton and the Ulster. (Courtesy Elwyn Roberts)

the cylinder liner, and this cannot be done without altering the crankcase throat." The problem arose in translating the F1 regs: "The original French says the crankcase material may not be altered," said Slinn, "while the English translation says the design of the crankcase may not be changed." The devil was, as ever, in the detail.

Nor was Sports' racing department alone in facing difficulties. Mocheck, among the stars of the 1978 series, was on the point of withdrawing from F1 for want of engines. Already struggling with the loss of Tom Herron to Suzuki's fledgling F1 team (using Dunstall GS1000s), the London outfit had wanted new CB900FZ-based engines from Honda Britain, but was offered instead some of Honda Britain's 20 costly race kits.

"We imported five engines, which because of the price didn't sell," recalls Symmons. "So instead we offered two each to frame builders P&M and Ron Williams (Maxton) in an attempt to increase the availability of F1 chassis for privateers." These engines were the least exotic in Honda's three-tier performance structure. Next were the 'Gempo' engines, used by national distributors, and then the full works kit, used only by the factory and wholly owned Honda subsidiaries such as Honda Britain and American Honda. Still waiting for its own bikes, Honda Britain stocked up on aftermarket frames, buying a P&M chassis each for Haslam and Grant, plus one spare – and, later, Harris frames as well. Meanwhile, David Dixon's F1 Honda for Charlie Williams got its Maxton frame, and Gilbert's of Catford recruited 1977 F750 World Champion Steve Baker to ride its P&M Honda in place of the injured Cowie.

COUNTDOWN

Honda said it wouldn't re-homologate the 31mm Keihin CR carburettors that appeared on Read's 1977 TT-winning 810. Whether it would have been possible with 1000 now required was a moot point, but as the CB900FZ came with 32mm CVs it didn't seem to matter. Honda Britain's new hardware arrived for tests at Donington in May, a couple of weeks before the first round of the '79 TT-F1 series, now co-sponsored by *Motor Cycle Weekly*. The new bike, officially designated the CB900 (modified) became known as the RS1000 for its origins in Honda's RSC workshops. The top end of the 16-valver had plenty in common with the road bike: valves of stock size, 26mm (inlet) and 22.5mm (exhaust), cams with comparable lift (8.5 and 9mm) and the stock Morse camchain, albeit with a stiffer tensioner. Bore and stroke were 67.8mm (from 64.5mm) x 69mm, giving a capacity of 996.5cc. Power was rated at 125bhp at 9500rpm with 10.5:1 compression. Like the sportster, the F1 bike used a one-piece crank with plain mains and big ends, but where the road bike had a wet sump the F1 lump went dry to

Mick Grant, pictured here at the Ulster GP, joined Honda Britain in 1979, winning the British F1 title in 1980, but TT-F1 success for Honda at Dundrod eluded him. (Courtesy Elwyn Roberts)

reduce oil drag, with a twin-rotor oil pump to keep lubricant circulating. In place of the roadster's 16-plate wet clutch a 14-plate dry unit transferred power to the close-ratio five-speed 'box. Like most competition bikes ignition was total loss, using a 12V battery, and the alternator was lopped from the right of the engine to shorten the crank, cut weight and improve cornering clearance. The frame was a straightforward steel double cradle with 26 degrees of rake and a wheelbase of 1440mm. Dry weight was given as 168kg.

Haslam gave the new bike its '79 FT/MCW TT-F1 championship debut at a Brands weekend overshadowed by events at the North West 200. The Ulster meeting cost the lives of Tom Herron, Brian Hamilton and, eventually, Frank Kennedy, and put several others, including Mick Grant and Warren Willing, in hospital with serious – in Willing's case career-ending – injuries. While Kevin Stowe, Kennedy and Willing all crashed at Coleraine in a one-off match race, Herron died at Juniper Hill while disputing third place with Jeff Sayle and Steve Parrish on the final lap of the North West 200. Grant suffered a cracked pelvis in the 500cc race when a broken chain adjuster jammed his back wheel and brought him into painful contact with a call box at York Hairpin.

Days later, a subdued racing community gathered at Brands. Charlie Williams rode Grant's Honda Britain RS1000 and Manship Parrish's GS1000. Haslam's toughest opposition came from an unexpected quarter. Graeme Crosby had recently come to the UK from the Australian Grand Prix meeting at Bathurst. There he'd put his TKA Kawasaki KR750 into second place between winner Ron Boulden's TZ750 and John Woodley's RG500 in an edge-of-the-seat thriller that was a genuine candidate for race of the decade. After 60 lead changes over 20 laps, it all came down to the last corner. Croz led through the plunging twists and turns across the top of the 3.8-mile Mount Panorama circuit, and Boulden wasn't quite as close as he wished at the top of the mile-plus Conrod Straight that closed the lap; but he held his Yamaha flat over the humps at the end of the straight and was near enough to out-drag Crosby from the last turn, the 90-degree Murray's Corner, on the final dash to the line.

Now Crosby was back with four-stroke power, on a bike he'd first seen in Japan in 1978. He'd been there to ride with Australian Tony Hatton in the inaugural Suzuka 8 Hours. Crosby relished taking on grand prix two-strokes with big, unruly four-strokes, and demonstrated his capacity to do so very effectively on the Pops Yoshimura-infused Kawasaki Superbikes put together by Sydney dealers Ross and Ralph Hannan. In Japan's steaming summer of 1978, Crosby and Hatto began doing business with another member of the Yoshimura family, Mamoru Moriwaki, who'd married Pops' daughter Namiko.

While Pops decided his business future lay in the US, and ultimately with Suzuki, Moriwaki stayed at home and made his name with Kawasaki and later Honda-powered motorcycles. The bike Croz and Hatton rode

*By 1981 Honda's RS1000s were beginning to struggle against the Suzuki XR69.
Pictured is Ron Haslam on his 999 (with mechanical anti-dive).
(Courtesy Elwyn Roberts)*

at Suzuka was an early example, and made the kind of 130+bhp power Crosby was used to with the Hannans' bikes. It too had a Kawasaki Z unit as its base, running 73mm pistons to give a capacity of 1105cc, 31mm Keihin smoothbores and Moriwaki cams pushing 1.5mm oversize inlet valves and 1mm bigger exhausts in the ported and polished head. The crank was stock, as was the clutch, albeit with heavier springs. Compression ran at 10.5:1.

Its frame was based on the stock unit – and not braced. "None of our frames were," recalls Ross Hannan. "It was unnecessary and offered no advantage." Suspension was from Kayaba: "Ralph changed the head angle and fitted Z650 triple clamps to change the offset, helping it steer better." Add Morris Mag wheels and straight bars giving a sit-up riding position and the result was, effectively, a Superbike of the type America was coming to know and love. At Suzuka the Australasian pair finished third after Hatto had run dry and undertaken a long, hot push in to refuel. Winners were Wes Cooley and Mike Baldwin on one of Pops' Suzuki GS1000s and second a Yamaha TZ750 ridden by David Emde and Isoyo Sugimoto.

Croz and the Moriwaki – albeit with 28mm carbs and 69.4mm pistons, dropping its capacity to 998cc – now stood alongside Haslam's Honda Britain RS1000 at the Brands Hatch opening round of the TT-F1 title. The new Hondas looked good and Haslam got a flier at the start from Steve Baker's P&M Honda, Manship's GS1000 third. Croz completed his first racing lap of Brands short circuit in fifth, but soon closed on the front runners, getting into third with three of the 12 laps done, while Charlie Williams fell at Clearways and Baker drifted back. The Kiwi passed Manship for second and then took the lead with two laps to go, as Haslam missed a gear on the run-up to Druids. But Crosby ran wide at the same spot a lap later, and Haslam nipped through to win despite a troublesome gear selector. Manship was third from Roger Marshall's P&M Honda while Baker completed his first and last F1 race in fifth. The American fell heavily at Paddock later in the meeting, breaking an arm and a leg. Coming so soon after his 1978 season-ending crash at Mosport Park, it was more than enough: before the season was out, Baker had announced his retirement.

Hailwood again stole the show during TT week, winning the Senior and, back on his RG500 for the Classic, taking his only second place on the Island after pushing winner Alex George (Yamaha) hard all the way. George also made the F1 TT headlines. Deputising for Mick Grant, he won on the Honda Britain RS1000 with a new lap record at 112.94mph. Charlie Williams ran second on David Dixon's Maxton-framed Honda, and Haslam third on an RS1000 that kept cutting out (later traced to fuel starvation) after a scrap with Hailwood.

The multiple world champion had, he said, "an enjoyable dice with young Ron. He's improved tremendously since last year." But for all his bonhomie, Hailwood had a trying week. His 1979 F1 bike wasn't a patch on the mount he'd had in 1978. Prepared by the factory, it was effectively a square-case 900SS "with an Imola cam," said Steve Wynne. It had a new frame that gave more cornering clearance and quicker steering, yet handled so badly the team put Hailwood's engine into a 1978 frame. His F1 race was then punctuated by problems, among them a fractured exhaust and a dead engine at Keppel Gate, which Hailwood traced to a loose battery lead. He restarted but then lost fifth gear on the last lap at Bray Hill, making things, he said, "distinctly inconvenient" and dropping him to fifth place behind Island debutant Crosby.

The wheel thing

Back in the mainland for the Mallory Park Post-TT meeting, Grant marked his return to competition by leading away the TT-F1 race and holding off Haslam until half-distance. The pack included Tony Rutter's 996 P&M Honda and Charlie Williams' Dixon Honda – but not Croz, who'd gone out on the opening lap with a broken first gear; nor Hailwood, whose ride on a Dunstall Suzuki ended, reported *Motor Cycle News*, "after he ran out of brakes." Hailwood quietly left the paddock and moved on to his next venture.

There was good news for British fans who were cultivating a taste for Crosby's frequent and lurid wheelies. Ross Hannan had been in conversation with British promoters, and put together a plan to help the Kiwi ride in the UK for the rest of the season. Mamoru Moriwaki had been asked to supply a spare engine.

At the start of 1980 the American Honda team received its hardware –
CB750F-based Superbikes and RS1000 F1 bikes. Ron Pierce (pictured) rode his
RS to seventh in the Daytona 200. (Courtesy Mary Grothe)

Croz had yet to put one over on Haslam, however, and it didn't happen
at the Donington third round of the FT/MCW series. There, in front of a
50,000-strong crowd, the Nottinghamshire rider beat a star-studded field
on his Pharaoh TZ750 in both legs of the Duckhams/*MCN* Superbike event,
making it three with the TT-F1 race. Both Haslam and team-mate Grant
(trying RG500 forks on his RS1000 in an effort to fix its poor handling)
started downfield while Manship got away and led until his engine seized.
After Charlie Williams crashed, Croz got into open country, but Haslam
caught the Kiwi at half distance, passing him and pulling away. Marshall
looked good until slowing with gearbox trouble and Grant finished third
from Rutter, Marshall and Moyce. Four rounds down: Haslam 55, Croz 32,
Grant and Charlie Williams 22 apiece.

The Kiwi tried again at Snetterton a week later when he and Haslam
diced hard, the Moriwaki man scooping up the Honda rider under brakes
only to lose point on the straights. During the closing stages Haslam got
a 30-yard break through traffic, which was too much for the Moriwaki's
brick-like aerodynamics. Manship was best in a furious dice for third from
Rutter and Williams, while Marshall finished sixth and Grant retired with an
RS1000 running on three.

Within a fortnight Crosby was back at Suzuka for another go at the 8
Hours, this time qualifying fastest, and setting the fastest lap before an

oil leak and a crash by co-rider Akitaka Tomie put the Moriwaki team out. Instead, the day belonged to Honda and its CB900F Superbike ridden by Australians Hatton and Mick Cole. Dale Singleton and Dave Aldana had tailed the Australian pair, but Aldana crashed on lap 46 and the team lost 25 minutes to repairs. British hopes rested with Haslam and double TT winner Alex George, who stormed through the field after early gearbox problems to finish a fine second. The leaders' most consistent opposition, the Yoshimura Suzuki ridden by Wes Cooley and Ron Pierce, threw a rod during the third hour.

Crosby got a little unexpected help at Silverstone, when light rain fell before the start of the TT-F1 race at the British GP. The Moriwaki man outbraked Grant at Copse on the opening lap to put his nose in front. Haslam, feeling secondhand after a crash in practice for the 250 race, retired early, and Grant crashed at Becketts. But George and his P&M Honda looked the goods, passing Crosby, who now had front brake problems and lacked the speed to hold the Honda on a drying track.

Haslam was back on form for the Ulster GP and in championship-winning mood, bruises and all. Bad weather cut practice short, making race-day jetting a gamble that didn't pay off for George, Haslam's closest challenger for the F1 world title. Croz was also struggling with set-up problems and while Haslam got away, he held an uncertain second until Rutter swept past. George, meanwhile, was scrapping with Marshall for fourth, and that's where he stayed: Haslam posted his fifth win in seven F1 races and collected a world championship into the bargain.

Suzuki drafted in more assistance a week later for the Oulton Park F1 race, giving Barry Sheene his first ride on a four-stroke since 1969, when he'd ridden a Kuhn Norton at Scarborough. He adapted quickly to the GS1000 – in Sheene parlance "the muckspreader" – ousting Grant from second and getting away in pursuit of a flying Haslam. He all but caught him too, but was shoved onto the grass at Esso by an unwary backmarker. Haslam headed for the hills, leaving Sheene in second from Grant, George, Woods, and a subdued Croz, his Moriwaki tired for want of spares and now battered from a practice tumble. Eight rounds gone: Haslam 100, Crosby 71, George 46.

Suggestions that Suzuki might be pushing harder in F1 for 1980 came in August with the news that Crosby was on the point of signing for Suzuki GB. Rex White had been chasing Haslam's signature, but when that came to nothing, declared himself "quietly confident" of signing Crosby.

The TT-F1 field got a little respite from the Haslam onslaught at Scarborough, where Grant, Croz and Marshall put on an exciting dice until Croz's brake lever started coming back to the bar. Grant pushed on in the lead until baulked by a backmarker, letting Marshall through for his first win of the series. But the inevitable could be delayed little longer, as Haslam took the title at Cadwell Park the following weekend with a round to spare. Riding with an arm hurt in a practice, Haslam challenged Grant until a spasm of pain forced him wide at the Gooseneck. He rolled it off to finish fourth while Grant won, fending off George and Croz. Job done.

As the season wound down Haslam had three factories chasing his signature. In the end he stuck with Honda, but would do up to 20 races on Mal Carter's Yamahas. Grant and George would likewise ride for Honda, though the big news came from elsewhere: Suzuki confirmed Crosby's signing for the team to do TT-F1, the TT, and 500cc races.

The last dance on Britain's domestic card was the Gauloises Powerbike International at Brands Hatch, where Barry Sheene, in his one ride of the weekend (on his XR23), took a last win for Suzuki in the title event and Potter beat Haslam by half a wheel to secure the Duckhams/*MCN* Superbike Championship. In the TT-F1 race Haslam tried as hard as ever, pursuing early leader Grant, then falling while pulling a desperate outbraking move at Druids. Marshall and Croz chased Grant home in second and third. Final points: Haslam 108, Crosby 101, Grant 74, George and Marshall 58, Williams 36.

CODE RED

Croz described it as a wrench to leave Kawasaki, especially since getting wind of the mooted KR500 grand prix bike back at Suzuka. It was poignant, too, that his last ride on the old KR750 triple, in the second race at the

Rare bird: Kawasaki's Z1000SR TT-F1 prototype went to Australia in early 1980, to be ridden by Gregg Hansford and Jim Budd (pictured at Oran Park) in two long-distance races. (Courtesy Ian Falloon)

Macau Grand Prix, should end with a crash on oil and a broken collarbone after he'd done so well in chasing home winner Sadao Asami's semi-factory Yamaha in the first race.

Suzuki's plans were well advanced, so far as the hardware was concerned. Crosby would be riding the new GS1000R – otherwise known as the XR69 – and an XR34 RG500. As yet Crosby had no team-mate. Talks with Kork Ballington hadn't borne fruit; Mike Baldwin's name had also been mentioned, but now there were doubts over his fitness. After a good AMA season in 1978 Baldwin had joined the renewed Kawasaki US team, primarily to ride Superbikes – but he'd also snared a KR750 ride, and it was from the triple that he fell heavily at the Pocono AMA national, badly breaking a leg. Now there was another name in the frame, that of the new American wunderkind, Californian Randy Mamola.

In February, Suzuki announced signing Mamola on a one-year contract, riding XR34s in grand prix and XR23s in some internationals – though a shortage of spares might limit the 652's appearances. It seemed likely that Croz would be going it alone for Suzuki GB, at least for the time being, in the season's 10-round FT/MCW TT-F1 Championship – and perhaps the Duckhams/*MCN* Superbike Championship, which was now open to four-strokes of any capacity, with bonuses for the top three four-stroke finishers.

More changes were coming among Britain's F1 fields, not all of them welcome. First, Peckett & McNab were no more. Peter McNab wanted to get back to racing and joined the George Beale team, leaving Richard Peckett to go it alone. Buying McNab's share of the business left Peckett little money for luxuries such as racing. "We did road bike repairs, stuff like that, and we made the odd frame," he recalls. "And then classic racing started ..."

Others too were tightening their belts. Moriwaki was gearing up to send four bikes to Daytona, but internal difficulties (Ross Hannan had been unwell) meant that Mamoru's outfit would be unable to mount a serious effort in the UK during 1980 and so capitalise on Croz's 1979 successes.

Meanwhile, Suzuki was making the headlines. Although Patrick Pons notched a seventh Daytona 200 win for the Yamaha TZ750 in 1980, the Florida meeting marked an early opportunity for the factory-backed American Honda and Yoshimura Suzuki teams to square off against one another, with the first round going decisively Suzuki's way. In the Superbike Production race Croz took one of Pops' GS1000s to a clean win, and, if the four-strokes generally made little impression on the 200, Aldana hustled his F1 Suzuki into sixth place behind a block of Yamahas and just ahead of Ron Pierce's Honda. Croz had, according to some, worked his way through five engines during practice, with ailments ranging from crank failure to ignition woes, and retired from the 200. He said the XR69 was fast and handled well, but parked it on lap 32 after running out of brakes.

British fans had to wait a while before getting their first glimpse of the new XR69. On the same weekend as the Scarborough opening round of the

TT-F1 championship, Crosby and Mamola were at Salzburg watching snow fall. Meanwhile George Beale's Granby Honda team-mates Marshall and Graeme McGregor fought through wind and rain to take first and second at Oliver's Mount, Marshall leading from start to finish. The Honda Britain bikes of Grant and George were third and fourth, having fitted straight 'bars to cope better with the filthy weather and then found, said Grant, that the Granby Hondas "had 10mph on my bike."

Ron Haslam rejoined the team at Donington on the first of the new RS1000s, overbored 0.1mm to give a capacity of 999cc, with a hefty alloy swingarm replacing the older bike's steel unit, 44mm forks compared with 37mm and new CV carbs that proved tricky to set up. More problematic to begin with, the new bikes came with a batch of suspect pistons and Haslam was asked to take it easy, which he did for a time, watching Marshall carve himself a seven-second lead. He then decided enough was enough, catching and passing the Granby man, who slowed with gearbox problems. Haslam won with team-mates George and Grant third and fourth. The last F1 stop before the TT was the third round at Brands, and with the Suzuki team yet again on GP duty, Haslam trimmed the lap record in an eight-second win over Marshall, Grant and George. Three rounds done: Marshall 39, Haslam 30, Grant 28, George 26.

Suzuki's XR69s finally materialised at the TT, and were impressive – Pops Yoshimura had, after all, been honing the GS1000 engine in American Superbike racing for two full seasons. The dohc two-valve engine shared but few numbers with the 1978 road bike engine it was based on: 70 x 48.6mm bore and stroke, 997.5cc. Beyond that came divergence: compression ratio measured 11:1 on the XR (GS1000E, 9.2:1); its carburettors were 29mm Mikuni smoothbores (with a restrictor ring). The bottom end was more like stock with its wet-sump lubrication, a wet, multi-plate clutch and five-speed gearbox. There was a new crankshaft, re-profiled cams, reworked and highly polished ports feeding oversize 39mm inlet valves and expelling spent gases through 34mm exhausts. Power was up from the road bike's 90bhp at 8200rpm to 130bhp at 9500 – more, explains Ray Battersby in *Team Suzuki*, than the XR34.

While Pops' men in the US had to make do under Superbike regs with a modified version of the stock double-cradle frame, the TT-F1 XR69 got a tweaked XR34 frame with Kayaba suspension. All up weight was 167kg, but the bike was potent enough to be competitive, as Croz demonstrated in an F1 TT remembered as much for its acrimony as for its racing.

The trouble started when Croz was given the number three starting slot, which he felt he didn't merit on his first visit to the Island. Team chief Martyn Ogborne agreed and asked the FIM jury that he be started further back. The authorities gave him number 11, putting him alongside Grant. Honda wasn't impressed and said so to the FIM jury, which reversed its decision and put Croz back at number three. But Croz wouldn't budge, so he and Grant howled off towards St Ninian's crossroads together, Grant's 999cc Honda spluttering a little from its persistent carburation problems.

Granby Honda man Graeme McGregor led early, but stopped at Kirkmichael with a broken clutch cable, leaving Grant and Crosby together with a 10-second break on Alan Jackson's ex-Crosby Moriwaki Kawasaki. Then, at half distance Grant got going, opening a 10-second gap. Haslam retired early, coping with a broken exhaust but then rolling to a stop with a broken chain; and with one lap of six left, Grant had done it for Honda and was 30 seconds up on Crosby – who picked up the pace to pull clear of Sam McClements' Honda.

Grant crossed the line 10.8 seconds up on Croz – and was confirmed as winner two days later. First, he was subject to a protest for running an oversize tank. Gordon Pantall, Alan Jackson's entrant, thought it odd that Grant had done six laps on one fuel stop, where most others (Jackson included) made two. Grant said the going had been damp in places, reducing fuel consumption; though he admitted that the tank measured 28 litres, reduced to the permitted 24 by shoving a plastic bottle and some ping-pong balls inside. Croz's suspicions had been raised after the race when he saw Grant give the tank a thump as he returned to the paddock. The jury then threw out the protest, making Grant the winner at last. At a stewards' meeting the following day Grant's tank was measured – at 23.7 litres. And, says Barry Symmons, the FIM still measures fuel by volume rather than weight.

The four-strokers fitted their big motors for the Classic TT – 1084cc for Croz, 1062 for Grant's Honda, 31mm carbs and all. But Croz was soon out, retiring at the end of the second lap after over-revving and bending valves. The Hondas fared better, Grant taking second after battling with overgearing and a broken tank-retaining strap, Haslam having a quiet run

Graeme Crosby's introduction to Pops Yoshimura's GS1000-powered F1 bike came at Daytona in 1980. He retired with brake failure after battling with Dale Singleton for sixth. (Courtesy Mary Grothe)

into third. But no-one was about to stop Joey Dunlop from staking an early claim on his kingdom with a storming win on his Rea Racing TZ750 Yamaha, holding a loose tank with his knees while posting a new lap record at 115.22mph. Joey's day was dawning.

THE HAKA

Honda and Suzuki finally got to take on one another in short-circuit territory at the Post-TT, but the developing battle between Granby and Honda Britain became the headline act, Grant and Marshall in the thick of it with Haslam, Croz and, making his four-stroke debut, Randy Mamola. Marshall got in front early, then Grant, then Haslam; but Croz, already battling with his suspension set-up, got no higher than third before the XR69 started puffing smoke from piston failure. As Haslam slid about in third with front tyre problems, Grant won from Marshall, with Mamola putting his XR69 into fourth behind Haslam.

While British F1 runners had only one another to contend with, the going was tougher across the pond. Formula 1 in the USA was more liberal in its rulings, allowing 750cc two-strokes to line up against 1025cc four-strokes, though with fewer restrictions on engine modification. The TZ runners formed a powerful group, never mind that the heavily promoted and growing Superbike class was now garnering most of the headlines. After Daytona, AMA national road racing moved to a circuit new for motorcycles at Elkhart Lake, Wisconsin, where Wes Cooley gave his GS1000R the first AMA national win by a four-stroke since Cal Rayborn at Laguna Seca in 1972. True, Singleton and Baldwin were absent, but as Cooley put it, "They (Suzuki, Pops and his merry crew) built a bike that runs faster than hell," in his GS1000R Suzuki. He battled with new star Freddie Spencer until the Honda man retired his Superbike with a loose exhaust. Cooley then eased away, reporting better drive out of corners than the strokers, while Richard Schlachter (with off-key ignition timing) and Miles Baldwin (coming through the field after a sight problem) wrestled to get the first two-stroke home.

American racing looked promising again: a burgeoning Superbike championship and a thickening calendar of road race nationals helped to attract fans: in June, Loudon had a record crowd of 40,000 at its AMA meeting. In Britain, however, things were heading south. Margaret Thatcher came to power in May 1979 with 1.5 million unemployed, and the 10 per cent inflation she inherited from the Callaghan government soared. In her battle for control Thatcher used monetarist policies that pushed up the value of sterling. Britain's exports fell with the closure of factories, mines and shipyards; unemployment surged towards 3 million, so it was little wonder race gates were slumping: Donington Park and Oulton Park were well down year on year, and the Mallory Park Post-TT international attracted about half its usual figure. Only Brands Hatch seemed to be holding its own. "It's a worrying situation," said MCD boss Chris Lowe.

Cuts to Britain's crowded calendar were coming, but for the moment the cavalcade rolled on, to Snetterton where Croz finally broke his TT-F1 duck, putting his XR69 in front of early leader Grant. McGregor moved into second and Grant held third while Haslam slowed with an oil leak and then stopped altogether when his motor blew.

The Kiwi won again later in the month, rejoining his Yoshimura partner Wes Cooley to win the Suzuka 8 Hours on the latest of Pops' mighty creations. This time Kawasaki took the fight to Suzuki with Gregg Hansford and Eddie Lawson on its Z1000SR. For the opening session Hansford and Cooley led the field, Haslam holding third for Honda Britain on an RS1000 with a developmental monoshock rear end. The Honda pair dropped to fourth after a tyre change but fought back until a broken drive chain gave Haslam a long, hot push. With the leaders still circulating within seconds of one another, the decisive moment came when '79 winner Mick Cole dropped his Honda in front of Lawson, leaving the Kawasaki man nowhere to go but straight over him. Lawson stopped to check on Cole's condition and lost two minutes in doing so. Both leading bikes pitted once more – Lawson handing over to Hansford, Crosby to refuel and keep going, pulling clear of Hansford and getting home by 40 seconds at the flag. Endurance specialists Marc Fontan and Herve Moineau took third for Honda, with Haslam and Marshall sixth, four laps down on the leaders.

Croz made it three in a row at the British GP. While team-mate Mamola cleaned up the 500cc GP from Roberts, Croz showed the Hondas the way home in the TT-F1 race, taking the lead on lap four of 15 and staying there. His team-mate for the occasion was Joey Dunlop, who took to his duties with enthusiasm, working through the field into a clear second place at half distance. The Hondas generally struggled to match the XR69s for speed, and John Newbold was quickest of them, holding third on his Harris-framed 996 from Haslam on the best of the Honda Britain RS1000s. Seven rounds done: Grant 72, Marshall 59, Haslam 48, Crosby 42.

After Crosby was crowned F1 world champion at the Ulster Grand Prix it was clear that signing Dunlop was Suzuki's master stroke of the season. As the crews arrived at Dundrod, Grant led Crosby 15 points to 12 in the two-round championship, but with Dunlop again on an XR69, and having a rare appetite for the ever-changing sun, rain and rolling mists of his native turf, the odds tipped Crosby's way, the more so as Grant was stuck between choosing big carbs that left him struggling for grunt out of the hairpin or smaller units that cost him top end.

Joey was fastest in practice and stormed away from the start, while Crosby challenged Haslam for second. Joey had a 30-second lead by the time Croz got clear of the Honda. With Grant then fourth, Croz led the title by a point; then Haslam began to slow, and with a lap and a bit left, Grant moved into third – and led the championship by a point. But Joey, too, slowed, and Crosby passed to win: Crosby 27 points, Grant 25. While Croz joined Hughie Anderson and Bruce McLaren in the roll of Kiwi world champions, Joey plunged away towards Leathemstown en route to winning

Freddie Spencer used his RS1000 to good effect during 1981, leading the Daytona 200 and winning at Elkhart Lake, then pairing with Dave Aldana for a crack at the Bol d'Or. (Courtesy Stuart Rowlands PR)

the Classic, using his XR69 to lick Marshall's TZ750 and Newbold's Suzuki.

In early September, Haslam tested a new F1 bike with a modified engine and suspension, drilled discs, lighter callipers and narrower forks. Grant, too, got the new goodies, with frame modifications from Ron Williams and an engine angled to bring the gearbox sprocket in line with swinging arm pivot. Honda deployed its new firepower at Donington Park for the eighth round of the TT-F1 title. It didn't help: Croz and Dunlop again flayed the Hondas, thundering home from Grant, McGregor and George after Haslam retired with gearbox woes: Grant 82, Marshall 59, Croz 57. With two rounds to go, Croz had an outside chance at another title.

The end of the season was more about Grant than Croz: all Croz could do was win, and that wasn't enough. At Cadwell, Grant led early but was soon in a titanic struggle with Haslam, Marshall, McGregor, Newbold and Kiwi Stu Avant. Croz pressed the go button after a bad start, taking the lead at half distance. Haslam stormed after him, breaking the lap record to take the lead. Then, going into the Hairpin for the last time Haslam missed a gear and Crosby slipped past to win from Noddy. Grant was third, Haslam trailed in eighth, and the title was going to Yorkshire. Grant 92, Crosby 72, Marshall 67, Haslam 51.

The F1 field took a break while Mamola won the Race of the Year on his XR34, instead lining up for the last race of the season at Brands for the Gauloises meeting, and while Grant led from the start, Croz won again, giving him five wins from six starts and 87 points. Grant won the title with 90 points, running second to Croz at Brands, with Noddy again third.

ALL CHANGE

Croz had had a superb season in Britain, and was starting to make his mark in GPs. Certainly he was now among the world's best four-stroke riders. Honda thought so, and invited him to join up for '81 and take on American Superbike as well as TT-F1 – but with no 500 offered, Croz decided to stay put. So did Ron Haslam, signing a two-year deal with Honda that this time contained a clause preventing him from riding for anyone else. Like Croz, he'd be riding F1 at world and British level, and would have a 'special bike' for the *MCN* Superbike Championship. Who'd be alongside him was, temporarily, a mystery. As the nights drew in, Mick Grant was still waiting to hear from Honda, and there were whispers Joey would be taking his place. Making life still more complex, a withdrawal of Castrol money forced George Beale to trim his team, leaving Graeme McGregor and Roger Marshall without rides in the bigger capacities.

News from the Malta FIM congress that the 1983 F1 and Endurance world championships would run a 750cc ceiling brought audible rumbles of discontent. Meanwhile, it was confirmed that Joey had joined Honda. That left Suzuki without a wingman for Croz in four-stroke events, though the betting shortened on Grant when Crosby himself said he'd like an IoM specialist on the strength.

What was certain by the end of November was that Britain's 1981 TT-F1 series would run to nine rounds and be richer than ever, with more than £2000 per round. Croz got his eye in by winning the Swann Series in Australia; running his XR69 in 1084cc guise, he shared wins with Steve Trinder's RG500 at Oran Park and with Greg Pretty's TZ750 at Surfer's Paradise, before securing the series with a double win at Adelaide International Raceway. Finally, at Sandown, Croz bent some valves, letting Ron Boulden in to win from Haslam, who at last seemed to be getting used to the sunshine.

All the hands were at last dealt – Mamola and Croz would lead Suzuki GB's grand prix effort with Croz leading the way in F1. He'd be backed up in F1 by Newbold, and for the TT and the Ulster by Grant, who'd ride his own Harris Suzuki in the UK F1 championship. Haslam and Joey would be Honda's main men, and the season's wild cards were united in a new Moriwaki team to be overseen by Croz. There'd be an F1 mount for Roger Marshall and a new iteration of Moriwaki's American-style Superbike for a new kid – Wayne Gardner.

Gardner came from Wollongong, an hour's drive south of Sydney. As he grew up he'd ridden some dirt, cut his teeth on TZ Yamahas backed by local dealer Karl Praml, and developed his name on Billy McDonald's NCR Ducati and Peter Molloy's Honda Superbike. Ross Hannan, who'd done so much to help Croz's career, kept an eye on Gardner during 1980 and invited Mamoru Moriwaki to the Sandown leg of the Swann Series to see Gardner win a national championship race, riding a bike fitted with rain tyres on a dry track. Moriwaki liked what he saw, and later, during a party at Hannan's home, the three of them retired to a quiet corner and worked out a deal that put Gardner on Moriwaki's rides at Daytona, and then provided him with bikes and parts, via the British Moriwaki agent, for the UK season.

There was talk of big four-stroke engines for open races, with Honda

Moriwaki and Wayne Gardner took Britain by storm in 1981. He's pictured at Donington on his 1105cc Superbike with Yamaha-mounted Barry Sheene doing the stalking. (Courtesy Mortons Media Archive)

Britain cooking up 1123s in '81 for Haslam and Dunlop, and more 1084s for the Suzuki men. As for the F1 bikes, the powerplant of the '81 spec Honda RS1000 was largely as before, but for 35.5mm CV carbs. Suzuki's XR69S, on the other hand, was now equipped with a Full-Floater rear end that Croz said was worth up to two seconds a lap during early short-circuit tests. And nor was that the end of it: the bike had gone on a diet with the addition of magnesium cases and covers. The clutch basket too was lighter, and all up, weight was trimmed to around 159kg. An assortment of carburettors was available, ranging from 31mm Keihins to 36mm Mikunis. Power was officially rated at 134bhp at 9500rpm.

With rumours that the new RS1000 was making 150bhp, Suzuki's 134 seemed a little light, but Grant said his Yoshimura engine had made 147bhp at the gearbox sprocket, and that the bike was the quickest he'd ridden. Now he was sampling monoshock units from DeCarbon and a trick F1 car strut from Koni. Small wonder, perhaps, that he had his sights set on the Shell/*MCN* Superbike Series. Meanwhile, the FIM postponed until 1984 the introduction of a 750cc ceiling for endurance and TT-F1 after copping a barrage of complaints from riders and entrants.

Despite drives by Daytona and the AMA to get four-strokes into the action, two-strokes still ruled the roost in American F1. After Wes Cooley's ground-breaking win at Elkhart Lake the TZ750s came back, winning the 1980 nationals at Loudon (Richard Schlachter), Road Atlanta (Schlachter again, Cooley second), Laguna Seca (KR on his 0W48) and Pocono (Singleton). The '81 Daytona 200 ran to a similar script after the leading four-stroke contenders all retired: Spencer's Honda with a blown engine after leading for 16 laps, Cooley with a sticking throttle followed by a broken camshaft and Crosby with gearbox woes. Dale Singleton had a good day, though, taking his Taylor-White TZ750 to victory for the second time in three years. Yamahas filled the first nine places, but among the better four-strokes were the Moriwakis: Gardner 11th, Marshall 13th.

Gardner did better in the Superbike race, finishing fourth and winning himself some useful coverage in the British press. Meanwhile, Honda Britain's new F1 bikes were expected to be on duty for the opening round of the TT-F1 title, for which Grant also got some much-needed cheer, with news that Granby Motors would back him for the series. At the end of March, however, the British press had an altogether more sombre story to tell, that of the death of Mike Hailwood and his daughter Michelle after their car collided with a lorry as they drove home after collecting fish and chips for the family's supper.

The Moriwaki team bikes came out of their containers on the Tuesday before the Cadwell Park F1 series opener and didn't need long to make an impression. Gardner, riding his high-bar Superbike with its 1105cc engine, began the final eclipse of the TZ750 Yamaha in British open-class racing by winning the first leg of the Shell/*MCN* Superbike event and finishing runner-up to reigning champion Dave Potter's Yamaha in the second. Croz, fighting niggling problems with his new XR69S, and Ron Haslam, losing damping from the new Koni shocks on his Maxton-framed 1123, posted solid results, but looked better in the opening round of the TT-F1 series. Haslam and then Croz took turns at the front, hounded by Gardner and Marshall, who was lucky to be there at all: he'd blown his motor in the second Superbike race and Moriwaki's skilled crew had done a heart transplant in some 40 minutes. Now he got past his new team-mate to take the lead, but while Haslam slowed with front-end patter Croz stormed through to win.

By the time they were unveiled at Cadwell, Honda's new F1 runners had lighter frames, trick Showa forks and laid-forward Kayabas in a redesigned rear end. There was a new exhaust system, and the ignition was now on the right of the crank. There were teething problems, however: "I think we'll have to get more speed out of it," said Haslam of his new mount.

In the faster going at Donington, Gardner's Superbike couldn't win but he stirred the crowd with wheelies, running second and third in the Shell/*MCN* Superbike races, while Yamaha runners Sheene and Graham Wood divvied up the wins. He fared better among the four-strokes, getting away well in the TT-F1 race to lead from Croz with Marshall closing in third. Haslam was riding his heart out in fourth but lacked the speed of the leaders. At half distance Crosby got going to win and set a new race record, the Moriwaki boys completing the podium from Haslam, Noddy's XR69 and Joey. Gardner later explained he'd lost fourth gear and agreed that Croz was fast. "Moriwaki have arrived," said Marshall.

Back in black

Laden ferries docked at Douglas to the usual background of bickering over TT start money, with the stars unhappy this year about the ACU's new allocation system and its 'guaranteed minima.' On the Island, Honda Britain hoped to regain some of the glory lost to Croz and to Joey in 1980.

The UK had licked a threadbare American team in the Transatlantic Trophy, with Haslam winning the opening leg to post his first four-stroke win at Mallory Park since 1973, underlining his belief that the damping problems with the Konis on his 1123 had been fixed. Yet there were concerns over the team's F1 performances, and Ron had been to Japan to test new bikes. "I hope they'll be faster," said Haslam. "Our Cadwell and Donington bikes are lighter than last year's and they have more speed and torque – but they're down on acceleration."

Honda flew a bike to the UK for more testing, along with conversion kits for two more. Haslam and Joey tried them at Brands and Oulton Park before pushing on to the Island. The new bikes were smaller and more potent. The oil cooler had been moved into the nose of the fairing, and an extra frame strut fitted between the downtubes. Ron Williams added bracing to the underside of the swinging arm, and the Showa forks now came equipped with anti-dive like that on the NR500. The engine gave Honda a new route to 999cc by using the CB750F's crank. The short-stroke, freer-revving unit measured 71.6 x 62mm and early comments suggested better mid-range than the old 69mm-stroke unit. During TT practice Alex George's Honda Britain RS was clocked at 161mph, Croz at 159 and Haslam at 158.

The F1 TT was settled for the second year running by an FIM jury. Crosby's bike was wheeled to the start after a last-minute tyre change with the wrong rear sprocket fitted: the mistake was spotted, the XR taken from the grid and the sprocket briskly changed. With everything given a final tweak, Croz got onto the grid 45 seconds late and the ACU ordered him to the back of the grid, giving him a start time almost five minutes later than originally allocated. An announcement via the PA then said Crosby's race time would be taken from his original start position, according to ACU regulations.

Joey led early, pulling seven seconds on Grant's Suzuki GB XR69 over a damp, blustery mountain. Croz was third on corrected time from Moriwaki-equipped McGregor, then came Haslam, followed by Sam McClements' Suzuki. Grant closed on Joey during the second lap and took a narrow lead at the first stops, only to retire at Ballacraine – he thought he'd bent a valve in a missed change and stopped when he heard "a dreadful rattling." McGregor was also out after falling in the pit lane on spilt petrol, making Haslam a clear second. Charging through the field, Croz would have had the lead by lap four on corrected time while Joey slowed with a chunked rear tyre and a misfire caused by loose plug leads, letting Haslam past on the clock. After six laps, ignoring Croz, Haslam got home 37 seconds clear of Joey, with McClements third from Noddy.

Ron Haslam, Alex George and Joey Dunlop (pictured) turned out in black for the 1981 Classic TT as a protest against the result of the F1 race. Croz won for Suzuki, but Joey set a lap record at 115.40mph. (Courtesy TTracepics.com)

The race was given to Haslam, but Suzuki team chief Martyn Ogborne had lodged a protest over Crosby's penalty, believing his start time had been calculated wrongly. Two hours later, after the FIM jury had convened to discuss the matter, Croz was reinstated, Haslam dropped to second and Joey to third, the jury saying Crosby's time should have started when he began the race. Honda was furious and team boss Gerald Davison put a forceful case, pointing out that Ron could have gone harder if he'd known Croz was still in contention – but the result stood.

Honda considered withdrawing from the meeting, but for the Classic TT ran Haslam, Dunlop and George and their bikes, Maxton-framed 1123s, decked out in black. "We felt we had a duty to race fans," Davison explained to *Motor Cycle News*. "So we withdrew our official identity."

For the opening laps of the Classic, Croz and Joey went toe to toe, Joey leading early by a couple of seconds, Croz coming back at him. They were still neck and neck when Joey ran dry at the Nook and started the long push in. Haslam, meanwhile, stopped at Sulby Bridge with a broken crank, and after Croz caught Grant on the road the two Suzukis did the last lap together for an emphatic 1-2, leaving George with the consolation of third place on the remaining black Honda. As for Joey running dry, Barry Symmons recalls Joey forgoing his second fuel stop for a crack at the lap record. 115mph laps are thirsty things.

With the Mallory Park Post-TT meeting reworked as the Sidecar Race of the Year, Crosby's march towards the domestic championship resumed at Snetterton. There, Haslam chased home Kork Ballington's KR500 GP bike in the *MCN* Superbike races, and Croz took another well-executed F1 win, leading early while Haslam took second from Grant and Gardner passed Noddy – then to be excluded for running his Superbike carbs. Four rounds down: Crosby 60, Haslam 42, Newbold 28, Marshall 24.

Marshall didn't add to his score at Snetterton. He didn't practice on Friday and a cracked piston on Saturday kept him out of the meeting for want of spares. Moriwaki director Graeme Crosby sought talks with the team's UK suppliers.

Croz's string of wins in the TT-F1 series came to a stop at Silverstone. While Grant fell after cornering too hard and Haslam worked through the field, Croz chased early leader Gardner, taking the lead and easing away. Haslam then passed Gardner while Croz over-revved, clipping valves. Two laps later he rolled to a stop while Haslam won from Gardner, Joey and Newbold.

Gardner's second place looked like being his high-water mark for a while. It seemed the British end of Moriwaki had run out of cash, and at a meeting with directors Rolf Munding and Crosby, Gardner and Marshall were told they'd only be supported at key championship meetings – TT-F1 for Marshall, *MCN* Superbike for Gardner.

Happier days lay ahead for Croz. Before the Ulster Grand Prix he had a three-point lead over Haslam in the two-round F1 world championship. On race day the weather was filthy, though the track dried a little before the race and Croz, Grant and Haslam all went for intermediates. Haslam bolted from the start, knowing he had at least to finish in front of Crosby. Grant, Croz, Noddy, and Dunlop gave chase, Croz pulling clear in second while Grant fell back a little, in pain from an injured shoulder. Noddy held fourth from Joey – by his own admission having an off day. Haslam won comfortably from Croz, but it wasn't enough: each ended the day with 27 points but Crosby won the title with a shorter combined time for the two races, taking his second world championship by one minute, 37 seconds.

Back on English soil, Croz began his Oulton Park visit with a crash in the opening Superbike race. He resorted to his spare bike for the second leg but retired early with carburation problems. Dave Potter looked like an overall winner, taking the first leg and leading the second before being badly hurt in a crash at Cascades. Haslam went on to win overall while Croz took the TT-F1 win after a scrap with Noddy. Haslam was third, saying his bike "couldn't match the speed of the works Suzukis," and Marshall fourth. Gardner withdrew with engine problems, but was still second to Haslam in the *MCN* Superbike standings.

A week later Potter was 'stable but critical,' on life support with serious neck injuries. Witnesses had begun to come forward saying he'd hit an unprotected barrier. Vernon Cooper, who'd been clerk of the course,

In 1981 Ron Haslam performed well on his 1123cc open-class Honda, winning a Transatlantic Trophy race at Mallory Park – the first four-stroke win in the series since Peter Williams' Norton in 1973. (Courtesy Mortons Media Archive)

began to receive threats, and a police guard was mounted on his Cheshire home. Potter died 17 days after his crash without regaining consciousness, leaving a widow and two children.

The factory teams withdrew from the Scarborough round of the series, saying F1 bikes were too heavy and potent for the tight, narrow track. In their absence, Marshall and Grant put on a show while Gardner came through from the back of the grid, chasing home his Moriwaki team-mate and collecting second place after Grant stopped to fix a loose plug lead. Though still coaxing maximum entertainment value from his straight-'bar Superbike in 998 and 1105cc guises, the Australian seemed unhappy with Moriwaki, and began talking to Honda and Suzuki.

MAN OF THE WORLD

Croz collected more pots at Mallory, snatching the Race of the Year from Barry Sheene, and then taking the TT-F1 championship with his sixth win of the season. Haslam again led early, then Grant, but there was no stopping Crosby who took the win from Newbold, Marshall and Haslam. Haslam had a happier time on his 1123, taking both Superbike races and a 28-point lead over Gardner, who added to his woes by crashing. Soon he was on a plane home, leaving behind him word that he'd signed to ride for Honda in '82.

There was no keeping Croz out of the headlines either. In October Mamoru Moriwaki said he would "almost certainly" run his team from Japan during the coming season, leaving Marshall without a ride. Croz sold his shares in Moriwaki UK. And then the big one: Croz and Suzuki were to part company. In late October, Maurice Knight invited Croz to Suzuki GB HQ and told him the team would have no GP bikes for him in 1982. F1 bikes would be available, but no 500s.

The announcement came as Croz prepared for the final British meeting of the year, at Brands, where for once he finished second in the TT-F1 round to sometime team-mate John Newbold's Suzuki. Grant finished third and Marshall fourth, but Haslam's race came to an end when he fell at Graham Hill Bend, his 999 catching fire. The Honda man again did better on his 1123, rolling home third in the *MCN* Superbike race behind Keith Huewen's RG and Ballington's KR to take the series, becoming the first four-stroke rider to do so since John Cooper in 1972. But Croz was the man in TT-F1. Final points: Crosby 102, Haslam and Newbold 75, Marshall 65.

As the year closed Suzuki's position became clearer. Crosby had won three titles for Suzuki in his second year with the team: the British TT-F1 and ShellSport 500 and the TT-F1 world championship; but where his GP team-mate, Randy Mamola, had won four 500cc GPs, Croz had yet to open his account. Said Suzuki MD Denys Rohan: "In Mamola we have a rider capable of winning the 500cc title." *Motor Cycle Weekly* pointed out that there was "no love lost" between Mamola and Crosby. In December, Mamola told the British press: "By the end of the season things were real bad between us, and I told everybody there was no way Croz and I could ride in the same team next year, and I guess Croz thought the same way."

Croz spoke to Gerald Davison at Honda with a view to riding in US Superbikes for 1982 and had a chat with his old friend Pops Yoshimura. He went home, thoroughly fed up, and then got a call from Giacomo Agostini offering a grand prix ride – for Yamaha.

Even without Moriwaki, the coming British TT-F1 season looked intriguing, with Gardner joining Haslam and Joey at Honda while Marshall joined Grant and Noddy at Suzuki. Before Gardner and Marshall could try on their new leathers, however, there was the Swann Series in Australia, this year with just two rounds, at Oran Park and Surfers Paradise. Gardner won on his Moriwaki, demonstrating the value of consistency by winning just one race of the four but gathering points from all the others. Gary Coleman won the remaining three on his McCulloch TZ750 Yamaha but lost the series by just two points to Gardner through falling in the second race at Oran Park. Marshall ended the series in fourth place. "They're hard men here," he said.

Britain's calendar for the coming season had an undernourished look commensurate with the nation's shrinking economy. The Post-TT meeting was gone, and everywhere seemed to be cutting dates except for Donington Park, where six internationals were planned for the year. The Shell/*MCN* Superbike Championship and the FT/MCW TT-F1 series were holding their own, though, with one important change to the latter – from the coming season F1 would run without its regulation limiting carburettors to road bike spec. "Along with our competitors," said Gerald Davison, "we can now use CR carburettors in F1."

On an international level, the view was a little different. The TT-F1 world championship took a modest step forward with the addition of a third round, at the Vila Real street circuit in Portugal. Meanwhile, competition in the US continued to strengthen with up to a dozen Superbike rounds planned, and six AMA road race nationals. At the first of these – Daytona – Honda's much-rumoured water-cooled V4 was expected to appear, ridden by Freddie Spencer and Mike Baldwin.

The new bike, the RS1000RW (aka FWS), has a hybrid look to it today – the first of Honda's superb V4 engines, but in a steel tube frame with hefty 43mm Kayaba forks, a rising-rate monoshock rear end, 16-inch front and 18-inch rear wheels. The 90-degree V4 swept its 1024cc volume from massively oversquare 78 x 53.6mm cylinders cast with the upper halves of the cases. Cam drive was by gear, there were titanium rods, and the hydraulic clutch that fed power to the five-speed 'box used steel and copper plates. Many details of the engine, heads in particular, are still hard to come by, but all-up weight was about 175kg and power output some 150bhp at around 11,500rpm.

As the homologating bike was the curious VF750S Sabre, launched in March '82, the RS-RW was never a candidate for British F1 racing as it would have had to keep its shaft final drive. Honda Britain's Gerald Davison remained confident, however, that Michihiko Aika, the driving force behind Honda RSC, would have something new for 1983. Joey would, however, ride one of the three million-dollar V4s in the Classic TT.

The FWS, as it became known in the US, soon proved its potency. At Daytona, Roberts qualified his 0W60 square-four fastest at 2m 1.84s (114.346mph) with the Honda V4s within half a second of his time, Baldwin leading the way. The race began with the three of them in close company until Roberts went out early with a broken crank; then the Hondas were in difficulties, pitting for fresh rear Michelins as early as lap 12 for Baldwin, a lap later for Spencer. Eddie Lawson (KR500) then led, bowing out on lap 28 with transmission problems, putting Graeme Crosby's YZR750 into the lead. The two Hondas were still the fastest bikes on the track, but a second stop for tyres ended their hopes of winning. Spencer used a harder compound for the remainder of the race, closing on Crosby at three seconds a lap, but

The first of Honda's V4s, the RS1000RW (aka FWS), appeared at Daytona in 1982 ridden by Freddie Spencer and Mike Baldwin. It was fast but ate rear tyres. (Courtesy Stuart Rowlands PR)

then had to stop again for fuel. Crosby took Yamaha's 11th straight Daytona 200 win by 11 seconds from Spencer. Roberto Pietri nabbed third on his Moriwaki-framed RS1000 after Baldwin slowed with ignition problems.

As the British season opened, Honda Britain was still awaiting its new 999s for TT-F1. They were on the grid at the Cadwell Park opening round but Haslam was plagued with a misfire that defied a change of battery and plugs, while Gardner's weekend was interrupted with two broken camchains. Marshall, meanwhile, led from start to finish, chased by Dave Hiscock's monocoque Suzuki and Grant, who missed a gear and slowed with bent valves, and Newbold. Today, Grant looks back on the XR69 with affection, but points to a problem: "At that time we didn't have rev limiters – just miss a gear and that's the inlet valves bent. I remember leading two TTs, and each time missing a gear because it was so bumpy and losing acceleration."

HOLDING THE LINE

Honda's new TT-F1 RS1000s featured a hydraulic clutch, rocker-arm suspension – and a reversion to wet-sump oiling; and, with an extra couple of weeks' sorting time, they looked more convincing at Donington, where Gardner scrapped with Marshall for the lead of the F1 race until the last lap when his ignition went sour, but still finished second through a determined last-lap pass on Hiscock at the chicane. Haslam was fourth from Grant but did better on his 1123, winning both legs of the *MCN* Superbike round while Marshall and Gardner (999) each took a second and a third.

TT-F1 took a break until June while the *MCN* Superbikes went to the NW200. With four-strokes at the head of the field the class looked ever more like US Formula 1. The double-points *MCN* Superbike race was new to the North West's programme, and got off to the worst possible start: Newbold, dicing with Haslam and Grant at the head of the pack, touched the back of Mick Grant's Suzuki and crashed flat in fourth at Juniper Hill, yards from where Tom Herron had fallen in 1979. He was pronounced dead on arrival at hospital. He was 29. Haslam, ignorant of Newbold's fate, went on to win the race, but the heart went out of the meeting. The name event was contested by a depleted field and won by Grant, who donated his winnings to the benevolent fund quickly established for Newbold's family.

For the TT, Grant used a crankshaft with full-circle flywheels in his XR69, in a bid to avoid over-revving. It looked like it was working too: in the F1 race he got away at a good clip, posting a new lap record at 114.19mph and building a 21-second lead by the second lap. Meanwhile, Marshall retired with the familiar bogey of bent valves, and Haslam moved past Dunlop into second. Joey was running his spare engine after a practice blow-up and, having to keep down the revs, was soon passed by Grant on the road en route to a 30-second lead. Haslam began closing, and by Ballaugh on the fourth lap had cut Grant's lead to 16 seconds. While refuelling for the second time Grant reported brake fade, but got as far as Ramsey Hairpin on lap five before a 'massive' oil leak ended his race. Haslam inherited the lead

Mick Grant was back in harness as a full-time member of Heron Suzuki in 1982, spending the season getting to grips with the XR69.
(Courtesy Elwyn Roberts)

with Joey, reported to be touring, still second. And that's the way it stayed. Dave Hiscock brought his monocoque Suzuki into third despite easing off for want of fuel, with Geoff Johnson's Kawasaki fourth. "This is one TT they won't be able to take away from me," said Ron. Three rounds of the British title done: Hiscock 32, Marshall 30, Dunlop and Haslam 23 apiece.

If second place in the F1 TT could be described as a disappointment, there was more on the way for Joey in the Classic. Honda's million-dollar RS1000RW had arrived, but what worked at Daytona couldn't do the job on the Mountain Circuit: as well as scraping the bottom oil cooler over bumps in practice, it broke a suspension linkage at Ballaugh. Nor was that the end of it: the bike was "incredibly quick," reported Joey, "but I had to knock it off on Sulby because of the handling." Reverting to his tried and trusted 1123, Joey led early in the Classic from Grant and Dennis Ireland's RG500, but by the end of the first lap Charlie Williams' TZ500 Yamaha was in front, with Haslam moving into second and then grabbing point while Grant retired with a misfire. Haslam was then gone, lasting only one more lap before pitting with a heavy oil leak from the base of the cylinders, prompting Barry Symmons to pull his man from the race. When Marshall retired with a split fuel line and Joey with a broken camchain, the Classic became the business of two-strokes and after Williams stopped with a terminal clunk from the gearbox, Ireland led home Jon Ekerold (RG500) and Tony Rutter (Yamaha). The FWS was likewise a failure at its only other British appearance, at Donington Park towards the end of June; while Franco Uncini, Croz and 1123-mounted Gardner claimed the spoils, Joey battled suspension problems and melting gearbox oil seals. It was, he said, "less than brilliant."

The second stop on the TT-F1 World Championship trail came at Vila Real in July, where the circuit was such a shock that Honda Britain and Suzuki GB felt compelled to drop a line to the FIM delegate at the meeting, suggesting that the track posed "a threat to the future of the series" and was "extremely dangerous." ACU chairman Vernon Cooper accused the teams of "destructive criticism," and said the track complied with the street-circuit spirit of TT-F1.

After griping about the heat and the slippery, sand-blown track surface, the riders for the most part just got on with it, and in another good day for Honda, Gardner won by almost three minutes from Joey. Both Suzukis looked good for a time, but Grant lost the front end on sand at the chicane, and Marshall retired with bent valves after a scrap with Gardner. In the end Geoff Johnson brought his Yoshi Suzuki into third from Hiscock. Two rounds down: Joey 24, Hiscock 18, Johnson 17, Gardner and Haslam 15 points apiece.

The recession continued to bite. Amid talk of up to 10 per cent of dealers going to the wall, Peter Hillaby told the press Scarborough's September meeting was being downgraded to a national because of Scarborough Racing Circuit's "ever-diminishing bank balance" – and a date clash with

Roger Marshall's first stint with Suzuki, in 1982, brought him the British TT-F1 title, the final MCN Superbike Championship and the British Championship. (Courtesy Elwyn Roberts)

the San Marino GP. The loss of international status took with it the TT-F1 title round. The Race of the Year was also called off: "it's difficult to get a class field, except by paying suicide money," said MCD motorcycle boss Chris Lowe. And that wasn't quite the end of it for Mallory Park: MCD soon said the circuit itself was to be sold at the end of the season.

While the row mounted over the causes of Barry Sheene's disastrous crash during open practice at Silverstone, racing went on. The TT- F1 field reconvened for its race on the Saturday of British GP weekend – though even that took on a political flavour when the privateers that dominated the grid threatened to walk out because the ACU initially refused to pay the 300 Swiss Francs start money minimum offered to GP riders. Barry Symmons from Honda and Rex White from Suzuki intervened successfully on the riders' behalf.

When the action started Haslam cleared off, leading from Dunlop, Hiscock, Marshall and Grant. While Dunlop faded and Hiscock slowed with the Suzuki curse of bent valves, Marshall and Haslam, now joined by Gardner, laid it on for the crowd; on the last lap Haslam led to Club, then Marshall through Abbey and into Woodcote, fending off a last challenge from Gardner: typically breathless stuff on a fast, simple circuit that almost guaranteed close racing. Marshall won by 0.09 seconds, his third win of the series bringing a handy eight-point break on Hiscock.

At Dundrod, Ron Haslam took his second win in the three-round TT-F1 World Championship, but Joey collected the title with his third runner-up spot. Suzuki took to the grid with a total of five works-supported riders, of whom only Dave Hiscock stood an outside chance of taking the title. Again, the weather looked patchy, but it began to clear for the F1 race, leading to tyre changes on the grid after the warm-up lap. Dunlop led away from Norman Brown's XR69 and Haslam, then a gap back to the Suzukis of Grant, Hiscock and Marshall. While Brown closed on Joey, Marshall pitted first, losing two laps while his crew fought with a seized steering damper that was trapping the throttle cable; then, at half distance, Grant, using his spare engine, toured in with a broken crankshaft. That left Haslam scrapping with Brown for the lead from Joey, who rode a strategic race, then Gardner and Hiscock. The race was decided on the last lap when Brown went down after touching Haslam's bike as they worked through the traffic. Haslam won and Honda took all three podium spots with Dunlop second from Gardner, and a 1-2 in the world championship: Joey 36, Haslam 30, Hiscock 26. Marshall got some recompense by winning the Classic, setting a scorching lap record at 119.91mph, with Joey again second and Haslam third after over-revving and bending valves; but he was more fortunate than Gardner, who found neutral entering a corner on the first lap …

The Shell-*MCN* Superbike series resumed at Donington a week later, where Gardner and Marshall took a win each, while Haslam struggled with flu and the recurrence of an old foot injury. Even so, the three of them put on a ding-dong scrap in the first race with Gardner and Marshall only pulling clear of Haslam in the closing laps. Gardner won by half a second, but was out of luck in the second leg, his RS stopping on the warm-up lap. Haslam and Marshall resumed a dice that was decided on the last lap when Haslam missed a gear coming out of the chicane. Grant added a third to his first-leg fifth, and Marshall was closing on Ron at the top of the table: Haslam 128 points, Marshall 122, Gardner 67.

After losing its dates at Scarborough and Mallory Park, the TT-F1 circus had a two-month break before Donington in early October, where it was a support race to the Donington World Cup (won by Mamola). The old firm went at it again in the closest race of the day: Gardner led from Marshall, Grant, Haslam and Hiscock, but then the Kiwi broke away to win. Gardner whistled straight on at the chicane, clearly with braking troubles, and Haslam did likewise. As the race wound down, Marshall slowed with bent valves, leaving Hiscock clear from a late-charging Haslam, Marshall and Grant. Five rounds done: Marshall 55, Hiscock 53, Haslam 45.

CLOSING TIME

Gardner took time out to win his second Castrol Six-Hour Production race at Amaroo Park in Sydney, this time with Wayne Clarke as co-pilot to lead a 1-2-3 for the CB1100R, taking revenge for the 16-valve Suzuki GSX1100's

1981 win. He was back for the final act of the British racing year, the Brands Powerbike International, but after one of the closest seasons in recent times, Marshall seemed to be in everything, vying for the TT-F1 and Shell-*MCN* Superbike titles. Word now had it Marshall would be joining Honda, no doubt enticed by the offer of two new £15,000 RS500 triples as well as a brace of F1 bikes. At Brands, though, his business was, for the last time, on 997 and 1023cc Suzukis.

In the event Marshall won only one race, the feature event, from his future team-mates Haslam and Gardner, but he did enough to take both championships. The F1 race was perhaps the star turn. Haslam led first, then Grant, then Hiscock, then Haslam again. Marshall squeezed into second and Gardner into third, relegating Hiscock. On the last lap Gardner was forced wide by a backmarker, giving Haslam the win from the Australian and new champion Marshall. Hiscock was fifth behind Grant. Final points, Marshall 65, Haslam 60, Hiscock 58, Gardner 42.

Marshall was the final *MCN* Superbike Champion as well, winning both races at Oulton, and the final at Brands Hatch after Ron's camchain let go. The series was being discontinued after a dozen years to be replaced, temporarily, by the *MCN* Masters, which wasn't so much a racing class as a series of events for riders invited to participate on the basis of their performances in other races on a given programme. Did that make Formula 1 the premier formula in the UK? Riders up and down the country pulling dust sheets over their TZ750s might have thought so – but if it was a victory, it looked distinctly pyrrhic. At international level, TT-F1 remained a marginal proposition. In Opatija, the FIM congress rejected the Vila Real circuit, and the Belgians withdrew their application for a round of the 1983 TT-F1 world championship, reducing it to its traditional homelands, the TT and the Ulster. The FIM General Council also withdrew the TT's 'protected status,' which meant other circuits could apply to run events at the weekends bracketing TT week. The offer from the Dutch to stage a round saved the title for the moment, but TT-F1 clearly needed a lift – and Honda looked set to supply it.

Back in August, Mike Baldwin had delivered Honda's first US F1 title, taking his FWS V4 to wins at Loudon, Pocono and Sears Point. Wes Cooley won Elkhart Lake for Suzuki and KR took time out of his GP campaign to deliver a masterclass on his 0W60 at Laguna Seca; but it had been Honda's season overall, and the remaining TZ750s were now in retreat. Although Honda hadn't enjoyed quite the same success in Superbike, help was on the way there too with the release of the VF750F, known as the Interceptor in the US. The new V4 street bike was revealed to dealers late in 1982 and launched early in 1983, in time to meet its homologation deadlines.

The VF-F – factory code RC15 – used a water-cooled 90-degree V4 with chain-driven double overhead cams and a 70 x 48.6mm bore and stroke, giving 748cc. Compression was 10.5:1, and included valve angle a narrow 38 degrees, allowing a flattish piston crown and a short, straight flame

After a difficult year with Moriwaki, Wayne Gardner joined Honda Britain in 1982, and enjoyed great success when he'd got his eye in. He's pictured at the 1982 Ulster GP where he finished fourth. (Courtesy Elwyn Roberts)

path. Carbs were 30mm CVs. Power was taken from the 360-degree crank via a sprague clutch (giving controlled slip that inhibited wheel chatter on hard downchanges) to a five-speed gearbox. Claimed power for the roadster was 86bhp at 10,000rpm, a 4bhp break on the best of the air-cooled 750s.

That the bike made an immediate and striking impression was largely due to its exposed, square-section frame, made from steel but painted silver to give it the look of aluminium – though the swinging arm was the real deal. The wheels were Comstars, 16-inch front and 18 rear, the 39mm front forks equipped with mechanical anti-dive.

As well as giving service in American Superbike, the VF750F would provide Honda Britain's motive power for its 1983 F1 machinery, albeit in significantly tweaked form. With Ron Haslam now on GP duties, Gardner and Marshall would form the A team for the domestic TT-F1 title, joined by Joey at pukka road races. At Suzuki, Grant would run alongside new recruit Rob McElnea, who pipped Norman Brown and Hiscock for Marshall's vacated berth. The team's new bikes were equipped with XR69 engines, which had dry clutches for the first time, in lighter, smaller square-section aluminium frames. The revised motorcycle was now designated the XR41.

Mick Grant said he preferred the rigidity of the steel frame. "I think the French endurance team had asked for aluminium," says Paul Boulton, a dedicated Suzuki man who has wrenched for Keith Huewen and Rob McElnea as well as Grant. "Suzuki had gone to an aluminium chassis in the second half of '81 with the XR35 and saved weight, so I think they were just going down the same route with the XR69 and XR41 – and anyway, the factory probably had the GSX-R750 in mind. I'm pretty sure the back end, the suspension, was just a straight swap; the front suspension was a straight swap in."

That the XR69 engine was still competitive spoke volumes about the worth of the six-year-old GS1000 design. The original magic Pops Yoshimura wrought on Suzuki's mighty two-valve lump was honed to a fine pitch of durable potency. "We just played around with the settings to give us what we wanted," explains Boulton. "We had a range of carburettors – 31s, 33s … one of the guys set up magnesium RG 36s to go on it."

Over the years, titanium and magnesium spread through the bike. "The cam cover and breather, ignition covers, sprocket cover, clutch cover, and clutch pressure plate were all magnesium," explains Boulton. "Then there were the triple clamps, sprocket carrier, rear disc brake carrier, rear disc brake calliper hanger …" Titanium had other uses: "almost every nut and bolt was titanium – all the studs and nuts, and everything inside was titanium or aluminium."

No engine is ever perfect, but that Suzuki went harder for longer than most: "To the end of '83 we didn't really have any failures; the few we had were from over-revving because there was no rev limiter – no effective rev limiter – and it was a big, heavy lump: once you'd got it spinning at the Isle of Man, North West, or Dundrod, and jumped over somewhere, it was very easy to over-rev it and bend valves." But then the mechanic earns his money: "I'd seen the guys beat the valves straight, put them back in and run the thing again – you'd stop at the Isle of Man for refuelling and it would be difficult to restart because you'd lost a bit of compression, so you pulled the choke on, flooded it, pushed and it would go again and you'd do another two laps."

TT-F1's last season of muscular, air-cooled litre bikes was about to begin – and Z1000J or not, there would be no official Kawasaki presence, despite recent noises to the contrary. So the 1983 TT-F1 series, now backed by Shell, looked like business as usual; and if Suzuki needed encouragement, it only had to look as far as the Swann Series down under, where Stu Avant (RG500) and Dave Hiscock on his Steve Roberts' monocoque Suzuki F1 bike bagged three wins apiece, the title going to Hiscock by a single point with only Andrew Johnson, on Team Honda Australia's RS1000, disrupting the procession of triumphant Suzukis.

Suzuki GB planned to have its new XR41s on the grid at Cadwell Park for the opening round of the TT-F1 title, but Honda Britain expected to be using its old RS1000s for at least the first couple of rounds. Before that, however, a mutiny in the class had to be averted. Veteran entrants Colin Aldridge and Ted Harris said they wouldn't be competing, for want of decent prize money for their runners. It was all very well offering a grand to the winner, they explained, but a tenner for ninth wasn't exactly pushing

Roger Marshall signed with Honda in 1983. After the RS850R's teething troubles had been overcome, he gave solid support to team-mates Dunlop and Gardner. (Courtesy TTracepics.com)

the boat out. *Motor Cycle Weekly* to the rescue, inviting the ACU and the works teams to talk through the issue, with the result that Gardner, Marshall, Grant and McElnea all agreed to a cut in prize money if it could be distributed through the ranks – so now each round winner could expect £600 with £25 each to ninth and 10th. "This is a wonderful gesture," said Shell Competition Manager Keith Collow.

GRAND SLAM

The opening meeting for the 1983 British season came at Donington on the first weekend of March, where Gardner won the 1000cc race from Grant and Marshall, who were logged as a dead heat for second. Gardner was riding his '82 RS1000. "We're having a few problems with the RS850R," he told *Motor Cycle Weekly*. "It handles and stops, but lacks a little jump out of corners."

The RS850R (factory code NC9), an interim measure for one season, added ideas from the FWS to the race-friendly design of the VF750F. Unlike the street bike, the racer used gear-driven cams and an oiling system that pumped lubricant from a split sump through an oil cooler mounted low on the front downtubes. Lightened reciprocating bits included titanium rods and valves that were larger than the stocker's. Compression ratio was lifted to 11.5:1 and capacity increased to 859cc by boring the stock liners to 75mm. Carbs were 32mm magnesium-body Mikunis, and power output around 130bhp.

The RS850R's racing ancestor, the Honda RS1000RW/FWS, made its last appearance at Daytona. While Team Honda number one Freddie Spencer rode an NS500, Mike Baldwin and Steve Wise wheeled out the V4s and qualified well but were unable to stop a rampant Yamaha team with KR bagging his second Daytona win, this time on the feral 0W69 square four, a 695cc version of the 0W60. Baldwin led early but slipped to fourth before retiring with a fried clutch. Wise collected third place behind Lawson's 0W69, and so the FWS became history.

Honda's other notional museum pieces, Honda Britain's RS1000s, were still winning. At the Cadwell opening round of the championship Gardner won the TT-F1 race and the Masters, Marshall and Grant behind him in both. A week later at a breezy Thruxton, Rob McElnea turned in a virtuoso performance to get Suzuki off the mark. Gardner gave chase until a massive slide forced him to back off, and Marshall was bouncing around with soft suspension; but they both did better than Grant, who fell, belting an ankle.

The RS850Rs took their bow at the Donington third round, where Grant won from Rob Mac. Marshall tried hard, running off at the chicane and crashing while chasing Grant, but at least had the consolation of setting the fastest lap while Gardner bagged third. Three rounds done: Gardner 37, McElnea 27, Grant 25, Marshall 24, Trevor Nation (Suzuki) 22.

Already there was talk of new Honda V4s coming during May, with revised engines boasting dry clutches and alloy frames that were 8kg lighter than the steel units. Barry Symmons was emphatic that the fresh bikes were not a result of the first RS850Rs' failure to match the performance of Suzuki's '83-spec XR69/41, but the team welcomed their coming – Marshall had dropped his RS850R during the Donington Gold Cup, and the team hadn't had enough spares to fix it. Gardner too was in trouble, pulling a hefty wheelie on the last lap of the same event and stopping seconds later by a broken crank.

"When Wayne did his crank at Donington, that was the only 850 still running," said Symmons. Nor was that the extent of the problem: the team's RS500s were likewise afflicted, as was the older stock. "We're even running short of bits and pieces for the '82 F1 bikes," he said.

The situation was remedied by the end of the month, when Ron Haslam was back in the headlines, using his NS500 to win four races of six in the Transatlantic Trophy (Mamola got a double at Oulton Park) and set the UK on course for an unexpected series win 245-198 from an American team that included KR, Lawson and Baldwin. Gardner was also in good form, rounding out the weekend for Honda with wins in the Shell TT-F1 races at Oulton, where he was chased by Marshall and Joey on their '82 RS1000s, and Brands, where Grant squeezed into third behind Marshall. All in all it wasn't much of a weekend for Suzuki, with Rob Mac out of action at Oulton Park after falling in practice and breaking a collarbone, and temporary replacement Barry Sheene there finishing an unexceptional seventh, saying he didn't like "the diesel." Five rounds done: Gardner 67, Marshall 46, Grant 37, Nation 36, Rob Mac 35.

The redrawn Honda team had no full-time place for Joey. He was supplied bikes and parts, but otherwise left to himself – "I'm happier doing my own thing," he said. But he was back in the team for the team and soon demonstrated why: come the F1 race, he set a new outright lap record at 115.73mph from a standing start, and cleared off, revelling in the first dry day for a week. Mick Grant ran second, but was fighting soft suspension and a sliding back tyre while team-mate Rob Mac, showing a rare aptitude for Island racing on his debut, fought clear of Marshall and then Geoff Johnson's GSX-powered Suzuki for third. Joey stopped for a minute at the end of lap four to have his rear cover changed, but still beat Grant home by 53 seconds. Mac was third a couple of seconds clear of Marshall at the flag while Johnson, who looked a cert to hold fourth from a flagging Marshall, rolled to a stop with a blown engine – an oil feed split and the head ran dry.

Rob Mac used his XR41 to turn the tables on Joey's V4 in the Classic, taking the lead when Norman Brown's flying Mk8 RG500 ran dry at the Creg on the third lap. While Dunlop and Grant each struggled with handling problems that cost them places – Joey with a hefty fuel load (and a misfire), Grant a rapidly wearing rear tyre – Mac won by nearly two minutes from Con Law's RG500, while 250 TT winner Brown at least had the consolation of breaking Joey's outright lap record, leaving the mark at 116.19mph.

By the time he'd visited the Dutch TT, Rob Mac was a genuine candidate for the TT-F1 World Championship. In front of a 100,000+ crowd the Humberside rider passed early leader Dunlop and pulled away. The race looked like a Suzuki 1-2 when Grant did likewise; but with only a couple of laps to go, Grant's XR41 went onto three and the catch tank filled with oil, later attributed to a holed piston. Dunlop took second with Marshall and Gardner close behind for Honda. Two rounds down: Dunlop 27, Rob Mac 25, Marshall 18. "You miss the 150cc," said Joey of his RS850R. "But it's certainly the best 850 imaginable."

The best 850 wasn't what was needed when the British Shell TT-F1 title resumed at Donington in July, where Mac was a clear winner, and Grant second with a new lap record. Gardner was third on his steel-framed RS850R, which wasn't quick enough – and neither was Joey's old RS1000 in fourth place. Gardner did better on an RS1000 at Snetterton, leading Mac home from Nation's Suzuki while Grant nursed a broken hand after running out of brakes in practice. Gardner's purple patch stretched to Silverstone as well. Back on his RS850R, he and Mac put on a race-long display that only came to an end when Gardner got away through traffic, taking the title with two rounds to spare. Grant got second in the closing stages with Joey behind Mac in fourth, and Marshall, struggling after a practice crash, fifth. Eight rounds down: Gardner 107, Rob Mac 72, Marshall 64, Grant 61.

After much speculation about the RS850R's revitalised performance

For 1983 the XR69 got a face-lift and became the XR41. This ex-UK team bike now belongs to Andy Smith. It was pictured at Castle Combe in 2018 running a GS1000 motor. (Author collection)

that went as far back as Assen, it now seemed Joey's mount would get a trick three-piece aluminium frame, its new cylinder liners and a 78mm bore to become a 928 in time for the Ulster, where he won in the kind of sodden going that brought out his best. By the time Rob Mac hustled into second Joey was long gone, securing his second world title. Mac waved Grant through to second on the last lap, unhappy in the wet going, but was still second in the championship. Final points: Joey 42, Rob Mac 35, Marshall 26, Grant 24.

Suzuki mopped up the last two rounds of the Shell TT-F1 series, Grant winning from Joey and Mac at Scarborough, Mac taking the grand finale at Brands. Gardner was out with a broken ankle from a fall at Donington but already had the TT-F1 title, as team-mate Marshall had the ShellSport 500. It was Honda's grand slam, and as the RS850R (and RS1000) and its great rivals, Suzuki's XR41 and XR69, disappeared into the pages of history, the team could look back on a full year's experience with next year's motorcycle.

6

WARRIORS FOR THE WORKING DAY

Ask Steve McLaughlin, the man who did so much to create the World Superbike Championship, and he'll say 'Superbike' was a term coined in the late '60s by Bob Braverman, publisher of the long defunct *Cycle Guide*, to describe the multi-cylinder sports bikes then starting to appear. The word was first attached to a road race series by *Motor Cycle News* in Britain: the *MCN* Superbike Series began in 1971 and you might remember Percy Tait winning it for Triumph back in Chapter 1. But the first racing series for Superbikes as we now know them – stock frames, hot-rod engines from roadsters – ran at Amaroo Park in New South Wales, Australia, for three seasons from 1973. True, the *MCN* series had roadsters at its core for a time, but from 1974 the Yamaha TZ750 began to dominate, as it did almost everything else – but not in the Chesterfield Superbike Series. Around rock-lined Amaroo, Len Atlee won the first series on a Norton Commando, and then the two-strokes – specifically the Kawasaki H2 – took over: Garry Thomas won in 1974, and Warren Willing the following season.

McLaughlin learnt of Sydney's Superbike racing while Willing was in California as a guest of his family. He thought it had an American ring to it, as well as being an apt description of the races he was himself riding through the American Federation of Motorcyclists – the club founded by his father John and a group of friends in 1954. AFM's race regulations were of the group's own devising, and fairly relaxed, reflecting the need of the club's members for a means of going racing cheaply. "Cook Neilson [editor of *Cycle* magazine] called them California Hot Rod rules," explains McLaughlin. "They were loosely production-based, but because there was just a small group of teams and riders – Yoshimura-Kawasaki, Neilson-Ducati, the Norton gang, and a few others – our agreement was that all would be legal except overboring." As four-strokes faded gradually and painfully from open-class racing elsewhere, Superbikes began to take root in California.

In the beginning: Kawasaki H2-mounted Gregg Hansford at Amaroo Park, Sydney, in the Chesterfield Superbike Series – the world's first. (Courtesy Ian Falloon)

In May 1973 the AFM held its first meeting at Riverside where McLaughlin on a Z1 scrapped with Reg Pridmore's R75 Beemer in the Heavyweight Production class. McLaughlin got the nod from Pridmore and Wade Killen (H2), Neilson putting his Ducati 750GT into fourth in just his second road race. The action was typical – and it was about to be put before a larger audience. British promoters Gavin Trippe and Bruce Cox added a Production race to the programme of Laguna Seca's 1973 AMA national; Pocono, the next stop on the calendar, did likewise. Some thought the technical regulations were stricter than they'd been used to, and certainly the bikes were required to look stock. "Inside, most anything was okay as long as it was carved from stock," observed *Cycle News*. That Du Hamel's winning Z1 was prepared by Pops Yoshimura underlined the point. Du Hamel rode an H2 at Pocono but won just the same, albeit from a slender, seven-bike field a long way from US Production racing's heartland. But it was a start.

There was little doubt that the Laguna Seca Production race had been popular with the crowd and would return; in the meantime, Du Hamel appeared more often and more prominently on Pops' Z1s at AFM meetings. Within a year of the bike's release, Kawasaki's big four-stroke had conquered everywhere, starting early in 1973 when Kawasaki's racing team – Du Hamel, Wilvert, Baumann and Carr – swapped their H2Rs for Z1s to set speed records on the Daytona banking, using engines that Pops had given cams and worked heads, the fastest of them enabling Du Hamel to set a one-lap record of 160mph. Weeks later John Crawford and Mick Hone gave the Z1 its first stock Production race win in Australia at the Adelaide Three-Hour; in October, Ken Blake, in one of the sublime rides that dotted his too-short career, won the Castrol Six-Hour single-handed on a Z1 – and did it again in 1974 with Len Atlee. All this potential could be yours for £1200 in the UK, $1900 in the US. Little wonder the big K was voted bike of the year in countries around the globe.

When Production racing returned to the headlines at Laguna Seca in 1974, Du Hamel again won the Heavyweight class on Pops' Z1. He kept company with McLaughlin's Z1 and Pridmore, until McLaughlin faded and the BMW man stopped – cracked ignition coils were blamed. Pridmore, now on an R90S, got his own back at the Ontario national and won going away while McLaughlin got the better of a slipstreaming duel with Du Hamel to finish second, the best of the Z1s.

That was that for 1974, and, as the year came to a close, the future of road racing in the US looked anything but bright. Crowds were down, just four AMA nationals were scheduled for 1975 (three after Atlanta was cancelled) and, back in August, Pops Yoshimura had left Yoshimura Racing and returned to Japan to start again, albeit with strong support from distributors David Dixon in the UK and Ross Hannan in Australia. There was good news, however: Daytona planned a Production race for its March 1975 speed week.

That first Daytona race was a 10-lapper and dominated by Kawasaki. Dave Aldana, complete with skeleton leathers, won on his Yoshimura Z1 from Bob Endicott's Action Fours Z1. Du Hamel, in pain from an ankle injury, completed an all-Kawasaki podium – though *Cycle* editor Cook Neilson, now Ducati 750 Super Sport-mounted, won the 750cc class. The win began a long campaign with the bike for Neilson and *Cycle*'s Editor-in-chief, Phil Schilling, details of which were published in *Cycle*, giving Superbike racing a useful publicity hike, as well as boosting the magazine's reputation for delivering much of the sport's best journalism.

It took a year for Pops to get back on his feet, but by mid-1975 he was back in California with a new business – Yoshimura R&D of America – and preparing a Z1 for Wes Cooley to ride at Laguna Seca. On that day, though, Yoshimura Racing, renamed Dale-Starr Engineering, had the upper hand. Du Hamel won again on one of its bikes, this time from Ron Pierce and Gary Fisher on R90S Beemers from national distributor Butler & Smith, and Endicott's Z1. Cooley got ninth while Neilson broke a bone in his left hand during a practice fall, helped the *Cycle* crew replace the broken rings in the rear cylinder and then stopped on the second lap of the final with a blocked fuel line. The 750 class win went to Triumph-mounted Dale Singleton.

The AMA now announced that a new 'Superbike Production' class would be run at AMA nationals from 1976. The class would allow bikes a maximum of 1000cc, four cylinders and six gears. First, though, there was the season-closer at Ontario, where it seemed likely Kawasaki's finest would

Bones on the banking: Yoshimura Z1-mounted Dave Aldana during his winning ride in the first Daytona Superbike race, in 1975. (Courtesy Mary Grothe)

again dominate. Ranged against Du Hamel's Dale-Starr bike were Cooley's Yoshimura Z1 and McLaughlin, back with Action Fours after a three-year break. In the early jostling, Ducati-mounted Neilson held off Du Hamel for a couple of laps around Ontario's combination of banking and tight infield corners. Neilson won the 750 class, sticking to Du Hamel's back wheel long enough to savour the Canadian's riding. Du Hamel then got free of a six-bike dust-up to win the open class, leaving McLaughlin second from Wilvert's Yamaha. Neilson was fourth overall, ahead of the short-geared R90Ss of Pridmore and Fisher.

NATIONAL TITANIUM
The AMA's vision for Superbike Production left the *Cycle* crew with an immediate problem – there was now no 750 class, but, encouraged by the 750's pace against bigger bikes at Ontario, collaborators Neilson and Schilling reached deeper into the SS and redeveloped it as an open-class bike.

The new rules reflected the silhouette principle of earlier seasons: chassis as stock (braced if required), though the steering head angle could be changed, as could the shocks, and the swinging arm strengthened; engines could be moved to help handling, and capacity lifted to 1000cc (plus a 1mm overbore); stock carburettor bodies, stock muffler bodies; overall stock appearance – including light shells.

Jerry Branch, the cylinder head wizard at Branch Flowmetrics, told the *Cycle* team the flow capacity of the Ducati heads could run to a 900cc ceiling. Branch increased valve sizes and reshaped the ports while the crew fitted 450 liners and machined the cases to give an 87mm bore – 883cc with the stock stroke. Venolia supplied the pistons, ZDS the rods, and a new crank came from Neilson's street SS. After problems with ring sealing, tests at Ontario showed the Ducati was at least competitive with the B&S BMWs.

The B&S Beemers, up from 917cc to 1001cc in 1976, got extra capacity from 95mm Venolia pistons that boosted compression from 9.5 to 12.2:1. The titanium Carrillo rods were shorter than stock, as were the cylinders – all to boost cornering clearance. In the twin-plug heads the ports had been welded and reshaped; the valves were oversize and carburettors bored out to 40mm; all up, the R90Ss were said to make 92bhp at the clutch, and could be spun to 9200rpm. The talking point of the BMWs built by, among others, Udo Gietl and Todd Schuster, lay not in the engine, however, but in the chassis, where the stock rear suspension had been replaced by a single Koni unit with the swinging arm suitably fortified. "It's within AMA Production machine rules," said Gietl.

The first championship round, Daytona '76: winner Steve McLaughlin (83, Butler & Smith BMW) leads team-mates Reg Pridmore (obscured) and Gary Fisher (24), with Cook Neilson's 883cc Cycle Ducati astern. (Courtesy Mary Grothe)

McLaughlin, a new recruit to the B&S team, got a surprise when he arrived at Daytona in March '76. "They're unloading these bikes and the third one, which had obviously been crashed, has my number 83 on it. It was a test crash, of course. And every day I practice, every time I got on the track, I came back in a truck – the bike never made more than two laps before something fell off. The reality was that Udo had never planned that bike to be raced; it was for spares. But somehow it worked for qualifying."

In the 13-lapper Neilson and Fisher got away first but were soon caught by Pridmore and McLaughlin. Fisher fell away from the tight quartet, suspension and gear change problems slowing him, and then a broken rocker arm stopping him. Before long Pridmore and McLaughlin were locked together with Neilson dropping off astern. Then, on the final lap, Pridmore led out of the chicane: "Daytona has great towing straights," says McLaughlin. "And as any NASCAR fan can tell you, it's all in the dash to the line. I practised the tow for two laps: I would pass Reg in the infield and let him by on the back straight, testing it. It was a close thing but it worked."

Coming out of the final turn for the last time McLaughlin yanked his BMW out of Pridmore's slipstream and across the line first by inches. Neilson was two seconds back in third and, with Du Hamel recovering from a leg broken in a snowmobile accident, the first Kawasaki home was Pops' "bucking, shaking" Z1 ridden by Wes Cooley. Mike Baldwin finished fifth on Reno Leoni's Moto Guzzi – and then carried on the good work at Loudon in June, the next stop on the national tour, using the Guzzi's fine handling to show the field the fast way round his home track. Neilson and Schilling sat this one out while putting the Ducati – now dubbed the California Hot Rod – on a weight-loss course. Fisher beat team-mate Pridmore for second, while McLaughlin retired with ailments that included a broken driveshaft and brake fade.

At Laguna Seca, Keith Code's Z1 led until the third lap when Fisher's BMW stormed past. It wasn't a good day to be Italian: Baldwin's Guzzi retired early with ignition failure and Neilson's Ducati began jumping out of fourth as he chased Fisher and Code. Gradually, too, the BMWs disappeared, Fisher's with a split oil tank, McLaughlin's flying out of contention rubber side up at the hairpin: "Pridmore and I were racing for the last turn and I misjudged his stopping distance, which was longer than mine," McLaughlin recalls. "As he cut across my line, I did, for all intents and purposes, the first recorded stoppie. But yes, it ended in failure." The decimation of the field complete, Pridmore won from Code and Mike Parriott's Yoshimura Kawasaki.

Pridmore made it two from two in the season-closer at Riverside but not until the old firm had done battle again, Cooley getting out of the gate first and finding he had Neilson, Fisher, Pridmore and McLaughlin for company. Neilson led for a time, then Pridmore, then Neilson again until a crankcase breather oiled the rear end, when Pridmore slipped past to win. Neilson kept faith with his rear Goodyear, and got the better of a late challenge by McLaughlin to hold second. Pridmore, the records would soon show, was the inaugural AMA Superbike Production champion, amassing two wins, a second and a third from four starts.

1977 looked much more promising than '76. Half a dozen AMA nationals were scheduled, plus the Laguna Seca world F750 round. If they proved successful, said AMA Competition Director Bill Boyce, he had another four or five up his sleeve for 1978. As preparations got under way for the season, Pops Yoshimura suffered a major setback when he was badly burnt in a fire

The best-laid plans: the result of Steve McLaughlin's bid to outbrake Reg Pridmore at Laguna Seca in 1976. McLaughlin walked; Pridmore won. (Courtesy Mush Emmons)

at the dyno room of his California workshop. Petrol fumes ignited while Pops was testing a Kawasaki engine intended for Cooley and Daytona. While Pops was taken to hospital, Fujio took over the racing programme, building a replacement engine in record time.

Pridmore's new mount for Daytona, prepared by Helmut Kern, was based on BMW's new R100S and looked more like the stocker than its predecessors, thanks in part to the AMA's new ruling that the swinging arm had to be as stock, braced if required. The champion's season beyond Daytona looked less than certain, however, with the news that the BMW factory was to withdraw its support for the team's Superbikes.

Over at *Cycle's* workshop, the California Hot Rod – renamed Old Blue in deference to its new paint job – was equipped for the new season with heads reworked by Jerry Branch, new pistons from Venolia, close-ratio gears from car transmission expert Marvin Webster – and trimmed to a slender 168kg. The 883's measured 90bhp propelled it to 149.5mph in practice at Daytona making it, as Neilson observed, one of the few bikes there that went fast and handled rather than one or the other.

Come the race, Neilson motored off more or less straight away, taking the lead at turn 4 and putting his head down. By the time he looked around several laps later, his rivals were in disarray: Cooley's Yoshimura Kawasaki had slowed for want of effective suspension damping, McLaughlin retired his Gietl BMW after losing third gear and Pridmore had his hands full with a wobbling B&S BMW and Baldwin's Guzzi. Neilson won by 28 seconds,

Cook Neilson retired the 883cc California Hot Rod at Laguna Seca in 1976 with gearbox problems. Their day soon came. (Courtesy Ian Falloon)

David Emde was second on a Mack Kambayashi Kawasaki and Cooley third from Pridmore and Baldwin. It was Ducati's best day yet, and Baldwin added to the Italian euphoria by leading Kurt Liebmann home in a 1-2 for Leoni's Moto Guzzis at Charlotte, the next stop on the AMA tour.

TURNING JAPANESE
Pridmore turned out on a Racecrafters Kawasaki at Loudon for the third round of the series. The new hardware seemed to suit him and the early laps of the race settled into a three-cornered scrap between Reg, Baldwin, and Ron Pierce's BMW. As the laps ticked by Pridmore slowed, leaving Baldwin and Pierce to settle it in the last corner of the last lap: Baldwin slid off and collected some hay bales while Pierce took his first national Superbike Production win from Pridmore and Liebmann's Guzzi. Baldwin reorganised himself to push in, and was with credited with sixth. Three rounds down: Baldwin 39, Cooley 26, Neilson and Pierce 20 apiece.

Steve McLaughlin was having a patchy season, retiring from the Daytona Superbike Production outing, and having only moderate runs on his Yamaha TZ750. All that was soon to change though, and in July it was announced he'd be joining the Yoshimura team. "Pops' bikes were the fastest on the track, but they hadn't figured how to cure the handling problems," McLaughlin recalls. "As everybody knows, the Z1 was a big wobble machine – but it never had a wobble it didn't like. It had three basic problems: one, the swinging arm pivot bolt was loose in the chassis as it was overbored;

two, there was not enough travel in the rear units, so torque wound up the rear end and locked the suspension; three, the engine mounts at the bottom of the frame were too thin and flexed under engine torque. Once you fixed those three things, okay it had long geometry and steered slowly, but it didn't wobble any more."

McLaughlin's programme of remedial work on the Kawasaki's chassis wasn't to last long. At Sears Point he kept pace with leader Neilson and Paul Ritter on Dale Newton's 860 Ducati, only surrendering second spot deep into the 16-lap journey when he pitted with a broken sparkplug cap. A lap later Neilson slowed with a broken clutch and Ritter won, while Pierce got his BMW past Pridmore's sliding Kawasaki after a struggle for third. So that was McLaughlin's race run with Pops' Kawasaki, though he had "laid out a plan to fix it."

At Pocono, Pops had taken a leaf out of the Hannans' book, supplementing McLaughlin's tweaks with Kayaba suspension acquired via Suzuki. Cooley was back on the bike, reported improved handling and led strongly until a dropped valve stopped him. Pridmore then took over, despite a crash in his heat, and won on his Pierre Des Roches-tuned Racecrafters K from Guzzi twins Baldwin and Liebmann. McLaughlin, meanwhile, was back in California working on Pops' new venture, a 944cc Superbike adaptation of Suzuki's superb GS750. He was pleased with what he found. "We spent several weekends with Pops and Suzuki technicians modifying the bike. It was a much more refined motorcycle than the Kawasaki. When we started development it was 85 per cent there already … the steering head, the swinging arm pivot. They needed a little help with suspension travel and some other stuff, and I was lucky there because some friends at Boge-Mulholland had a shock dyno that gave a lot of very interesting information."

As for the bike's Laguna Seca debut: "We just kicked it – I had one of those rare things in racing: 20-30 more horsepower than the competition and a bike that could put the power to the ground." The Superbike Production field, guests at the Monterey track's world F750 round, offered impressive action on a two-stroke-dominated programme. The usual suspects opened the bidding: Suzuki-mounted McLaughlin took the lead from Neilson, Pridmore and Cooley. Pridmore slowed with a misfire, and Cooley's Kawasaki broke its chain, but McLaughlin and Neilson went hard at it. McLaughlin rode so hard he scraped a hole in his alternator cover (already bevelled), and coated Neilson with a fine oil mist. He didn't let up though, and ran out the winner from the oil-begrimed Neilson, Pridmore, Ritter and Pierce.

If McLaughlin was pleased with his win, so was Pops; and the Suzuki, he said, offered more potential than Kawasaki's hardware, because it weighed less and handled better. Details of the bike were yet sparse, but to get to 944cc Pops opened the GS750's bore to 73mm. He fitted 'punchier' cams and an oil cooler, and bored out the carbs. Chassis work included Kayaba forks and lay-down rear units, as well as bracing to frame and swinging arm. The bike was put together in seven weeks.

Despite switching from BMW to Kawasaki, Reg Pridmore had managed to stay ahead of the pack for much of the season and collected his second Superbike Production title at Riverside. Not that he contributed much to the race, stopping on the opening lap with a loose battery lead. The pre-race betting was about McLaughlin and Neilson, in his last Superbike Production race. The fates were against them though: McLaughlin was out on the first lap with a broken clutch hub, to leave Neilson and Ritter chasing Cooley's weaving Kawasaki. As Baldwin slowed with gearbox problems, Neilson passed Cooley for the lead, losing it again on the last lap as the Kawasaki man won a dash to the line for his first Superbike Production win. Final points: Pridmore 71, Neilson 68, Baldwin 56, Pierce 53, Liebmann 50.

Glimpsed in Paris, tested in Japan, and finally released early in 1978, the Suzuki GS1000 threatened to knock Kawasaki off its perch as the dominant four-cylinder Japanese engine in Superbike Production. As Pops had shown, the Suzuki chassis had potential, and now there was a powerplant to match. By the time Pops had finished waving his magic wand over that first 70 x 64.8mm engine, he'd boosted power from a claimed 90bhp to 130+. This engine, the forerunner of the lump that would do so much for the careers of Graeme Crosby and Wes Cooley, used Pops' own cam grinds and oversize valves in his trademark highly polished ports. Slipper pistons ramped up compression to 11.5:1. The roller-bearing crank was stock, as were the rods, though polished to eliminate surface flaws. The mixture was fired by CDI ignition and delivered via a stock clutch with heavier springs to Pops' close-ratio gear cluster. Carb bodies were stock, as per AMA regs. But, recalls Kevin Cameron, that wasn't necessarily the case right through the field: "I remember people in the tech line posting someone up at the head to report what carbs were being passed as legal, and then get all the gear to change as needed – without anyone losing their place in the line." As for the chassis, Kayaba provided suspension at both ends, the forks running through a steepened steering head fitted with taper-roller bearings; the downtubes were braced, as were the shock mounts and the underside of the swinging arm. Brakes were plasma-coated discs with Lockheed callipers and braided lines.

Like the 944, Pops' GS1000 Superbike came together in good time and much of its testing happened on the Daytona banking, says McLaughlin. "We went to Daytona with several engines, and the last of them threw a rod from number four-cylinder in my heat, so I had to start from the back of the first wave.

"The race was just hours later, so Pops stood on a milk crate, grouped the team around him and said he would build an engine – but that I had to go to the AMA and buy time. 'Steve-san,' he said, 'you big wind in AMA. Now you must make typhoon get some delay.' I don't remember what I did but it was enough – they got me a bike on the line."

McLaughlin started 34th and while Cooley got his Yoshimura Kawasaki out into the lead, the Yoshi Suzuki man was up to 12th through the infield, fourth a couple of laps later, and then passed Cooley for the lead on lap six. Cooley repassed him, and, as Pridmore's '77-spec Racecrafters Kawasaki and John Long on a Gietl/Schuster BMW disputed third, it looked as if the leaders might likewise mix it. But Cooley took a stone through the oil cooler and that was more or less that. McLaughlin won comfortably from Pridmore, Long and, in a lonely fourth, Baldwin's Guzzi Le Mans. But McLaughlin just made it: "When I stopped to pick up my mechanic to ride to victory lane the transmission seized."

Early GS1000 problems included excessive camchain tensioner wear, and damage to the alloy clutch hub caused by steel plates; but these were soon fixed and the Yoshimura GS1000's transition from competitive to dominant was swifter than its rivals might have wished. Daytona marked high tide for McLaughlin's time with the team. Within weeks of his win he'd been sacked by Yoshimura, and the team now hired Pierce to ride alongside Cooley. Neither party wanted to go into details of the divorce but a difference in policy – which didn't directly concern racing – at least gave McLaughlin the chance to reconsider his future.

Yoshimura Suzuki made it two from two when the circus reconvened at Loudon in June. Cooley, beginning his long and successful association with Pops' GS1000s, again took an early lead from the pack, headed by Yoshimura East-sponsored John Bettencourt and Cooley's team-mate Pierce, with Pridmore, Baldwin and Long not far adrift. Pierce was the first to go with clutch failure, while Bettencourt put his 944 Suzuki past Cooley for the lead. Baldwin was next out, crashing at three-quarter distance and Cooley retired with an oil leak two laps later; but Bettencourt motored

Coming through: Leoni Ducati-mounted Freddie Spencer leads Richard Schlachter's Ducati at Loudon in 1979. Schlachter won and Freddie was fourth when the race was red-flagged. (Courtesy Mary Grothe)

on with Harry Klinzmann's BMW looking set to follow him home – until stopped by cracked cases with a lap to go. Long then steered his Beemer into second from Pridmore – his Kawasaki now backed by Vetter fairings – and the new rider of Old Blue, Paul Ritter.

THREE

Grids were slowly growing, as were crowds; and at Loudon in 1978, five different marques were represented in the top five finishing spots of the Superbike Production race. By contrast, the top five spots of the open national (won by Skip Aksland) were taken by Yamaha TZ750s, with five more making up the top ten and five more behind those. The merit of a near-monopoly in the nation's premier racing class was doubtful. Add to that persistent worries over tyres coping with the explosive power delivery of Yamaha's all-conquering rocket, and perhaps it isn't surprising the AMA was contemplating changes at the top level of the sport, perhaps by featuring Superbike Production.

The diversity of marques struggling for Superbike dominance wasn't so marked at Sears Point, but the race was interesting enough, Ritter this time coming out on top for Ducati after tracking Cooley for most of the journey. Suzuki-mounted again, Cooley got into a good lead from Ritter and Pridmore's Kawasaki, while Baldwin scythed through the field, putting his Leoni Guzzi into fourth before ignition failure and a broken steering damper stopped him. Cooley then stopped, his drive sprocket pulling off its magnesium hub, letting Ritter in to win – as he'd done in '77 – Pridmore into second, and Harry Klinzmann third from Code and Long. Three rounds done: Pridmore 45, Long 36, Ritter 31.

Though it was not immediately clear which way the AMA might jump, Mike Baldwin was proving himself as adept in Superbike Production as F750, and so might have been happy with either class in pole position. After winning the F750 national at Sears Point he did it again at Pocono as well as going toe to toe with Cooley's Yoshimura Suzuki in the Superbike race. Now on one of Leoni's Ducati 860s, Baldwin chased Cooley all the way, with Long's BMW for company until it threw a rod. It was a familiar story: Suzuki's raw power versus the Ducati's handling, Cooley bagging the points on the drag to the line. Baldwin said he might have won but for a late slide that gave Cooley just enough leeway; but he then had bigger problems to contend with, facing disqualification for running what some thought were illegal cases.

Baldwin's next port of call was Japan, where he underlined his versatility by joining Cooley to win the inaugural Suzuka 8 Hours on Pops' GS1000R. Then they were back at Loudon, where Baldwin again made headlines by finishing second to Dale Singleton in the F750 race and then ran hard in Superbike Production until stopped by a seized piston. Cooley didn't start as the Yoshimura team was preparing his Suzuki for Laguna Seca, and Pridmore was out as well, having damaged a shoulder in a fall at Suzuka.

That left David Emde's Kawasaki and Klinzmann's BMW at the head of a depleted field, the BMW man crossing the line first with Suzuki-mounted Bettencourt, who'd started last, hustling up to claim third. Long's Beemer would be the last twin to win an AMA Superbike round until Doug Polen's Ducati at Laguna Seca in 1992.

Come the grand finale at Laguna Seca, Pridmore became AMA Superbike Production champion for the third year in a row, tying on points with Long but getting home by posting two second places to Long's one. The six races of the series had produced five different winners, with only Cooley winning twice, at Pocono and in the final race of the series. And the last was perhaps the hardest: Cooley led every lap, but had McLaughlin, back on a Racecrafters Kawasaki, and Ritter's Ducati in close company for most of the contest. Everything seemed stacked on the last lap – but with no last-lap flag shown, Cooley crossed the line unmolested from Ritter. McLaughlin was third and Long fourth, a point shy of wresting the title from Pridmore, who finished behind Klinzmann in sixth place.

As the curtain came down on another season Pops announced he'd be building Cooley replica engines for sale, while American Honda hinted at plans for AMA Superbike, saying Honda RSC was building 120bhp, 997cc engines for a new team. Lashings of magnesium and titanium adorned these motors, it was said, and the bore and stroke measured 70 x 64.8mm – which surely made the lump a descendant of the long-serving and highly successful RCB endurance engine. Would that be eligible for Superbike Production? No: all eligible bikes "must be based on complete motorcycles currently available," the AMA reminded everyone.

The FIM's decision to terminate F750 at the end of '79 gave fresh impetus to the AMA's discussions over the future of its racing. By mid-December it had a draft plan on the table: there would be races for 250s, sidecars, 500 GP, and Superbikes – though which of the bigger solo classes would lead the way wasn't yet clear. The calendar, meanwhile, was back to three nationals when Loudon lost its second date and Pocono was rained off – though the Superbike Production would get one extra race, again being included in the Laguna Seca world F750 programme.

There was encouraging news, however: Kawasaki Motors Corporation was back, signing newly crowned American Road Racing Champion Mike Baldwin and providing him with KR250s and 750s, and a new Superbike based on the new KZ1000 Mk II – and perhaps, somewhere in a hazy, distant future, a KR500. The class regulations, meanwhile, were revised: a homologated model's stock number of gears was stipulated, as was the type of primary drive. The stock seat silhouette had to be retained along with working brake lights. External oil lines were to be of stainless steel, and catch tanks for crankcase/gearbox breathers were compulsory. The carburettor regulations were overhauled, too, with any type now permitted up to a given choke diameter for different numbers of cylinders: twins 43mm, triples 35mm and fours 31mm.

Mike Baldwin made a handful of starts for Kawasaki in 1979 before his disastrous fall at Loudon – but the KZ1000 Mk II Superbike was a winner. (Courtesy Ian Falloon)

Pops had a busy start to '79. At the end of January it seemed Yoshimura R&D of America would provide Suzuki-powered Superbikes for Cooley and Pierce, and a Kawasaki for David Emde, with help provided for Mike Baldwin on the KMC team. Kawasaki would help Pridmore on the Pierre Des Roches-built Vetter Fairings KZ and Steve McLaughlin at Racecrafters. Two weeks later, plans had changed again and Pops would now back only his Suzukis for Cooley, Pierce and Emde. The KMC team, headed by Randy Hall, carried on building its own bike.

In the event, Baldwin didn't start the now 100-mile, Bell Helmets-sponsored 'Superbike 100.' He'd crashed in practice for the 200, damaging his left wrist and collarbone. Emde was another casualty after falling from his 250 but, despite not competing in his heat, was allowed to start the 100 from last on the grid.

Cooley and Pierce got away into the lead, with third place disputed by Venezuelan Roberto Pietri (Suzuki) and a Leoni Ducati ridden by 17-year-old Freddie Spencer, who'd been given time off from school for the meeting. After the compulsory pit stops, the speed bowl began to take its toll: Cooley slowed with brake fade, handing the lead to Pierce; Spencer retired with gearbox problems and Pietri with a broken chain. Reigning champion Pridmore also broke a chain, while 1978 race winner McLaughlin stopped with a puncture.

Nothing could stop the Yoshimura boys: Pierce won impressively while

Cooley held on for second and Emde howled through the field to complete the podium for the team. Long got his BMW into fourth from Klinzmann (Kawasaki) and Bettencourt (Suzuki), but the day belonged to Pops.

SPECIAL K

Baldwin was back on form for Loudon and looked set to give the Mk II its head after winning his heat. Much of the new bike was not available for public scrutiny, particularly in the top end – though Yoshimura cams and 10.5:1 pistons together with a sturdier camchain were on the list of modifications along with, it was said, titanium valves. Carbs were the 31mm Keihin CRs now breaking box office records everywhere, and the exhaust plumbing was from Kerker. Crank and clutch were both stock as were the forks (in a steepened steering head), but Kayaba rear units were fitted along with Morris mags. Trick bits of the chassis included KR750 twin discs up front. The KMC engine was said to make 147bhp.

The Loudon final began with Cooley leading the Kawasakis of McLaughlin, Baldwin, Klinzmann and Pridmore. Pierce was last away after missing his heat, while his Suzuki's broken crank was replaced. Cooley suffered tyre troubles and was soon passed by McLaughlin and Baldwin as Ducati men Spencer and Richard Schlachter closed on the leaders. McLaughlin was in trouble a lap later as he moved to lap Dan Chivington, who fell and was hit by the Racecrafters Kawasaki. While Pridmore retired with brake problems, Schlachter passed Baldwin for the lead, the Kawasaki man apparently content to tuck in behind and bide his time. With four laps to run, the race was red flagged so help could reach the injured Chivington. Schlachter won from Baldwin, with Cooley third from Spencer, and Pierce was eighth.

Baldwin's season came to an end in the F750 national. While contesting the lead with Romero and Aksland, he unloaded in a high-speed right-hander and broke his left femur, the inch-thick thigh bone. The Connecticut rider decided he'd rather heal in traction than undergo surgery and plating. He would be out of action for more than a year. In mid-July, Kawasaki signed Schlachter and Spencer to pilot the Superbikes built for Baldwin.

The season closed with two dates in California, where Spencer got an opportunity to demonstrate his genius. At Sears Point he cleared out from the start, new team-mate Schlachter astern from Klinzmann. McLaughlin, still sore from Loudon, was a non-starter and Cooley got rolling last after collecting a puncture in his heat. Even so, he made contact with the leading group by half distance – though not Spencer, who was long gone. With a lap to go, Pierce had passed Klinzmann, then Schlachter for second, while Cooley squeezed into third. Coming home seventh was Pridmore, bagging his last Superbike points before retiring. As Reg bowed out, Freddie arrived; with one race to go he had an outside shot at wrecking everyone's plans. Three races done: Cooley 42, Pierce 36, Schlachter 34, Spencer 31.

Laguna Seca ran to a similar script: Spencer ran away, this time with

Cooley in a secure second while Pierce, Schlachter and Klinzmann argued over third. And that's how they finished, with Cooley's second place enough to secure him the title from team-mate Pierce, 58 points to 55. Spencer, third with 51 points from three finishes, was now the hottest act in town.

It wasn't long before McLaughlin was back in the news. At the AMA ball that closed the 1978 season, he had put forward a formula for the Daytona 200 that would allow in 1000cc four-strokes, and so break the Yamaha TZ750's effective monopoly of the event. This was hardly new territory for McLaughlin. As far back as 1975 he'd collaborated with Hurley Wilvert and journalist John Ulrich on a formula for the future of American national racing that would allow 1000cc four-strokes to compete alongside the mighty TZ. And he had a new employer: after long negotiations he would join Ron Pierce in American Honda's new Superbike Production team and act as team co-ordinator with a budget for mechanics, equipment – and an outside PR firm.

The final piece of the Honda puzzle fell into place when Spencer signed a two-year contract early in the New Year. Spencer had been reluctant to turn his back on Kawasaki and its potent Superbike, but Dennis McKay and McLaughlin intervened to help the 18-year-old (Spencer's birthday is on

Team Honda at Daytona 1980. From left: Ron Pierce, Roberto Pietri, Steve McLaughlin and Freddie Spencer. Spencer was second to Crosby's Yoshimura Suzuki, Pierce third. (Courtesy John Froude)

19 December) into red leathers, by stressing the long-term possibilities of joining the world's biggest.

After Honda signed 'Louisiana Lightning,' Randy Hall came up with a fall-back plan that would bring Kawasaki unparalleled success in coming seasons. Eddie Lawson, then 21, was a seasoned performer on the dirt. Like Kenny Roberts before him, Lawson was a regular at Ascot on Shell Thuet's Yamahas, and fought the same battles against Dick O'Brien's XR Harleys. He'd also made a name for himself in lightweight road racing and, late in 1979, had had a trial run on Kawasaki's Superbike at Willow Springs. Lawson was fast, clinical, and seemed never to crash.

At Suzuki, Cooley had the impression he was to be replaced by Aldana, and so was considering an offer from Suzuki GB to ride TT-F1. Certainly Aldana and Crosby would be joining Cooley at Daytona; but if Suzuki's plans didn't look quite solid, Mamoru Moriwaki's were: Lawson and Masaki Tokuno were to ride his Kawasaki-powered F1 bikes in the 200, while American Pat Eagan would join Tokuno in the Superbike race. Lawson, riding the 'Black Beauty' Superbike for Kawasaki, would have Gregg Hansford for company.

Honda's line-up, too, had been finalised, with Roberto Pietri becoming the fourth rider alongside McLaughlin, Pierce and Spencer, with Udo Gietl as crew chief, and mechanics Mike Velasco, Dave Langford, and Jyo Bito joining fabricator Todd Schuster, Brian Uchida, Mike Crompton, Dennis Zickrick, R&D rider Jeff Haney, and machinist Ryder Adams among others behind the scenes.

Honda's hardware began to arrive around the turn of the year. Honda RSC would supply F1 bikes for Pierce and Spencer, but the major point of interest was the CB750F-badged Superbikes. These began life as RSC creations but grew into American Honda's own hot-rod project. The base unit was very similar to the air-cooled dohc engine found in the first Honda Britain RS1000s: plain bearings throughout, four-valve heads with pent-roof combustion chambers, 11:1 pistons – though the Superbike engine started out with wet sump lubrication, changing to dry after Daytona, with oil from an under-seat tank circulated through an oil cooler mounted on the lower fork yoke or on the front downtubes. Using the CB900's 69mm stroke, the Superbike engine had a bore of 68.7mm to give 1023cc. Cam and primary drive were both by racing-grade Morse chains. To begin with, the CB-F came with 31mm Keihin CR carbs, and the electronic ignition unit mounted at the left-hand end of the crank. The chassis featured Gold Wing forks and rear units from Mulholland. Wheels were Morris mags, and the front brakes were twin 320mm slotted discs, mounting Lockheed callipers at the front, and a single 9in drilled disc at the stern.

The RSC four-into-one exhaust system could perhaps be identified as the starting point of the AHM project. Rumours of Kawasaki and Suzuki engines making close to 150bhp were current as the team went testing at Willow Springs. "We could live with power in the low 140s, as we had

Team Kawasaki's KZ1000 Mk IIs were the fastest Superbikes at Daytona in 1980, but Lawson (oil leak) and Hansford (pictured, loose filler cap) both bowed out. (Courtesy Ian Falloon)

Freddie," explains McLaughlin. "And don't forget I had won the Daytona Superbike race in '78 and Pierce in '79. So we knew what we were doing.

"We received 22 engines for our eight bikes, and all had sheets stating they'd made 141 to 145bhp on the RSC dyno. To have a look, we put the first engine on Jerry Branch's dyno and got 117bhp. After that we dynoed all 22 engines and got a range of 117 to 119bhp. This was a problem. We could race with 135 but 120 gave us no chance."

Experimentation with carburettors was of little immediate help, but Mike Velasco came up with an improvement in the exhaust collector box just weeks before the team was due to leave for Daytona, making the numbers encouragingly fatter.

"I had been told not to touch the engines, but I wasn't going to Daytona with 30bhp less than the others," recalls McLaughlin. "A week, maybe 10 days before we left for Daytona, Suzuki-san the vice president shows up. The chassis are gone, but he can see a bunch of the engines are apart. I don't know how he did it, but the next day Aika-san, president of RSC (later to become head of Production racing at HRC), arrived just as Mike Velasco was bringing in our newly cut, polished and balanced, don't-touch million-yen crankshafts." There was tension in the air, but the crash development programme worked, and the AHM crew had found much of the necessary power: at the start of the season the CB-F Superbikes made 135bhp, delivered between 9000 and 10,500rpm. In any event, "Freddie and Roberto blew past the faired RSC F1 bike on the Daytona back straight in practice."

The presence of the AHM team at Daytona was a major achievement, having gone from zero to full realisation – motorcycles, sponsorship, team branding – in six weeks. With Freddie on board, it could hardly fail to give Superbike a new appeal.

PRESSURE

So the most exciting American season in a decade began: no fewer than nine AMA nationals made the provisional calendar for 1980, and an impressive ten rounds of the Superbike series. At Daytona, the opening Superbike race of the season got away to a controversial start. Yoshimura Suzuki men Crosby and Aldana qualified well, despite having lost engines to crank failure and bent valves, but failed to pass the timekeepers at the end of their qualifying runs and had to start from the back of the second wave. While Croz worked up from 48th on the grid, Spencer and Cooley swapped the lead. Cooley stopped with a dropped valve on lap nine and Spencer pitted for fuel a lap later as Crosby swept into the lead. Both Kawasakis were in trouble early, despite being the fastest bikes in the race, each clocking more than 160mph. Lawson, running twin-plug heads, started with one of the eight working loose, then stopped with clutch trouble. Hansford lasted longer, but retired with a loose filler cap that let fuel overflow under brakes.

Spencer resumed the lead after Crosby pitted for fuel but began to slow with a misfire and a loss of acceleration. Crosby took the lead, building a comfortable 10-second buffer with Pierce a minute adrift in third from Tokuno and Eagan on the Moriwakis. Aldana had got up to sixth before stopping with a front tyre puncture, and McLaughlin stopped early with ominous noises coming from the bottom end of his CB-F. First blood to Suzuki.

Before the circus reconvened at Talladega, Aldana signed for Kawasaki. The veteran was unhappy with his Yoshimura Suzuki deal, and Randy Hall snapped him up in a move that immediately paid off. While the Honda team struggled with mechanical problems during qualifying, Kawasaki had it right almost from the off, with Lawson leading early. McLaughlin stopped with a fried clutch and Spencer with a chunked tyre, while Cooley, now secure in his spot at Yoshimura Suzuki, slowed with ignition problems. Aldana came through the pack to lead the final lap, with Lawson popping out of his slipstream just before the line to win. Cooley was a distant third from Honda's leading survivor, Ron Pierce.

A week later, and a little further north in the former Confederacy at Charlotte, North Carolina, Cooley was back on top while Spencer's season grew dramatically worse. Aldana struggled through from the back of the grid as Spencer got into a strong lead and was orbiting Charlotte's tight,

Jimmy Adamo took the fight to Japan on Reno Leoni's Ducatis (Pantah and bevel) in AMA Superbike, and campaigned successfully in Battle of the Twins. (Courtesy Mary Grothe)

steep banking at 130+, according to some, when the Honda gave a puff of smoke and Freddie took to the lifeboats: the aluminium bolt holding the oil filter had sheared at the head, and out popped both filter and oil. "The bike started to move and I jumped off to the left – best decision I ever made," said Freddie. McLaughlin, soon to become team manager, stopped in his last AMA race to help a dazed Spencer, noting that the teenager's bike had cartwheeled in the crash, and torn its engine from the frame. Cooley, meanwhile, won from Lawson and Aldana. Three rounds done: Lawson 36, Cooley 34, Pierce 33, Aldana 29 … Spencer 16.

Cooley looked like doing it again at Elkhart Lake, but ran dry on the last lap to let in Spencer, struggling with a lack of front brakes and cornering clearance problems, from Lawson, who'd wrestled with a sliding, pattering front end, then Aldana and Pierce – who finished with a dead engine. Spencer then made it two at Loudon, again taking an early lead while Cooley and Aldana scrapped for second. Lawson, for once running sluggishly, said later that work was needed "to get the bikes off the corners better." Even so, he got third after Aldana crashed and restarted to finish fourth.

Revised cam timings and throttle settings did the trick for Lawson. He was back on top of the podium at Road Atlanta, leading home Cooley, who'd been late onto the grid after a hasty engine swap and Aldana yet again, now perhaps in the most consistent form of his career. Spencer retired with ignition problems after winning his heat. Six rounds done: Lawson 85, Cooley 72, Aldana 66, Spencer 59.

As spectators slipped away from British racing, so American fans found new reasons to believe. At Elkhart Lake 40,000 crowded the fences, Road Atlanta was back on the calendar for the first time since 1974 and when battle rejoined at Laguna Seca, one of the most popular circuits on the tour, the faithful got a weekend's top-notch racing. While KR motored away from Spencer's Kanemoto-tuned TZ750 in both legs of the open national, no one bested Freddie in Superbike: Cooley led early, but Spencer passed him and then spent the last three-quarters of the race getting away in front. Of Lawson there was little sign: the gearbox of his better motor broke, and, after circulating for a few laps with Aldana's spare, he retired when it went onto three and began making "serious mechanical noises." Aldana was third for Kawasaki behind Spencer and Cooley, with Pietri's Honda fourth.

In mid-August Mike Baldwin got back onto a racing motorcycle for the first time since his heavy fall at Loudon in June 1979. He'd already been water-skiing and riding dirt, and now tested a Honda Superbike at Willow Springs, saying while his injured knee meant a GP bike was beyond him, a Superbike could be okay (though it would be fitted with a stock, padded seat to ease his leg). Sure enough, he agreed to ride for Honda in the final three rounds of the 1980 series, filling in for Pierce who'd hurt his back in a practice crash at the Suzuka 8 Hours.

So Baldwin lined up with Spencer and Pietri at Pocono, where Lawson's Kawasaki was equipped with S&W rear units and Pappy Edmonston's Blue Magnum flat-slide carbs. The Kawasaki number one also had a new Branch-flowed cylinder head, reprofiled cams, and a better-scavenging exhaust. The race looked like running to a familiar pattern: Cooley ran away from the start with Aldana and Lawson giving chase. Spencer worked through the field from the back of the grid, having stopped in his heat with 'electrical problems,' but by lap four had passed Cooley for the lead. Aldana ran off and dropped to sixth, Cooley stopped with piston failure (later traced to poor fuel) – and then Spencer too was in trouble, sliding and looking down at his engine. He thought he'd seen oil, but later analysis said the problem had been his soft rear tyre breaking up. Lawson won from Spencer and Baldwin, who'd had a steady ride into third: Lawson 105, Spencer 95, Aldana and Cooley 88 apiece.

With two races to go there were four contenders for the title. Spencer was the first to drop out, at Atlanta: his good motor threw a rod on the last lap of his heat and his spare threatened to do something similar, putting Honda's number one out of the points. The CB-F engines needed generous running in if they were to give their best, but sometimes a tight racing schedule just didn't allow it. Cooley was also in trouble after crashing in his heat; but he got going in the final to win handsomely from Lawson. Pietri's engine, too, ran a rod, but Baldwin, gradually recovering form, finished third for Honda from Aldana: Lawson 121, Cooley 108, Aldana 99, Spencer 95.

And then there were two: returning to Daytona – Kawasaki's jinx track – for the last round, the championship came down to a straight fight between Lawson and Cooley, though the race turned into a scrap between Cooley and

Typical AMA Superbike action at Road Atlanta in 1980: Eddie Lawson (Kawasaki) leads from Spencer, Pierce (Hondas), Aldana (Kawasaki), and Roberto Pietri (Honda). Lawson won while Spencer slowed. (Courtesy Mary Grothe)

Spencer. Cooley got away first, Spencer passed him under brakes, Cooley got him back. Lawson, who could take the title by finishing seventh if Cooley won, meanwhile developed an oil leak from a broken coupling, and fell at the chicane on lap six. After a dozen tight, tense laps, champion-elect Cooley won by inches from Spencer. Kawasaki team manager Gary Mathers then protested against "excessive frame modifications" to Cooley's bike. AMA referee Charlie Watson upheld the protest, disqualifying Cooley and giving Lawson the title. Suzuki counter-protested and AMA racing Commissioner Mike DiPrete ruled that because Lawson had ridden a different bike in the final (Aldana's – his own had a jammed valve) to the one he'd used for qualifying, he wasn't a "legal entrant" and couldn't protest. Cooley was champion again: Cooley 128, Lawson 121, Spencer 115, Aldana 99.

JUST ADD POLISH

McLaughlin's tenure as Honda team manager ended with the 1980 season, when Ron Murakami took over. There was little doubt the team's debut season had been a success. McLaughlin had built a winning team, and the CB-F was developing well. "For the time it was a good bike," he says. "It was

Race face: Venezuelan Roberto Pietri served Honda for many seasons in Superbike. (Courtesy John Froude)

a bit slow steering, and we worked both in the gearbox, undercutting the dogs, and in the engine – fixing the camchain tensioner with an Erikson Teflon device, and replacing the first rods with titanium Carrillos.

"We looked at the heads too. From RSC they flowed 87cfm [cubic feet per minute] and when I left we had 130. Jerry Branch had a jig for the engine – he could take the head off, mill it and the engine would be running again in 45 minutes. And while he was doing all this dyno work, he and Pappy [Edmonston] worked on flow and they developed this thing called the Turbulator – basically a restrictor on the carburettors to bring them down to 31mm that, when modified, gave higher flow …"

Edmonston's flat-slide, jetless carbs appeared on AHM bikes almost from day one: Blue Magnums that evolved into Black Bombs and then Qwik Silvers, reduced from 38 or 40mm via the Turbulator to comply with AMA regulations. They weren't for everyone: Spencer liked the sharper power of Edmonston's carbs while Mike Baldwin preferred Keihins' more progressive delivery. McLaughlin, however, was sure Pappy's were better: "They gave better pick-up and 10 horsepower on the top end."

Development continued throughout the three-year competitive life of the CB-F. There was plenty of scope in the AMA's rules for modification within the stock castings, to the extent of altering the included angle of the (titanium) valves. Handmade chrome-moly frames and swinging arms, factory anti-dive Showa forks, and gas-charged Ohlins rear units all found their place, as did Dymags – with a 16in front before the end of 1981 – and Nissin and Spondon callipers. The engine used both 62mm (CB750F) and 69mm (CB900F) cranks, and US aftermarket components that included Crane cams and Wiseco pistons. There was even a special projects department at American Honda that made covers and castings, including a bronze oil pan that dropped the bike's centre of gravity. With improved tyres came the need for extra cornering clearance, so by 1982 the Krober ignition was sometimes shifted from the end of the crank to become a belt-driven unit behind the right of the cylinder block. "The bikes," said Velasco, "changed constantly."

Innovation was something Kawasaki knew about, too. For 1981, the KMC team's bikes were based on the new KZ1000J, with bigger ports and valves than the old KZ1000. In Superbike form the new engine would keep the '80 model's twin-plug ignition, reducing advance, and minimising the possibility of detonation. Internals were surprisingly stock, including the lightened cranks and the rods, which were polished to remove surface flaws; but new crew chief Rob Muzzy put plenty of work into the ports and combustion chamber. Edmonston's Blue Magnum carburettors were used, and, at the other end, a new Kerker exhaust system that boosted torque. Ignition was by magneto. By season's end, the lump was rated at 150bhp at 10,250rpm. The frame was gusseted but otherwise as per the J design, albeit with a purpose-made aluminium swinging arm. Forks were Kayabas (with different yokes available for changing offset), the rear units Works Performance, and the wheels Morris Mags. Front discs were 330mm cast iron, and, to satisfy Lawson's demand for more braking power, came with four-piston callipers from the KR500 GP bike.

Of Wes Cooley's new GS1000S, Fujio Yoshimura said that the bulk of its components were listed in the Yoshimura catalogue. Special bits included one-off Kayaba anti-dive forks and rear spring/damper units. Capacity ran to 1023cc using a 70.9mm bore and Yoshimura pistons giving a compression ratio of 11:1. The top end was all Yoshimura, from cams to the oversize valves (of unspecified material) and double valve springs. The wet, multi-plate clutch had a steel hub, replacing the aluminium unit of earlier bikes. Electronic ignition was provided by Kokusan and Dymag wheels and brakes from the RG500 GP bike completed a potent package.

While the three stars – Cooley, Lawson, and Freddie Spencer – stayed put, there was movement elsewhere in the leading teams. At Honda, Pierce's contract was not renewed for 1981 and Mike Spencer hired in his place. Baldwin, hired for the final rounds of the 1980 Superbike series, would join Aldana – released by KMC – for a full season of European endurance racing with Honda France.

First into the headlines was Wes Cooley, giving Yoshimura Suzuki its fifth straight win at Daytona. With around 150bhp available, improving tyres and sturdier chassis, the Superbikes were now lapping at speeds

Freddie Spencer starred throughout the AMA Superbike series in 1980 and 1981 but lost out in both: in 1980 to Wes Cooley and in '81 to Steady Eddie. (Courtesy Mary Grothe)

comparable with good F1 bikes; Cooley and returning victor Crosby were most impressive in sharing a qualifying time of 2m 7.83s, 108.67mph. Freddie Spencer was next, his '81 bike wearing CB900F bodywork, with Lawson's apparently sluggish KZ1000J fourth.

The two white Vetter-backed Yoshi Suzukis led away, and diced with Freddie Spencer's Honda for the opening laps. The leading trio was still intact when fuel stops began: Spencer dived into his pit on the 12th lap of 26, and promptly abandoned ship when overflowing fuel ignited. Smartly deployed fire extinguishers prevented critical damage, and Spencer was soon on his way, although too far behind to bother the leaders. Cooley and Crosby pitted, and so did Lawson, looking doubtfully at his oil-streaked motor. With four laps to run he pulled in and parked the bike, its coating of oil making it difficult to handle. Cooley led the final lap expecting Crosby to pass out of the last turn, but it didn't happen, the Kiwi running home less than a second in arrears. Spencer was third, and Wayne Gardner an impressive fourth on Mamoru Moriwaki's latest.

Freddie claimed his first win at the second of the eight rounds: Talladega. In Alabama the banking again took its toll with Lawson's good engine throwing a rod in his heat, and Pietri's Honda likewise crying enough as he led the first lap of the final. Spencer took over, swapping the lead with Cooley until the Suzuki slowed. Lawson meanwhile closed up through the infield section and beat Cooley for second. Honda's new recruit Mike Spencer was fourth from Racecrafters' Harry Klinzmann.

Eddie's run for the title began at Elkhart Lake. Freddie was lightning fast and cleared out to a good lead until a jammed throttle slide put him down and out; and with Cooley losing his clutch early, Lawson was a comfortable winner from Mike Spencer, Cooley and Klinzmann. At Loudon, Freddie's luck was no better: carrying a wrist injury from a crash at the Indy Mile, he led the wet race until forced off the track by a backmarker. Down he went, up he came and got going again, passing David Emde's BMW for third and almost catching Cooley in second. But there was no stopping Eddie Lawson and his winning streak continued at Laguna Seca. With Muzzy's magic now having a real impact on the bike, Eddie outdragged his principal rivals in a straight fight, leading from flag to flag while Cooley and Spencer argued over second, each suffering from oil leaks that had them sliding: Spencer from dragging his cases through turn 1, Cooley's from a loose clutch cover. By the chequered flag Lawson was 16 seconds clear of Cooley. Mike Spencer and Pietri took fourth and fifth for Honda, but with five rounds done, Lawson (78 points) and Cooley (76) comfortably led the two Spencers, Freddie (59) and Mike (57).

Three straight was good, but it wasn't enough. At Pocono Freddie revived his flagging season with storming wins in both F1 and Superbike. He ran away in Superbike, opening up a four-second lead, while Eddie overshot at turn 1 and worked his way back. Cooley ran as high as third, but then stopped with a dead engine while Lawson charged back into second from Pietri.

Wes Cooley won the AMA Superbike series in 1979 and 1980 for Yoshimura Suzuki, going toe to toe with Lawson and Spencer. At Loudon in 1980 (pictured) he was second to Freddie. (Courtesy Mary Grothe)

SLOW BURN

If Spencer lost the title in 1980 at Atlanta, Lawson certainly won it in 1981 at Seattle's combination of drag strip and road circuit. This was perhaps the race of the season with Lawson and Spencer going head to head. Yet it was Cooley who led from the off with Lawson and Spencer reeling him in after he'd ground a bolt head off and the Yoshi Suzuki began leaking oil. Starting the last lap Spencer was in front, but going into turn 10 Lawson lined him up, passed on the outside and won the drag to the line. "I'd get him going into the corners and he'd get me going out," said Lawson. "I had a little motor on him but we were riding equal." One race to go, Lawson 112, Freddie Spencer 95, Cooley 91, Mike Spencer 68.

Back at Daytona, where it had all begun seven months before, Lawson's 17-point break on Spencer meant he could relax in the final race of the season, and came home an unflustered third while Freddie won from Mike Spencer. Eddie hadn't crashed all season. Freddie had his 'killer engine' fitted and rocketed away to set a new race record. Cooley didn't get there at all, having fallen in practice and broken his pelvis. Hondas filled the places with Doug Polen's private bike running home fourth, but Eddie and his crew – Muzzy, Steve and Mark Johnson – got the champagne: Lawson 125, Freddie Spencer 115, Cooley 91, Mike Spencer 84.

NEW BLOOD

Freddie would soon be gone; his genius would now see him on the mighty FWS at the Daytona 200, then with the NS500 and Kenny Roberts in Europe. Meanwhile, Baldwin and Aldana were back from their season's endurance racing for Honda France, a season that brought them a win at the Suzuka 8 Hours, and points finishes at Nürburgring and Donington among retirements elsewhere. Baldwin was a perfect fit for AHM, however, and joined the team before the end of the year. Mike Spencer had gone and talented all-rounder Steve Wise was recruited to complete AHM's riding strength with ever-present Pietri. The team also had a new manager in Udo Gietl.

There were changes at Kawasaki as well: Californian Wayne Rainey climbed into green leathers and took delivery of one of the 30 new KZ1000S Eddie Lawson Replicas. These came without Muzzy's headwork or Edmonston carbs (instead having 33mm Keihin CRs), but were competitive and rated at 135bhp out of the box. Rainey was no stranger to Kawasaki, having put in in a season of club racing on the marque's street bikes in 1980, getting a ride on one of Lawson's 250 GP bikes on the strength of it. Only now he was getting his first taste of the big league, with the remote but dedicated Lawson as team-mate.

Freddie Spencer won the Daytona Superbike race at his fourth attempt, leading a Honda 1-2-3, and holding the lead even when he pitted for fuel. Baldwin opened his account with second despite an oil-misted visor, and Pietri was third as rival teams wilted in the Florida sun. Cooley limped into fourth on his old GS1000S, down on power with his feet sliding off the

188

Mike Baldwin's crash at Loudon in 1979 kept him out of racing until the second half of 1980, when he filled in for the injured Pierce on Honda Superbikes, bagging two thirds and a fourth. (Courtesy John Froude)

pegs from leaking oil, while the team's new 16-valve Katana-based bikes, intended for Wes and the returning Aldana, sat in the team garage after a spate of seizures. "We were having crank and piston problems," said Cooley. Lawson, visibly slower than the new Hondas, got up to second but then slipped back. He decided not to stop for fuel and rolled to a stop in turn 7 on the last lap, still credited with sixth, behind new team-mate Rainey.

On the Sunday of speed week, Graeme Crosby again entered the history books by outlasting Roberts and Spencer to take the 200, so giving the Yamaha TZ750 its ninth and final win. In open-class racing Yamaha's big two-stroke, largely deprived of development since 1977, was in retreat. Honda's mighty FWS almost won Daytona at its first attempt, and soon the TZ would be released from its intake restrictors yet still struggle to match the better four-strokes; Cooley would win again on his F1 GS1000R at Elkhart Lake, and Eddie occasionally chose his Superbike over his KR500 in F1.

Lawson's first win of '82 came at Talladega, taking the flag 30 seconds clear of Wise and Rainey. Honda's ambitions ended in clouds of dust after early leader Pietri and Baldwin both crashed during the opening laps, while Cooley, reunited with his Katana, broke a valve in his heat and seized a piston in his spare engine during the final. Lawson was still on top a month later at Riverside, outpacing Baldwin and Rainey, even after slowing with his rear tyre going off. Cooley got his Katana into fourth, reporting that it wasn't yet a match for Lawson's missile in the top end, from Pietri's Moriwaki-famed Honda. Eddie made it three at Elkhart Lake, this time from the back of the grid after crashing in his heat. Cooley's Katana was still improving, finishing second after passing Rainey, but the best Honda was Pietri's, in fourth. Four rounds done, Lawson 69, Rainey 49, Wise 40, Cooley 38, and the future looked green.

First the master, then the apprentice: Kawasaki's dominance went unchecked at Loudon, but where Lawson faltered after choosing the wrong front tyre, Rainey worked clear of Baldwin to take his first national Superbike win from Lawson, Thad Wolff's Suzuki and Cooley, while Baldwin faded with brake problems.

Lawson was on top at Laguna Seca, in a virtuoso performance that might have been better still if Spencer – back for the occasion with his NS500 to take on KR's 0W61 in the F1 event – hadn't blown an engine in his heat, and then stopped with a broken fuel line as the grid formed up for the final. Eddie led from flag to flag with Baldwin a lonely second and Cooley getting the better of team-mate Aldana for third. Rainey fell at the Corkscrew but remounted to finish 10th. Six rounds done: Lawson 105, Rainey 74, Baldwin and Cooley 62 apiece.

Lawson didn't do quite as well in the F1 event. While Spencer and Roberts shared the wins, Eddie's KR500 seized in the first race and he crashed in the second, cracking a vertebra that put him out of the Pocono Superbike race. There, Baldwin won from Rainey – and found himself in hot water for using a Goodyear front that hadn't received AMA approval, though the result stood. He had a good meeting at Sears Point too, taking his favourite bike, the FWS, to its last win in the F1 race (and taking the title), and then, with Eddie still convalescing, winning the Superbike round after Rainey fell, breaking a collarbone, on the last lap.

Eddie was back in business at Seattle, and, while he wasn't able to take the title there as he had in '81, he did all he could, leading from start to finish while Baldwin fell from second place and Cooley took over, his 195kg Katana now sporting high 'bars that gave him more leverage: "We've got the power now," he said, "but I'm not the biggest guy you ever saw." Baldwin fanned the dying flames of his title bid with a win at Daytona, scrapping hard with Lawson all the way. For once Kawasaki had appeased the Daytona gremlins, and Lawson finished a good, if outpowered, second from Wise and Rainey. Cooley blew another motor: "the third in two days," he noted grimly.

The big bruisers rolled out for the last time in the unfamiliar territory of Moroso Motorsport Park in Florida. Honda fielded no fewer than five factory bikes in a bid to cut Lawson's 19-point series lead: along with the usual suspects, Sam McDonald rode Steve Wise's second bike and John Long hopped onto Baldwin's spare. To be certain, they needed Eddie out of the points altogether, and a fast rider on a dependable bike argued persuasively against that outcome. Come the race, Baldwin and Cooley

Texan all-rounder Steve Wise (pictured) starred on dirt. He began road racing for Team Honda in 1982, becoming a winner in Superbike and collecting podiums in F1. (Courtesy John Froude)

scrapped for the lead, and after Rainey stopped with clutch trouble Lawson cruised into an unflustered fifth to collect his second title, with race winner Baldwin runner-up overall: Lawson 151, Baldwin 142, Rainey 114, Cooley 109. Steady Eddie indeed.

And that was that. Ten long years after that first AMA-sanctioned Superbike Production race at Laguna Seca in 1973, the air-cooled, litre-class big bangers were wheeled back into their trailers for the last time. The FIM had for a couple of years wanted to reduce the capacity ceiling of four-stroke racing to 750cc, notably in European endurance racing and TT-F1, being haunted by the possibilities of ever-increasing power outpacing frame and tyre technology. While the ACU in Britain had bought a year's postponement after heavy lobbying by teams and privateers who'd spent the kids' inheritance on 1000cc bikes, the AMA had decided to introduce a 750cc limit from 1983 – despite a petition to retain the 1025cc top limit for Superbikes signed by 30 of the biggest names in the sport, Spencer, Baldwin and Cooley among them.

The era of the water-cooled 750 was just around the corner – and Honda was bringing it.

7

WELCOME TO THE JUNGLE

If Ross Hannan's relationship with Pops Yoshimura had a visible starting point, it's probably the CB750 he and his brother Ralph built for Ron Toombs to ride in the 1973 Chesterfield Superbike Series at Amaroo Park in Sydney. Under its bodywork were many of the goodies Pops had used in his bikes at Daytona in 1971, including CR Keihins and a factory close-ratio cluster. Although the Hannans' Honda didn't dominate the series, it certainly added spice – but while Superbike racing gradually gained prestige and support in the USA, it was an uncomfortable inclusion in Australia's racing calendar during the mid-1970s. The national championships were about grand prix two-strokes, and a growing calendar of long-distance stock Production races had no use for heavily modified four-strokes; and there seemed little room for anything else.

The Chesterfield series petered out in 1975; after that, Superbike racing came in individual races – often described as 'Improved Touring' – added to a given programme at the organising club's discretion. For all that, Hannan was keen to get another Superbike built and Sydney dealer Ian Cork did the pioneering work on the first of their Kawasakis, using as its basis a Z900 that Tony Hatton had jumped off early in the '76 Adelaide Three-Hour after having his front wheel taken out at the end of the main straight.

Another key ingredient in the Hannans' early efforts was Graeme Crosby. The Auckland maverick was trying to build up his CV and worked at the Hannans' Sydney shop while racking up impressive performances on the Kawasaki built by Cork. The bike ran 998cc, boasted Pops' ported cylinder head and oversize valves, Bonneville cams, and the inevitable CR Keihins, that all contributed to a horsepower boost rated by some at 50bhp over stock. By the time Croz had done the 1976-7 Marlboro Series in New Zealand – "it handled like a roller skate in gravel pit," he noted – Crosby and the Hannans' Yoshimura Kawasaki – the Beast – had become well-known on

Croz on 'Son of Beast,' the Hannan brothers' Z1R Superbike that did so much to popularise the class Down Under, pictured here at Bathurst in 1978. (Courtesy Phil Aynsley)

both sides of the Tasman. 'Son of Beast,' the Hannans' famous Z1R, would soon follow.

Gradually, the number of races grew, and the term Superbike gained currency again. An abiding problem, however, was the lack of common rules. Different states, even different clubs, applied their own limits to four-stroke racing: some regulated brake components, others tyres or wheels.

Mick Hone, a pioneering figure of Australian Superbike racing who would go on to establish perhaps the most successful team in the class, remembers how the strengths of Superbike overcame early difficulties. "Unlike GP racing, in Superbike you could choose from a dozen different bikes and get your bits from a dozen different suppliers, and the guy who made his bike work the best could be very competitive. The riders wanted it, the fans all jumped to the fence when it was happening, but there was no direction from Motorcycling Australia.

"The Pommies were puffing round on their TT-F1 bikes and American Superbikes were more radical than ours; but we went Superbike because we didn't want free frames and free everything else. Our basic concept was that anybody could start a Superbike. And that meant you had to have the original frame, original crankcases, cylinders, cylinder heads – but you could put on a pipe and carbies, you could do internal work.

"The bike's profile had to be the same; but then it started getting confused with stuff like brakes – originally, you could use any brakes the factory used. Well, the world endurance teams had factory bikes and might be using Lockheeds or Brembos, so if you could find a picture of any factory bike running them, you could use the same thing. We had people taking advantage of that and it was decided you had to run an Australian Design Rules compliance plate on the bike to show it was an Australian model."

In Melbourne, the Superbike Steering Committee, comprising manufacturer and dealer reps, accessory importers, the press and the riders, began to shape a future for the class south of the Murray River. The immediate result was the Victorian Superbike Championship that ran over five rounds in 1980 and laid the groundwork for bigger competitions in seasons to come. New South Wales contributed the three-round Bel-Ray series run at Oran Park, to the south-west of Sydney, also during the 1980 season.

Hone already had his bikes. In 1977 he'd bought one of Croz's old Kawasakis from Ross Hannan, and a chance encounter with aircraft engineer Alan Pickering accelerated the process. By the beginning of 1980 they'd developed a Suzuki GS1000S.

"We were in touch with Pops Yoshimura who helped us with the right set-up, and Pickering and his merry men from Ansett got us working to aircraft-industry standards of preparation," explains Hone. "We based it on Wes Cooley's bike, so we got Yoshi cams, valves and pistons, and Keihin 31mm carbs. It was a '79 model bike so that's when we started building it. Rod Tingate made the exhaust – did a beautiful job – and we basically ended up with a Wes Cooley replica."

Hone campaigned the GS in 1980, but he and Alan Pickering were soon eyeing up Suzuki's new 16-valve GSX1100. Although ineligible for TT-F1 in the UK because of its 1074cc capacity, and not homologated in the US, the new model looked good for Australian Superbike and its 1300cc ceiling. They were also looking for another rider: Hone had opened a Suzuki dealership in suburban Melbourne, and hadn't the time he might have wished to lavish on racing.

Meanwhile, Sydney rider Tony Hatton was getting an insider's view of Honda's burgeoning Superbike/TT-F1 programme, while it was no more than a rumour in the northern hemisphere. After he'd ridden Mamoru Moriwaki's Kawasaki into third place with Croz at the inaugural Suzuka 8 Hours, Honda invited Hatton to Japan in early '79 to test its new CB900-based Superbike. "It was great round Suzuka," he recalls. "It was typical Honda, built for that track. I could hardly fault it except that the suspension was a bit hard for me in some places – but I got round there way faster than I had on Moriwaki's bike the year before.

Rare bird: Australian Ken Blake could ride anything, being at home on hot four-stroke and grand prix two-strokes. He's pictured here at Bathurst in 1975 on that rarest of Ducatis, the 860SS. (Courtesy Phil Aynsley)

"They brought the bike to Bathurst for the Arai 3-Hour [later the Arai 500km] – one for me and another for Mick Cole. I told Honda Bathurst would be different, and to bring more rear springs. Sure enough, the thing went round corners fine, but the hardest part of Bathurst is down Conrod, where it was smacking everywhere – it was too hard on the initial hit and getting really light. I wanted stiffer springs with less preload – to soften it up by going harder. At Suzuka everyone suffers from front-end chatter so they set the bike up really soft. Take 'em anywhere else and they're bloody hopeless."

Hatton won the Arai 3-hour race, marking the beginning of a good season: he and Cole won the Suzuka 8 Hours, and at the Bol d'Or, Hatton – riding with South Australian Ken Blake after Cole had broken a leg in practice – was handily placed as the race wound down. "The bloody exhausts broke at the flange again [a Suzuka problem], but we were still trying to get on the podium in the last hour. Then the engine started vibrating. I knocked the revs off to eight or so – it was running a big end or a main. Blake started the final session with third place still possible. But then "it threw a conrod and Blakey had no choice but to put it into the undergrowth. Fuel went everywhere and it burnt out."

Hatton's racing days were almost over. In 1979, Ron Toombs, one of the Australian racing community's most celebrated sons, died at Bathurst after he clipped a bank with his shoulder, went over the concrete track wall and into the trees on the inside of the circuit. Hatton was among those lobbying for improved track safety, and thought the measures taken for 1980 were unsatisfactory. "I said, 'I'm never coming back here again' and once you say that, well, you retire."

BUILDING FOR THE FUTURE
After knocking back an offer to ride for Honda France, Hatton agreed to help with Honda's Superbike programme in Australia. There would be four bikes, two each for Honda's Victorian and New South Wales distributors, to be ridden by Hatton's old sparring partner Mick Cole, Alan Decker, Roger Heyes and Dennis Neill.

The factory Hondas ran 1062cc engines, and clearly had bags of potential even if they were a little unruly out of the crate. "They didn't carburate through the range," recalls Clyde Wolfenden, who ran the Victorian branch of the Honda team. "At Honda they got them to carburate when they were running flat out on the dyno, and we had to retune so the guys could ride them and keep up with more powerful bikes; we got them pulling from 6500-7000rpm to around ten-five."

While costly RSC Superbike/TT-F1 conversion kits came to Australia for a select few, others built to their own recipes, among them Sydney engineer Peter Molloy, who planned a Honda Superbike with collaborator Lindsay Walker, then Avon tyres distributor. Some aspects of the engine's design had him scratching his head: "It had huge, oddly shaped ports that gave low gas velocity," Molloy recalls. "So we filled the ports and reshaped

Neville Doyle was the architect of much Kawasaki success, turning out the world's most reliable H2Rs and managing Team Kawasaki Australia. He's pictured refuelling the Z1000SR TT-F1 bike at Bathurst in 1980. (Courtesy Phil Aynsley)

them, then worked on piston acceleration." He added his own cam grinds and Lucas Rita ignition. The bike ran to 996cc.

Initially, Molloy wanted John Pace, then Roger Heyes to ride the bike; but both were tied up elsewhere. Then Billy Hill, who ran Mentor Motorcycles in Sydney's inner west, made a suggestion. "I've got this kid from Wollongong," he told Molloy. "His name's Wayne Gardner."

For all the interest in the new 16-valve Honda and Suzuki, the durable two-valve Kawasaki engine was still a favourite among private builders, Gavin Cosway, Peter Van Meurs and Graeme 'Gyro' Carless among them. Van Meurs' background was in two-strokes – "I gave up tinkering with bits that had holes in them, to tinker with bits that leapt up and down," – whereas Carless and colleague Barry Spiller had drag-racing in their blood. Melbourne Kawasaki dealer Cosway built his 1197cc Z1000 Mk II and offered it to Andrew Johnson to ride – and he ran it in, open carbs, four-into-one and all, by riding it on his daily 25-mile ride between his home in Preston to Sugarloaf Reservoir, where he drove a bulldozer.

The Carless/Spiller bike – the Syndicate Machine – was very much a Melbourne special and less reliant on the contents of the Yoshimura parts book than many contemporaries. It ran 1160cc and boasted Gyro's own cam profiles, which were said to be similar to the Cosworth DFV's. "The crank was undercut and welded, but it was a standard Mk II," Gyro adds. "It ran a close-ratio Mk II gearbox, standard clutch, Yoshimura pistons, standard rods and, huge for the day, 38mm Mikunis.

"Once we got it going we realised it wasn't the best-handling thing on earth, so we built a swinging arm for it. We just kept developing. When we started, the bike weighed 212kg so we decided to lighten it and got it down to 227kg: we used larger engine bolts, larger bolts for the heads and barrels, larger bottom end studs … we kept breaking them. But twice we got 158bhp at the countershaft."

Before the two Superbike series got under way, the 1980 season opened with two long-distance races – the Coca-Cola 800 at Oran Park in March, and the Arai 500 at the Bathurst Easter meeting. Both events catered for Superbikes, prototypes and stock production bikes. At Oran Park, Honda Victoria riders Cole and Decker teamed up on one of the outfit's 1062 Superbikes (based on the new CB1100RB) to win outright. Dennis Neill and Ken Blake were warm favourites and ran well on a Hatton-prepared 1062 Honda until Blake fell on oil, bending the bike's crankshaft. Rob Phillis shared Mick Hone's GS1000 Superbike until carburation problems stopped them.

Cole won again at Bathurst while Neill stopped with a broken camchain. Hone, riding alone, went out with a broken gearbox while Phillis rode a production GSX1100 – and retired with a loose alternator. Gardner meanwhile had his first ride on the Molloy Honda and found it to his liking. "I love Superbikes," he said. "I was made for them."

The 800 and the 500 both featured that rarest of beasts, the factory

Andrew Johnson (1197 Cosway Kawasaki) exits the Calder hairpin during the second round of the 1980 Victorian Superbike Championship. No one gave more than Ajay. (Courtesy Rob Lewis)

Kawasaki F1 bike, the Z1000SR. It was shared at both events by Gregg Hansford and his Team Kawasaki Australia team-mate Jim Budd (hired primarily to ride the outfit's Z1R Mk II Superbike). Alas, after showing a good turn of speed the SR was gone. "That was a full prototype, the only one then in existence," recalls Peter Doyle, son of Neville and a gifted engineer in his own right. "It was sent to Australia to get miles on it. It did a head gasket at Bathurst and broke the taper off the crank at Oran Park. It was probably the dominant bike in both races, but we were told not to work on it beyond basic maintenance." The SR came with a spare 998cc engine, which went into Budd's Superbike. Kawasaki, meanwhile, built more SRs. "We went to Japan where Gregg and Eddie came second in the 8 Hours. Then we went to the Bol d'Or where two of our three engines suffered detonation and blew up – caused by poor fuel."

At the beginning of 1980, Robbie Phillis was new to the class he would soon make his own. After spending 1979 riding a TZ750 for Victorian Yamaha distributor Milledge Motorcycles, he quickly adapted to the demands of the equally potent but much heavier litre-plus Suzuki four-strokes he'd ride in the seasons ahead. "Superbikes taught you rolling speed and I had more than most. Lots of guys got it stopped to turn but I didn't, I had both ends sliding; and when radial tyres came you could brake deeper and go in tighter."

Superbike racing started in earnest at Oran Park in May 1980 with the opening round of the Bel-Ray series. There it was Honda all the way with Neill taking over from early leader Heyes, Gardner, Cole, and Decker snapping at their heels. Gardner, down on power with the early 996cc Molloy bike, came into his own when rain fell, passing Neill and Cole to win with 20 seconds to spare. Neill did better the following weekend at Winton for the opening round of the Victorian title, leading home Johnson on Cosway's 1197 Kawasaki, Cole, Hone's GS, and Scott Stephens on the 1170 Powerflow Kawasaki built by Peter Van Meurs.

Johnson took the lead in the Victorian series after the second round at Calder Park, a four-turn, one-mile loop west of Melbourne. Still on Cosway's bike, he ran second again, this time to Stephens with Decker third for Honda. Three weeks later at Oran Park, Johnson made his debut on the fearsome Syndicate Machine in the second round of the Bel-Ray series, leading for a couple of laps but then slowing with a misfire. Gardner won on the Molloy bike, now running Venolia pistons that ramped capacity to 1050cc, and an RSC dry sump – "the only thing Honda has given us so far," growled Molloy. Mick Cole again ran second from Decker and Phillis.

Neill led strongly but bowed out of the second Bel-Ray event with clutch failure and did the same at the third round of the Victorian series, again at Calder. While the other Hondas seemed down on power compared with the fast-developing opposition, Neill's, running Moriwaki cams, was fast enough if short on durability. Meanwhile Robbie Phillis got another taste of life at the head of the field. Riding Malvern Motorcycles' GSX1100, he retired from the preliminary race with ignition failure, but then led the title race before crashing, leaving Stephens to win again from Johnson on a wobbling Syndicate bike, Decker, and Cole.

Dennis Neill on one of Team Honda's RSC 1062s at Winton. Neill looked set for a promising debut at the TT in 1981 but was stopped by a freak accident at Bathurst. (Courtesy Rob Lewis)

Neill was back on the top step of the podium at Winton after the fourth round. Johnson again led but slowed with a sliding back tyre. Still, he clung to second place to maintain his overall lead while Cole and Decker filled the places for Honda. Four rounds done: Johnson 48, Stephens and Cole 36, Neill 34, Decker 32.

The Bel-Ray series wrapped up at the opening round of the 1980 Swann Series. Mick Cole took the laurels for the race and the series, passing Gardner's misfiring Molloy Honda to win from Neill, while the future world champion dropped back to fourth behind Budd's Kawasaki and so lost the title to the Victorian Honda man by a point, 39-38.

Johnson took the Victorian Superbike Championship at Sandown in the final meeting of the series, and the year. While XR69-mounted Graeme Crosby wound up the Swann Series itself, Johnson, riding with a broken shoulder from a crash at Oran Park, was third behind Neill and Hone to claim the inaugural Superbike state title, and show that in one corner of the world at least, private horsepower was as good as the factory variety. Johnson 58, Neill 49, Cole and Stephens 36 apiece.

ROBBIE

Andrew Johnson was the embodiment of determination, a force of nature who could rank alongside the toughest in the sport – Bob McIntyre, Gary Nixon, Wayne Gardner. Anyone who saw AJ tapped out down Conrod Straight at Bathurst, head shaking slowly, angry with himself for having made some minor mistake, is unlikely ever to forget it. In that sense, he and Robbie Phillis – so often disputing the lead in the early '80s – represented the opposite sides of the same coin; Phillis was a natural, touched with artistry. Mick Hone, for so long Phillis's manager and mentor, perhaps explained their attributes best in an offhand remark to the author: "Imagine a rider with the determination of Andrew Johnson and the talent of Robbie Phillis," he said.

Phillis joined the Hone team early in 1981. "I considered two blokes," Hone recalls. "My first choice was Graeme 'Goose' Muir. I wanted a Victorian guy because we were based in Victoria, and the Sydney guys seemed to get a lot of breaks the Victorians didn't. But Goose told me he had a ride – Geoff Taylor's TZ750 – and said if I were you I'd take Phillis. So I did." Phillis, however, came with a reputation: "Picky [Alan Pickering] and John Harvey [the noted touring car driver] who were in the team, asked: 'How are we going to keep the bikes up to him? He's a lunatic.'"

But Robbie understood the team and its values. "We just had to tell him we were focused on racing, that we were representing Suzuki, that we were looking for sponsorship – and he just fell into line. It was already there, he just had to stop being a dickhead sometimes. But he couldn't have been any better. He was impeccable."

Phillis became the Hone team's leading rider as the GSX1100 Superbike – the team's famous black bike – was under development, though the GS1000 was still front-line equipment, and after Sandown got new Yoshimura race crank with improved roads, and straight-cut primary gears.

After back-to-back tests the team decided to go with the GSX. "Ross Hannan told me I'd find the four-valve quicker," says Hone. "And with some of Pops' stuff fitted, it surpassed the GS pretty quickly. At Bathurst that year Robbie told me it didn't feel that quick, but he was flying; because it was so smooth he didn't realise how quick it was."

While Kawasaki withdrew its support for Australian Superbike, the class received a boost from an unexpected quarter – Yamaha. Mal Pitman in South Australia broke new ground when he and his Adelaide crew adapted an XS1100 tourer for Superbike racing, complete with chain final drive. A countershaft sprocket from a TZ750 proved, according to Sydney journal *Revs Motorcycle News*, an easy fit onto the splines of the final driveshaft once the bevel gear had been removed. Other modifications included twin-plug heads and reground cams. Carburation was stock, although the suspension and cast wheels changed with experimentation. A useful 45kg lighter than the catalogue bike, Pitman's creation was ridden to victory by Greg Pretty and Gary Coleman at the second and final Oran Park Coca-Cola 800, to the surprise of many and the consternation of some.

The bike was successful again at the Bathurst Arai 500 a month later, this time piloted by Pretty alone, from the production CB1100Rs of Glen Taylor and Vince Sharpe, and the Mick Hone GSX1100 Superbike ridden

Johnson (Syndicate Kawasaki) leads Graeme Muir and Trevor Flood (both Yamaha TZ750s) through turn 1 at Winton, Robbie Phillis giving chase. (Courtesy Rob Lewis)

by Phillis. But Bathurst had bad news to share yet again, with Dennis Neill's career brought to an end just four laps into the Arai 500. As his Honda's front end lifted over the high-speed hump on Mountain Straight, its front wheel dropped out and in the ensuing crash he suffered head injuries and a broken arm. At the time it was thought the wheel had been torn from the forks after a ferocious wheelie, but witnesses said the wheel had simply dropped out, and it was thought the quick-release axle clamps had let go. Neill eventually recovered, but his racing days were over.

After bickering over venues and ticket prices, the Victorian Superbike Championship, now with naming rights going to sparkplug manufacturer NGK, got going again in May 1981. Over five rounds again (though now with two races at each meeting), the action opened at Winton with John Pace, replacing UK-bound Gardner on the Molloy Honda, winning overall. Johnson was racing in Asia and Pretty crashed the Yamaha early in the opening leg, leaving Stephens and Team Honda's lone runner Mick Cole to chase Pace home. Phillis, his GSX now running to 1132cc, was fourth in the first leg, and went for taller gearing in the second race. It worked. After a race-long scrap with Pace he won by half a wheel, with Cole again third after Stephens had fallen.

Pace bagged another first and second in the opening round of the Bel-Ray series at a sodden Oran Park, this time giving way to Bill McCulloch's Suzuki in the opening leg. A notable non-starter at Oran Park was Greg Pretty. He'd been due to ride the Pitman's XS1100 but in the week between the NGK and Bel-Ray openers he and Yamaha Pitman had gone their separate ways, Pretty wanting to return to Europe. Then came the worst news of all, of Ken Blake's death in the Senior TT, his TZ350 losing traction at high speed through a wet Ballagarey on the fifth lap of six. Blake had been to the TT each year since 1978, notching a best result of fourth in the 1980 250 TT. Admired by fans and respected by rivals, he was perhaps best known for his heroic performances in the Castrol Six-Hour. Blakey had talent in abundance, could ride anything, and delivered his skills with a modest civility that placed him high among Australia racing's favourite sons. He was 35.

Johnson was back for the second NGK round at Winton, while Cole was in Britain and Pace in Japan for the Suzuka 200km TT-F1 race. Phillis, Stephens, and Hone were on hand, but none saw which way Johnson went. He cleared out in both wet races, while Phillis worked on his points tally. A month later at Calder the wet weather was back, and Johnson bagged another double, while Phillis and Stephens took a second and a third apiece. Pace was back in the fray with a couple of fourth places, but Johnson was closing on Phillis with two rounds to run: Phillis 48, Johnson 40, Stephens and Alan Mills (Kawasaki) 34 apiece.

Back at Winton for round four, Phillis was under instructions from Hone to pile on the points, but took a double win anyhow. The Syndicate had its problems, both with ignition and a cracked cylinder head, but a loose gear linkage slowed Johnson off the grid. Still, he was up to fourth at the end of the first lap while Phillis passed Stephens for the lead. By the flag Johnson had closed to within seconds of Phillis while Cole, back from the UK and waving the Honda flag vigorously, fought through the field for third. And that was as good as it got for Johnson. Rain came in the second leg, catching the bulk of the field on slicks. Johnson was among them and lost the front end in a fast right-hander, while Phillis won from Paul Feeney's Hannan-prepped Moriwaki Kawasaki and Suzuki-mounted Paul Walkley. The title was all but Robbie's with a 19-point lead and one round left.

Robbie, low-flying on Malvern Motorcycles' 1132 GSX1100-propelled Superbike at Winton; Graeme Muir in pursuit. (Courtesy Rob Lewis)

Sydney-based Kiwi Neville Hiscock now rode Peter Molloy's latest venture, a 1166cc GSX1100 Superbike – Molloy thought the Suzuki's cylinder head offered better flow and flame propagation than Honda's Pentroof design – and used it to wrap up the two-round Bel-Ray Superbike Series at Oran Park with a couple of podium places behind Phillis. Johnson meanwhile decided the time was right to sever his ties with the Syndicate, and at Sandown for the final encounter of 1981 he rode one of Honda Australia's 1062s, knowing the odds on keeping the NGK title were heavily against him. Phillis, having his first competitive ride on a Pickering-prepped Katana, rode to a measured third in the opening wet race while Johnson led, fending off Feeney's Hannan Kawasaki. With the title secured, Robbie took the fight to Feeney in the second leg, finishing runner-up while Johnson settled for third, taking second place in the title: Phillis 85, Johnson 67, Feeney 53.

As the New Year opened to the first tentative noises about a national Superbike championship, the Hone team, now with Cole riding alongside Phillis, was working up its Katanas for the new season. "We were very careful," says Alan Pickering when asked to explain his magic.' "I tried to be meticulous with assembly, cam timing, piston-to-head clearances ... we had great reliability and great results. There was nothing secret or very special about it.

"We used Pops' stuff and really weren't modifying it much. When we got a chance we went to a circuit and put a day in. I'd just make Robbie ride round and round at 3000 revs for a quarter of an hour, switch the motor off and let it cool down, then go out and go up to 4000 for a while – build it up gradually until after a couple of hours you could go round at max revs. I was a firm believer in that, even with our Production bikes.

"A lot of guys mixed stuff up and tried to do different things where we just built very reliable, rideable, quick motorbikes. We didn't chase horsepower. Probably the only bike I did a bit extra on was the black GSX11. I modified the head myself at home – opened it up, ported and polished, fitted valves one or two millimetres bigger ..."

METHOD

While Pops Yoshimura began a troubled season with his 1000cc Katanas in AMA Superbike, the Hone team carried on from where it left off in '81 – but not until Kiwi Rodger Freeth made his mark at Bathurst with a near-stock GSX1100 (E24 Katana cams, carbs and a pipe) in a Ken McIntosh frame. Freeth won the Arai 500 after the faster Superbikes of Pace (Molloy Suzuki), Johnson (Honda), Cole and Phillis had all bowed out. But Phillis was back in the winning groove at the opening round of the new Can-Am Series at Oran Park, taking a pair of wins from Pace's Molloy bike and Cole.

Robbie was just getting his eye in: he proved unbeatable in the first two rounds of the NGK series (running an 1100cc maximum in '82, dropping to 1000cc for 1983) while Johnson fell at the Winton opener, damaging a hand. Indeed, when the field got to Calder for the third round Honda had been hard hit with Pretty nursing a broken collarbone from a Surfers Paradise crash, while Johnson and new recruit Glen Taylor both fell in practice. Stephens was also out, his Kawasaki putting a rod through its cases in practice, but Katana-mounted Neville Hiscock, runner-up behind Phillis at the Winton second round, won at Calder after a race-long dice with Cole and Phillis in the opener, and did it again in race two, this time leading Phillis home from Dave Miller's Powerflow Kawasaki. Three rounds gone: Phillis 82, Hiscock 60, Cole 58.

By the time Robbie had returned to Winton to win the first race of round four, the NGK title was again his, in all but name. While Cole saw off Hiscock to bag second in both races, Phillis was in a class of his own. Johnson was again a non-starter, this time with gearbox problems.

Come season's end, Phillis claimed not one Superbike crown but two. Visiting Oran Park for the second round of the Can-Am series in mid-season, Phillis finished runner-up to Hiscock in both races and had an 11-point break over the Kiwi and his monoshock Action Suzuki Katana going into the final round. Phillis led for most of the opening race while Hiscock battled soft suspension, but then hit a kerb, damaging his ignition and rolling to a stop. Hiscock won and looked like doing it again in the second race, but fell on the penultimate lap trying to avoid a wayward backmarker. Phillis retained his overall lead, and added the Can-Am title to his plunder, 69-58.

The NGK series moved closer to full national status in 1983 with Victoria's regular five rounds supplemented by three at Oran Park. The opener, at Calder in January, brought its share of changes. Neville Hiscock had gone to South Africa and, sadly, his untimely death; Pace was to campaign in Europe, and while Cole still had his Katana, it was now in different colours. No longer part of the Hone team, Cole had backing from Dunlop and Grimshaw Suzuki. Johnson had no bike at all to begin with. His new VF860R V4 hadn't turned up, his interim warmed-over CB900F developed bottom-end troubles, so, as a last resort, the team gave him Pretty's old CB1100R. Change of bike or not, Johnson joined the old firm in the first race, getting away behind Phillis and fending off Cole's attempts to pass. In the second race Cole made the better start and held off Johnson. Feeney took both fourth places for the Hannan Kawasaki outfit, but again there was no stopping Robbie; with 30 points in the bag it was business as usual.

Johnson kept his points tally ticking over at Oran Park with the old 1062, but Bathurst looked altogether better with the new VF860R now ready to go. The water-cooled V4 was Honda's third combination of race and road components for a third continent, using the 859cc engine shared by Honda Britain's TT-F1 bikes with much of the street-derived VF750R chassis aimed at AMA Superbike racing. It was certainly fast enough: Johnson was favourite to win the Arai 500 until slowed by his sump grounding through McPhillamy and an unscheduled stop for a flat tyre. Phillis, guest riding on Honda's old RS1000 TT-F1 bike, took up the running to win from Johnson and Paul Walkley's Katana Superbike.

The amity between the Hone and Honda teams didn't last long. At Winton for the third round of the NGK series, Johnson's appetite for victory was piqued by the stated intention of Phillis and Cole to protest over the VF860R's legality. The Suzuki pair believed the Showa anti-dive forks fitted to the Hondas were specially designed, limited-production racing components, and so were illegal within Australian Superbike regs. ACU stewards allowed the Hondas to race and Johnson took two strong wins from Phillis with Honda's new recruit Mal 'Wally' Campbell, on the team's second VF860R, fighting clear of Cole for third in both races.

With three rounds down, Johnson led the NGK series on 77 points from

Team Honda's RSC 1062s in formation: Mick Cole leads Alan Decker at Winton.
(Courtesy Rob Lewis)

Phillis (74) and Cole (58) – but only for a matter of days. ACU Victoria upheld the Phillis/Cole protest, stripping Johnson and Campbell of the points they'd scored on the VFs and cutting Johnson's tally to 47. Team Honda Australia then decided to withdraw from the following weekend's Oran Park NGK round, citing insufficient time to swap the trick Showa units for stock VF750F forks and make the necessary changes to wheels and brakes. "It has pretty well blown our chances in the series," said Team Honda Australia boss Clyde Wolfenden. By the time Robbie had taken two more wins from Cole and Manny Blanco's Kawasaki at Oran Park, much of the spice had gone from the series: Phillis 110, Cole 90, Johnson 47.

Nor was there much likelihood of Johnson's early return. As winter took hold, news came that he'd suffered a neck injury at work, with surgery needed to relieve a pinched nerve. "It was more than a slipped disc," Johnson told *Revs.* "Two vertebrae were fractured." His doctors were talking of a three-month recovery period.

With Johnson and Phillis both missing from the following round at Winton (racing at the Suzuka 200) and Campbell crashing his VF in the first leg, Cole took both races and a 10-point lead in the series. Robbie pulled it back again at Oran Park, but only after some tough opposition from Campbell's VF-R. Hampered by a couple of muffed gear changes in the opening race, Wally got up to fourth while Phillis cleared off into a winning lead. Cole chased him home after getting the better of a long scrap with Paul Walkley's Powerflow Kawasaki. A poor start from Phillis let Walkley get away at the start of leg two, though this time Campbell had the V4 percolating well and used its grunt to take the lead. Cole and Walkley then went at it again but both crashed. Meanwhile, a sliding Phillis caught Campbell, but had no answer to his last-lap pass to the line, Rod Cox getting a good view of the action in third. Six rounds done: Phillis 137, Cole 132, Feeney 59.

Johnson, pawing the ground in frustration, got going again – not on his Superbike, but his RS500 triple, making a brave effort to win the 500cc Australian Road Racing Championship in just the last three rounds of the six. He almost made it too, running second at Adelaide and winning at Wanneroo and Sandown; he finished just a point short of Queenslander Tony Veitch's winning tally, 43-42. The ARRC now seemed to be in decline, with Australia's TZ750s having disappeared, like the rest of the world's, into the history books to leave the premier class – now 500cc – to a tiny clutch of eye-wateringly expensive grand prix 500s in a sea of TZ350 Yamahas.

The bulk of Honda's headlines were still being made by Wally Campbell on the team's V4s: by the end of the season winning three major production races on the VF750F (including the Castrol Six-Hour with Rod Cox) and, as the season closed, three of the last four NGK Superbike races. Heading back to Winton for the seventh round of eight, Campbell and his VF860R – now with a dry clutch – topped both races, but were pressed hard by the usual suspects, Phillis and Cole, as well as Jeff Thynne and the precocious talent of Kevin Magee, on Bob Brown's 674cc Ducati Pantah. Campbell's first journey became that much easier when Phillis didn't start, Alan Pickering just failing to fit the Katana's new cylinder head in time, but Magee and Thynne (Kawasaki) pushed him hard, while Cole's efforts were limited by a new combination of exhaust and carburettors that limited power below 6000rpm. In the second race, Campbell got away cleanly and though chased by Phillis and Cole, it was Honda's day.

Going into the final round a Calder, Cole led Phillis 152-149 with Paul Feeney a distant third on 71, but while Cole was caught up in a furious scrap in the opening leg and could finish only fifth, Phillis led Campbell home. Phillis cleared out again in the second leg while Campbell made another sluggish start, but this time the Honda man caught him and took the lead, Phillis in a secure second while Cole retired: the NGK title was Robbie's for the third year in a row.

Campbell ended the final day's campaign with fifth place in the NGK tally, but ended the year with a bigger prize: Honda sent the team one of its tiny handful of RS920 TT-F1 bikes for him to ride in the Swann Series, and while Johnson and Rob McElnea took two wins apiece in the six-race series and Campbell just one, he did enough to win overall.

NEW WAVE
Sponsored by insurance firm Western Underwriters for 1984, the now seven-round Superbike series would include rounds in Tasmania and South Australia in the season ahead.

Meanwhile, the class lost one of its star performers. Mick Cole decided he'd had enough. "I don't like production racing or racing at Bathurst," he told *Revs*. "I always thought the best would come, that I would crack it overseas. But with the recession, well, that's the way it goes."

The Superbike field reconvened at Symmons Plains in Tasmania for the first round of the '84 series, and Phillis, new Katana and all, was immediately back on top, though harassed in the first race by local favourite Campbell and Johnson, battling gearbox and suspension problems. Setting a record-breaking pace, Phillis staved off Campbell's last desperate lunge to win by half a wheel. "I came under Robbie sideways at the hairpin, sliding straight at him with the front wheel in the air," explained a breathless Campbell. Johnson, third in the first race, was left behind in the second as Phillis and Campbell shot away, Phillis again holding on by half a wheel in the last corner.

Johnson took a solid win in the Arai 500 and the 500 GP at Bathurst, beating home Freeth's McIntosh in the long-distance race. He said later that the wind blast down Conrod was causing pain from his old neck injury, and that he might be forced into retirement by his physical problems. "Look at me," he urged a *Revs* reporter. "I've got more wrinkles at 27 than you'll have when you're 40. That's what racing has done to me."

A double win at the Western Underwriters' first visit to Winton must have helped. While Campbell recovered from a crash in the Malaysian GP and Phillis struggled with a bike that wobbled badly after he'd crashed in practice, Johnson won comfortably in both races, and was well placed in the opening race at the Calder third round until he and Phillis both went down on oil. Johnson's new bike, running a warmed VF1000F engine (with 36mm magnesium-body Keihins) in an '83 VF860R chassis, was damaged in the crash, and, for the second race, team boss Wolfenden put Johnson on Campbell's identical mount. Race officials were advised of Johnson's switch and away they went, with Johnson taking the flag comfortably from Phillis's battered Katana and Simon Jones's Kawasaki. However, Johnson was disqualified because, said officials, the team hadn't notified the clerk of the course of his bike switch early enough, so contravening the General Competition Rules. It all seemed painfully familiar, and Team Honda Australia returned to barracks contemplating a withdrawal from the series.

Three rounds down: Phillis 60, Johnson 50, Mark Lithgow (Suzuki) 48. Clyde Wolfenden's new selection of Honda motive power was vindicated. "The 860 was a really good engine," he recalls, "but it wasn't fast enough against 1000s and 1300s. So when we got the VF1000F we put the engine straight in the 750 chassis; it had the same mounting points. So we ended up running pretty much stock 1000 engines for the last couple of seasons before the RC30 arrived."

Campbell would've been in the thick of it at Oran Park had it not been for a crash in practice, when a rider pulled onto the track without looking and straight into the path of Campbell and Johnson. No bones were broken but Campbell was packed off to hospital for observation. Johnson played a

Rob Phillis on Mick Hone's Katana at Bathurst in 1982. He would take five Superbike championships on Hone's Pickering-built Suzukis. (Courtesy Phil Aynsley)

lone hand, sharing the wins with Phillis but suffering with a badly overheated rear wet on a drying track in the first race, finishing fifth and dropping a little further astern of Phillis in the points.

Wet going also had a part to play in the fifth round at Winton, with Campbell and Johnson both sliding off – though not before Johnson had won the first race – and Phillis doing well to keep his head above water with a second and a third, Team Honda newcomer Chris Oldfield likewise. Kiwi Mark Lithgow won the second race and ran third overall with two rounds to go: Phillis 107, Johnson 86, Lithgow 72.

Phillis only needed one. Johnson crashed heavily in practice for the ARRC race on the Saturday of the Adelaide round, writing off his RS500 (valued at AU$26,000) and putting himself in hospital with eight broken ribs. Team-mate Campbell was recuperating from a hand operation in Tasmania, leaving Team Honda Australia represented by Oldfield and Rod Cox. Phillis led the opening race, while Oldfield high-sided in the pursuing melee, breaking an ankle. The race was stopped when Oldfield's bike caught fire, but the restart barely checked Phillis's momentum; he won the race and his fourth straight title, repeating the formula in the second leg with Cox again tailing him home. And so the series came to an end at Winton, where Campbell rode his way back into form and won the last two races, Phillis was second in both, with Lithgow and Honda's new recruit Ben Middlemiss sharing the third places. Johnson was on hand and took the holeshot in the first race, but his gearbox seized within a lap and down he went, this time hurting an ankle. It was all too much, even for AJ. As much as he loved his racing, it was the end of another wearisome season full of crashes, injury and disappointment, and he announced his retirement.

The series kept growing. For 1985 one round of the nine would be staged in Queensland, there would be television coverage and an AU$24,000 prize purse – and that rarest of things, a Superbike based on the Kawasaki GPz900R, prepared by Neville and Peter Doyle, and ridden by Warren Willing's younger brother, Len.

"We had six or seven weeks to build it and there were no bits available, so we had to make everything ourselves," explains Peter Doyle. "We adapted bits from the KRs – wheels, fork internals. But we did the porting, cam profiles, exhaust ourselves. To get the capacity up we had to knock out the liners, put in new ones with a bigger outside diameter and rebore all the liner holes, then redo all the O-ring grooves. We ended up at about 980cc.

"But we did it and went to Calder for testing the day before we had to catch the boat to Tasmania. We got it run in, made sure everything worked, then headed back to the workshop to get organised for the boat. But on the way back a tie-down snapped and the bike came off the trailer …"

After pulling another all-nighter the bike performed well, in spite of limited tyre selection for the 16in front wheel and then an elusive misfire. "Like most others we were running total-loss ignition," recalls Peter Doyle. "We also had surface-discharge sparkplugs that required a pretty high voltage to fire – more than a 12V battery then could handle. So we made 14V batteries, first with an extra cell glued onto a 12V battery. That gave us about 13V all the time, which cured a lot of things."

For the first round of the new Western Underwriters Superbike Series, however, different names took the headlines. Glenn Middlemiss and younger brother Ben finished first and second overall at Symmons Plains, Glenn (VF860R) topping the points with third in the opening race and a win in the second, Ben (VF1000F) running home with two second places. Willing also had cause to smile, taking his Kawasaki to third overall while the favourites fell away: Phillis with a seized engine and Campbell with a broken radiator hose in the second race after winning the first. For Phillis there was glory of a different kind, when he gave Suzuki's new GSX-R750 its first major win in the Western Underwriters Three-Hour at Adelaide.

By the time the Superbikes had visited Adelaide – after Dr Freeth had again put his McIntosh Suzuki on top of the heap at the Bathurst Arai 500 – the established performers, Mick Hone Motorcycles, Team Honda Australia (with a new crew chief in Mick Smith, lately returned from service with Suzuki GB) had stiffening competition: Yamaha Pitmans was back, now with Michael Dowson and a 1000cc bike based on Yamaha's new super-tourer, the FJ1100, and Team Kawasaki Australia's GPz900R. There was also fresh talent for Suzuki, with Robert Holden riding a GSX1000EFE for Action Suzuki – the new GSX-R750 wasn't yet homologated for Superbike use.

In the event, the newcomers were eclipsed by Phillis and the Honda crew, the Middlemiss boys again riding well and pressuring Robbie. Come

WELCOME TO THE JUNGLE

Bathurst 1984: McIntosh Suzuki-mounted Rodger Freeth leads Mal 'Wally' Campbell's VF860R Honda during the Arai 500. (Courtesy Phil Aynsley)

the last lap, though, Robbie swung wide on the exit from the speedbowl and might have pipped Campbell but for rubber on the dragstrip causing a momentary loss of traction. Ben Middlemiss was third from his brother, and clearly impressed by the way Campbell and Phillis went about their business. "I'm not really experienced enough to try passing the way Wally and Robbie do," he explained. In the second race Phillis had a good lead, but the Hondas remorselessly hauled him in. Robbie squeezed home by a length from Campbell, Ben and Glenn, with Willing and Dowson repeating their first leg fifth and sixth.

It was Phillis's turn to suffer at Oran Park. Plagued by a misfire, he finished second in the opener on the newly resurfaced track but crashed in the second race while trying to pass Glenn Middlemiss. Ben likewise fell, putting himself out of the day's action. Meanwhile, Campbell took two wins, the first from Phillis and Glenn Middlemiss, the second from Glenn and Willing. Three rounds done: Campbell 72, G Middlemiss 63, Willing 48.

Glenn Middlemiss parked his VF860R at Winton and jumped onto the more potent VF1000F usually ridden by brother Ben, who'd broken a toe at Oran Park. The field was now strengthened by John Pace on a new FZ750-based Yamaha and Dowson likewise, parking the FJ1000. But after Phillis had stopped with – of all things – sheared drive sprocket bolts, Kevin Magee on Bob Brown's minuscule TT-F2-framed Pantah did the most effective job of harassing Campbell, at least until he took to the grass after trying to nose through on the inside. Campbell got home from Middlemiss, Willing, Dowson, and a fast-recovering Magee. Phillis won the second leg from Campbell after a vintage duel, with Magee this time third.

HEAD TO HEAD

While Willing and the Kawasaki crew struggled to find a race tyre compatible with the 900's front end, Campbell dominated at the fifth stop on the tour at Surfers Paradise, leading the first race home as Phillis fended off Dowson's FZ750 while battling an intermittent misfire that started after he grounded the ignition cover. He held his position but faced the same problem in the second leg, again coming in behind Campbell with Dowson third from Willing.

By the time the circus reconvened at Calder, the Hone team's new firepower, a Yoshimura GSX-R750, was ready to go and Phillis, with Campbell and Magee on Trevor Flood's FZ750, staged one of the best scraps of the series in the opening race. Magee was away first from Phillis, Willing – with new triple clamps on his GPz900R changing offset – and Campbell. After half a dozen laps Campbell caught Magee and Phillis. The three spent the closing laps side by side, but Campbell made a little headway through lapped traffic to win from Phillis, Dowson, and Willing. The second race lacked the sparkle of the first, though a scrap for the lead this time went to Phillis from Campbell and Willing. Six rounds down: Campbell 156, Phillis 105, Glenn Middlemiss 101.

If Campbell couldn't quite claim the trophy after Calder, he certainly could after Oran Park. Another pair of wins in the seventh round put him 65 points clear at the head of the table with just 60 points left to claim. Phillis's GSX-R750 came to Sydney with a new close-ratio gear cluster and a dry clutch and as the bike went well, Robbie blamed himself for a pair of lacklustre fourth places. "I should have ridden better," he said. "Maybe I'm getting too old." He was certainly well adrift of Campbell, who led home Willing and Robert Holden's GSX-R750 in both events. The four-time champion recovered some lost territory at Winton, beating Campbell home to win the first leg. In the second, Wally led well and looked like ending the day on top until coming together with a lapped rider on the last lap. Down he went and through came Willing for his and Kawasaki's first win of the series, the 980's extra puff helping him hold off Phillis in second. Still, Robbie got his first round win in a difficult series, beating Willing overall, while the Middlemiss boys struggled to match their early season results.

It was Willing's turn at the Winton finale, winning the round and completing an impressive run of 18 points finishes in as many starts, taking another win in the first leg after early leader Phillis lost the front end, and Campbell high-sided while challenging for the lead. Home came Willing, followed by Holden and Ben Middlemiss. Phillis made amends in the final race of the season, closing remorselessly on early leader Willing to win going away while Campbell sauntered into fourth behind Holden. Final points: Campbell 198, Phillis 163, Willing 160, Glenn Middlemiss 128.

King Robbie had been deposed, and Australia's unique breed of fire-breathing open-class bikes had gone with him. Phillis battled the last of the old breed in the closing races of the 1000cc championship, beating them in the final race of the year on the first of the newcomers: the 750s had arrived.

8

ALL TOGETHER NOW

Honda's intention to dominate the AMA's new 750cc Superbike class came over loud and clear as early as January 1983. AHM's core team would comprise Mike Baldwin and Steve Wise on VF750R Superbikes (plus an FWS or RS500 for F1), with a five-rider support team that included Dave Aldana, John Bettencourt, Sam McDonald, Fred Merkel and Roberto Pietri, also on VF750Rs.

As the newly formed Honda Racing Corporation delayed delivery of the first RS500 triples while a gearbox fault was fixed, it was full steam ahead on the Superbikes with Mert Lawwill minding Merkel's bikes and tuning house Vance & Hines offering support for Pietri. The AMA's Superbike regs had been revised, but the changes largely applied to chassis: the stock tank, fairing and frame were to be retained; material could be added to frames but not removed, and the steering head could no longer be cut out and replaced.

All of which suited AHM well. The engines of its new bikes were, broadly, similar to those Honda Britain used in its RS850R (see Chapter 5), with gear-driven cams and oversize valves. Rods were titanium and the piston blanks supplied by Honda could be machined for the required compression ratio. While running a 13-plate dry clutch, magnesium-bodied 34mm Mikuni CV carbs and a low-slung oil cooler, the illusion of running close to stock was helped by the stock steel frame and swinging arm, albeit with a trick Showa rear suspension unit – and the Showa forks that cost Australian team boss Clyde Wolfenden much of his little remaining hair. But the bike's 120+bhp was a healthy 50 per cent up on the stocker's, and its weight, at 180kg close to the AMA minimum, was a useful saving on the roadster's claimed 220kg.

It was no surprise then that Spencer led a 1-2-3 for Honda in the Daytona Superbike race, taking the lead when Baldwin slowed with a leaking fuel cap. Aldana was third for Honda from Wayne Rainey's underpowered Kawasaki, while Team Green's new man, Wes Cooley, stopped early when his clutch failed. Round one to Honda.

Cooley was in green leathers as a result of Suzuki's withdrawal from US racing after the 1982 season. Some of the team's hardware went to Team Hammer for endurance racing, while Cooley and team-mate Aldana ended the year looking for rides. Pops Yoshimura was, meanwhile, preparing a Superbike for 1984, leaving Rob Muzzy's Kawasaki outfit, now without GP-bound Eddie Lawson, as the most viable opposition for the AHM team in '83.

On the face of it, Kawasaki's air-cooled two-valve GPz750 seemed unlikely to rival Honda's technology-laden VF for Superbike honours, and looked even a little unfashionable with its 18in front wheel, Uni-Trak rear suspension or no. But Kawasaki again had Rob Muzzy, Steve and Mark Johnson to run the show, and they knew how to win in Superbike, as did Rainey after a season spent running with Lawson.

With the familiar combination of home-brewed cam profiles and valves, twin-plug heads worked by Vance & Hines, and careful preparation of the plain-bearing bottom end (and 66.4mm pistons that bumped capacity up from 738 to, ah, 748cc), the Kawasaki delivered better than 100bhp and so could keep the rampant Hondas in sight. At Talladega, Rainey, playing a lone hand while Cooley recovered from a collarbone broken in the Daytona 200, finished second to Baldwin and in front of Wise's factory Honda. He followed that with second overall at Riverside, and even after crashing at Mid-Ohio (a new track on the AMA circuit) where Wise won from Merkel, the Californian held second in the standings: Baldwin 56, Rainey 43, Merkel 39.

Kawasaki had its problems early in the season, notably breaking valve springs while Honda, led by Baldwin, continued its winning ways. Wise crashed heavily at Elkhart Lake, breaking ribs and puncturing a lung, as Baldwin won again – though from Rainey and Cooley, while Merkel stopped with a broken valve. Baldwin was not likely to be beaten at Loudon, his home track, though Cooley came second and harried him all the way. Rainey, slowed through traffic with gear-selection problems, still beat Merkel for third, so when Baldwin fell in practice at Pocono, breaking a wrist, and Merkel stopped with "undisclosed engine problems" Rainey won and trailed Baldwin by just four points after six of the 14 rounds: Baldwin 96, Rainey 92, McDonald 63.

Rainey won again at Laguna Seca. While scrapping hard with a recuperating Baldwin he spotted that the Honda man couldn't brake hard into turn 6 and made his move there. Merkel ran third and did better still at Portland, winning both races, while Rainey stopped in the opener with his engine making "all kinds of internal noises." Muzzy's crew swapped motors and Rainey followed Merkel home in the second leg while Baldwin, taking second and third for second overall, bumped his points lead: Baldwin 128, Rainey 114, McDonald 86.

Cooley crashed at Laguna Seca, breaking an elbow, but was back at Sears Point to win the F1 race on his old 1025cc Superbike. Baldwin, still in pain from his wrist, got his RS500 into second despite suspension problems and looked like doing the same in the Superbike race, running behind

Honda's RS750R was all but unbeatable in TT-F1 during 1984. Joey Dunlop and Roger Marshall (pictured) proved fierce rivals in the world championship while Gardner cleaned up in the British Shell TT-F1 title. (Courtesy TTracepics.com)

Rainey's revitalised GPz750 until his VF developed a misfire. While Rainey won his fourth round of the series from Merkel and Cooley, Baldwin faded to sixth: Baldwin 137, Rainey 134. At a wet Brainerd, Rainey broke clear of Baldwin to win with Cooley third from Merkel; at Seattle Rainey blew his good engine in practice, but worked deftly through traffic to ease home seconds clear of Baldwin, Cooley, and Bettencourt: Rainey 174 Baldwin 169. Then, at Willow Springs, Baldwin and Cooley both blew engines in practice, and Baldwin, running Merkel's faster motor on race day, led the opener until crashing heavily at turn 7 on just the second lap. While the F1 champion went to hospital with broken ribs and a punctured lung, Rainey collected an untroubled win in the first leg and inherited the second when leader Merkel crashed. Cooley was second overall and the title was Rainey's. The series ended back at Daytona where Merkel got a consolation win for Honda. Rainey tailed him home, his Kawasaki better through the infield while Merkel had the grunt on the banking. Final points: Rainey 210, Baldwin 169, Merkel 135, Honda's support team packing the places.

Kawasaki had taken five of the eight AMA Superbike titles run so far and now took another temporary leave of AMA national road racing. While Rainey would spend the 1984 season in Europe, getting his eye in at 250cc GP level under the watchful eye of KR, Cooley was again looking for a Superbike ride at home. Nor was he alone. Shortly after Kawasaki's withdrawal, Honda shut down its support team, streamlining its effort for the 1984 season to just Baldwin in F1 and Merkel on Superbikes.

Cooley was soon developing and riding Pops' new Suzuki, based on the new, light, compact – and stop-gap – GS750ES (GSX outside North America). Everyone knew Suzuki had a ground-breaker in the wings, a new 750 that would blow away everyone else's rickety offerings; but, for the moment, the air-cooled GS750ESR was all there was. It shared its 747cc, 67 x 53mm engine with its predecessor, but little else – the stock engine was 16kg lighter, for a start. With the usual wiles and stratagems – head work including oversize valves, titanium rods, high-compression (12.3:1) forged pistons, and those all-important smoothbore carbs (33mm, from Mikuni) – Cooley's bike was said to give 118bhp, put to ground via straight-cut primary drive, a wet clutch and close-ratio five-speed 'box. The forks were Kayaba, the rear Full-Floater unit a Fox and wheels were five-spoke magnesium alloy with front brakes from the old GS1000R.

Honda sold its 1983 bikes – Sam McDonald buying one – and Merkel received new hardware, substantially unchanged from the previous season; but 'Flying Fred' had Merlyn Plumlee and Mike Velasco in his corner, who added a range of capabilities to his cause. In any case, the '83 VF's 120+bhp would no doubt have been good enough. In 1984, Honda dominated AMA Superbike the way it never quite managed the season before: of 13 rounds, Honda won 12. Cooley won at Sears Point for Suzuki after Merkel crashed and he took the flag first at Laguna Seca, only to be disqualified for running under the AMA's 390lb (176kg) minimum weight. And that was that: of the other 12 rounds, Merkel won 10; Spencer took his third straight Daytona Superbike race when Merkel's engine blew, and his principal opposition, Cooley and Graeme Crosby, said their Yoshimura Suzukis had "engine problems" and sat out the race; at Loudon, McDonald won from a sore Merkel (the result of a long slide on his backside) after Dale Quarterley's Kawasaki blew, adding a little more lustre to his solid season of second and third places. Baldwin again won the F1 championship, leading home a clutch of RS500s and underlining the point that US national road racing during 1984 was neither the time nor the place to be riding anything but a Honda.

The racing landscape looked only a little more diverse in the UK and the '84 season opened with a barney over whether the new RD500LC (RZ/RZV elsewhere) would be eligible for TT-F1. Honda boss Gerald Davison went to the FIM Spring Congress to push for a ban on "500 replica racers" in a class intended for hardware derived from roadsters. Yamaha, meanwhile, was said to be putting together an F1 kit for the water-cooled 50-degree reed-valve V4 for five grand sterling. Steve Parrish was up for it, having bought an RD he hoped would be ready for Donington at Easter. Alas, the RD didn't make the list of homologated models, with frame-welding troubles slowing production.

Suzuki GB had its F1 engines, which were largely the same spec as Wes Cooley's Superbike lump (later in the season with a dry clutch instead of the American bike's GS750-derived unit), and these went into '83 XR41 aluminium chassis. "Japan sent engine plates that let us bolt the 750 into a 41 chassis without having to work out where the engine was supposed to be," recalls Paul Boulton, mechanic to Mick Grant and Rob McElnea. "The important thing was the position of the sprocket in relation to the swinging arm pivot." Horsepower, or the lack of it, was also important. Of four engines – two from the factory, two kitted – the best figure early in the season was 112bhp.

Honda Britain, too, had a new 750, its powerplant again derived from the long-proven VF750F. Reworked plumbing at both ends resulted in two radiators smaller than the 860's hefty unit, and a rerouted exhaust system. But where the RS850R used a double-cradle steel frame, the RS750R (factory designation ND6A) used square-section aluminium. Rake was 25 degrees compared to the 850's 24.5, the wheelbase millimetres shorter, and dry weight down 11kg to a claimed 162.5kg. The engine was 60mm further back in the frame, allowing for the better-tracking 18in front wheel. If the GSX750ESR was trimmer than its predecessor, the 125bhp RS750R was both trimmer and faster – and took Honda a long stride closer to its own vision of perfection.

Honda Britain's allocation was two bikes (from a total of eight) plus a spare engine. One bike was Gardner's for the British championship and Dunlop's for the world title; the other was for Marshall in both. Gardner would soon rate the bike high on his list of favourites, making good use of it to clean up the first five rounds of the Shell British TT-F1 Championship. He led home Rob McElnea's GSX at Cadwell Park and Thruxton, while Marshall and Joey did their best on race-kitted VF750Fs, won again at Donington where Marshall finally got acquainted with his RS to finish second from McElnea (Joey was sidelined by ignition problems). Then, on the 2.36-mile Island Circuit at Oulton Park, the Hondas again broke away, though Rob Mac ran well until missing a gear and touching valves. This time Joey finished second from Marshall, Grant waving a slightly limp Suzuki flag with fourth. Gardner then made it five from five at Snetterton, where he posted a new lap record and won again from Marshall, Joey, Mac, and Grant. Gardner 75, Marshall 48, Mac 42, Grant 34.

Mac had a good TT week, bringing his RGB500 home triumphant in the Senior after a mighty scrap with Joey that ended when the Ulsterman's RS500 ran dry on the last lap. He had a slightly easier run in the Classic.

Joey, now on a Honda France endurance-spec RS920, struggled to get to grips with the bike, and, after leading early, lost point at the first of his two fuel stops and never got it back. Mac's 998 Suzuki needed just one top-up; he took the lead at Ballacraine on lap three, and posted a new lap record at 117.13mph to beat Joey by 14 seconds. "The bike was too heavy for me," said Joey. "I don't know how anyone rides them for 24 hours."

The Classic was Mac's swansong TT win, and his fastest; and it offered a rare glimpse of a Katana engine in British racing. "It had been used at Daytona and was shipped to us," recalls Boulton. "They said don't open it, don't touch it, just run it at the Isle of Man. So we whacked it into a 69 chassis. I fixed a cambox leak with a gasket cut from a cereal box, and it ran in the race – and that was Rob's Classic win; that was his last TT win."

So the troublesome GSX1000S engine finally passed muster. "I think it lacked midrange, which is strange because it should've breathed better than an eight-valver," says Boulton. "But it was set for Daytona, so would've had huge great camshafts and ports to make fast in a straight line. So that probably explained why it didn't pull out of corners so well; but it was fast enough to win – and reliable."

The same wasn't true of the 750 F1 lump. Joey ran away from the start of the F1 TT to win by 27 seconds from Roger Marshall, after stopping to kick a bent exhaust clear of the back tyre, Suzuki GB was in trouble from the off, Grant retiring on the first lap with gearbox trouble, and Mac stopping to replace a broken steering damper. He got going again and worked up to fourth before his engine seized at Crosby on the last lap.

The team was in the doldrums. McElnea wanted to go GP racing and Grant was musing about retirement. True, Mac had scored three podiums in British F1, but the GSX engine was troublesome. "We always felt it didn't make much horsepower," recalls Boulton. "We did a lot of development work with different oils but that didn't fix it: we seized camshafts, we seized pistons; sometimes the riders didn't even know. They'd say 'I think it's gone off a bit.' So we'd pull the plugs and find flecks of aluminium on them." Experimentation with oil went on, and the team was hoping to receive a new engine later in the season. In the meantime, said Heron Suzuki Sales Director Derek Cooper, "we soldier on."

Meanwhile, the TT-F1 World Championship moved on to Assen where Marshall won from Joey but failed to stop his engine during refuelling, breaking rules and raising hackles. He and Dunlop had scrapped hard early in the race but Marshall got away after the stops and Joey wore his pads down to the carriers trying unsuccessfully to catch him. Grant limped home third after missing a gear and bending valves. After the event, words were spoken but the result stood. Marshall then increased his lead with a win at the third round in 40-degree heat at Vila Real. Joey hung on for second but was then taken to hospital with heat stroke. Grant lost his front wheel trying to catch the leaders, putting Trevor Nation (Ducati) into third. Three rounds done: Marshall 42, Joey 39, Tony Rutter (Ducati) 22.

The RS750R was successful everywhere: Baldwin and Merkel won the Suzuka 8 Hours, leading home Guy Bertin/Dominique Sarron and Gerard Coudray/Patrick Igoa in a 1-2-3 for the RS – and that after Wayne Gardner had reeled in the Americans only for co-rider Raymond Roche to fall while passing a backmarker. The failure scarcely checked Gardner's stride. He returned to the UK and took the Shell British F1 Championship with wins at Silverstone, leading Marshall and Joey home while Grant retired with a seized big-end; at Carnaby, where, after coming together with Marshall he beat Rob Mac; and at Brands, where Marshall came in second from Mac. Suzuki's sole win was at Scarborough where the Honda Britain crew hadn't entered, and Grant showed his team-mate how they dance in the North Riding. Final points: Gardner 120, McElnea 84, Marshall 82, Grant 65.

Gardner also collected the tinware for the British 500cc Championship, winning four out of five in another emphatic performance. But he left them to it in the TT-F1 World Championship, and in the fourth round at the Ulster GP Joey and Marshall again went toe to toe, and came away from the meeting level on points. Dunlop won the 250 and 500 races, but the TT-F1 made the headlines. Joey and Reg stormed away from the start, swapping the lead while Grant, in third, did his best on the "slowly improving" GSX. As the race wore on, the leading Honda pair were nose to tail. Marshall led at the start of the last lap, but Joey whistled through

Joey Dunlop kept a clean slate in the 1985 TT-F1 world title: started six, won six. He's pictured at Whitegates in the F1 TT, leading home Tony Rutter and Sam McClements. (Courtesy TTracepics.com)

on the inside at the ultra-fast Windmills and won. Marshall wasn't happy and told team boss Barry Symmons as much, wanting a protest lodged against Dunlop for dangerous riding. "When Joey went through I lost the front end and got in a lock-to-lock tankslapper," said Marshall. Ray Swann was lapped by the Honda pair near Windmills and saw the incident. "It sure was a hairy moment," he told *Motor Cycle News*. "Roger was in all sorts of trouble. I thought he was down." Joey was unperturbed: "We didn't touch," he said. "I passed Donny Robinson there in the 250 race and he didn't complain."

The man with the plan

Mick Grant started favourite in the fifth and final round at Zolder. He qualified fastest and the GSX, full of fresh oil, seemed to be behaving. By the time he'd recovered from a poor start, though, the Hondas were long gone, Joey leading for five laps and then Marshall taking over. With 11 laps of the 36 done, Reg slowed and dived into the pits. The crew found nothing amiss, topped up the tank and sent him on his way. He got to the end of the pit lane before the head gasket blew, marking the RS750's first mechanical failure. Joey got a 'Marshall out' sign and slowed to take his third TT-F1 title in second place behind Dutchman Mile Pajic, who gave Kawasaki its first TT-F1 win. Grant likewise passed Joey … but then the Suzuki began misfiring. Final points: Dunlop 66, Marshall 54, Rutter 36, Pajic 23.

The wind seemed to be changing. While some in the UK still rankled over the loss of their 1000cc TT-F1 bikes, in the US the growing dominance of Superbike seemed likely to get official endorsement. In May, there was news of a Superbike series being planned to run worldwide with perhaps 15 rounds, starting at Daytona. The group behind the plan would become known as MCC – Steve McLaughlin and two Brits, reporter Chris Carter and Bob Cox, who worked for Champion. It all began, says McLaughlin, while he was working for the France family who ran Daytona, and wanted the 200 to be a Superbike race. "They needed me to take the change to the American public, and, since about 50 per cent of the Daytona entry was from Europe, to find out how that would be affected. In Europe, I found only Germany was running American-style Superbike racing, so we decided the way forward would be to propose a new Superbike world championship to the FIM. We expected opposition, but thought the publicity and the bikes then coming from Japan might help the FIM get behind the idea." That plan did however present the FIM with new and unfamiliar concepts – that the promotion and marketing of the series would be centralised in McLaughlin's enterprising and flexible hands; and that worldwide television coverage would be essential to its wellbeing. The new world had come knocking on a very old door.

In August Daytona announced that the 1985 200-miler would indeed be a Superbike race, with the F1 race run as a national on the Friday of race week. Opinion on the change was predictably divided. Wes Cooley thought "it's probably the best thing that ever happened to the sport," while two-stroke ace Doug Brauneck saw the writing on the wall: "I guess we can make our TZ750s into coffee tables," he told *Cycle News*. Eddie Lawson, too, spoke against the plan, saying: "they've turned the world's biggest motorcycle into the smallest."

The argument was still in the headlines two months later when McLaughlin, together with colleague (and interpreter) Philippe Debarle, went to the FIM's autumn congress to lobby delegates and move the Superbike world title one step closer to reality. They already had draft regulations for the class, like those the AMA already used: 750cc fours, 1000cc twins; major engine castings, numbers of gears and frames as per homologated model. Although receiving expressions of interest from circuits across Europe, and from as far away as Australia and Canada, McLaughlin had objections to overcome and relationships to build. He expected a development period of years – with much of the impetus coming from the AMA – before the championship came under starter's orders.

For one thing, McLaughlin saw that British four-stroke racing, with its evolving tradition of TT-F1, might be an obstacle, but then Britain itself took a step towards Superbike racing with the introduction of *Motor Cycle News'* Superstock series for 1985. The new series would replace the *MCN* Masters, run to ten rounds and be open to street bikes up to 750cc (including the new two-strokes, Yamaha's RD500LC and Suzuki RG500) and while "some chassis modifications" would be allowed, along with racing tyres and exhausts, racing kits and engine tuning would not.

Suzuki's newcomer, the GSX-R750, would slot straight into Superstock, as it would into TT-F1 and AMA Superbike. The thought processes began, like the mills of God, slowly: with equipment common to most major championships outside FIM grand prix, might it not be possible to combine common interests, to develop a strong single championship representing a powerful worldwide bloc of manufacturers, entrants and riders …

If Rome wasn't built in a day, it was certainly founded on one: "Mike Trimby and Paul Butler told me how difficult they found the FIM when they were planning IRTA [International Racing Teams Association]," explains McLaughlin. "But remember Yamaha had stopped making the TZ750 in the '70s and pukka 500cc racers were few and expensive – the world was going to go four-stroke sooner or later, and I have always been a man with a plan." McLaughlin soon gained support: from Luigi Brenni, the head of the FIM's Road Race Commission, from Vernon Cooper and Bill Smith, a key figure at both the ACU and FIM.

Word of the GSX-R750 – R for Race – Suzuki Chief Engineer Etsuo Yokouchi's lightweight, air/oil-cooled masterpiece, appeared in the British press as far back as May '84: of 100bhp power outputs and 180kg dry weights; of bigger valves than the GSX, and a reworked TSCC combustion chamber design. The engine's major advance over its predecessors lay in its oiling system, which used twin pumps to circulate a hefty five litres of lubricant. A high-pressure pump lubricated main bearings, big-ends and gudgeon pins, as well as delivering jets of oil to cool the undersides of the piston crowns. Meanwhile a high-volume pump sent oil to eight galleries feeding the head, cooling the outer surfaces of the combustion chambers, returning to the 5.5-litre sump to pass through a high-volume oil cooler. The system was so efficient in reducing operating temperatures that Suzuki used lighter, smaller components, giving weight savings of around 20 per cent in the crank and rods.

The engine's basic numbers were standard for the time: 70 x 48.7mm for 749cc, dohc with four valves per cylinder. Compression for the street bike stood at 9.8:1 with a claimed output of 100bhp at 10,500rpm aided by its 29mm smoothbore Mikunis, and delivered via a wet clutch and six-speed gearbox. The crank ran in plain bearings and plenty of aluminium (and a bit of magnesium alloy in the head cover) kept engine weight down to 44kg. The square-section aluminium frame, at the very least inspired by the XR41's, mounted a Full-Floater rear end and 41mm forks with 18in wheels. Rake and trail were moderate at 26 degrees and 107mm, and the wheelbase likewise at 1435mm; but a much more interesting number was its claimed dry weight, at 176kg.

Suzuki's new cat was officially released from its bag at the 1984 Paris show, as was Yamaha's – the FZ750. After a succession of slightly offbeat four-strokes with shaft final drive, Yamaha had at last entered the four-stroke sports market. Though markedly less a ready-made racer than the GSX-R – it was significantly heavier at 209kg dry and used a steel tube frame – there was no denying the worth of its engine, which offered more tractable power than the Suzuki and, bottom line, around five per cent more in total. The jury stayed out for a long time on the merits of its five-valve head, though Yamaha claimed higher flow and a lighter valve train; but either way, the bike was a welcome addition to a rapidly developing market sector.

Moods were lifting. Suzuki and Yamaha both reported increased production in 1984 over the previous year. Honda's VF750F had sold well and worldwide sales of Kawasaki's GPz900R had topped 14,000, making it the fastest-selling Kawasaki of all time. AMA Superbike racing, too, was strong, with a dozen rounds scheduled for 1985 while the TT-F1 world championship ran to six rounds. Interest in British TT-F1 seemed a little down with just seven rounds planned, but perhaps the new bikes would reverse the trend. Certainly Yoshimura Suzuki seemed to be setting new standards. Graeme Crosby, putting the TT-F1 GSX-R through its paces in pre-season testing, described it as "already miles better" than the old GSX, with a claimed 137bhp on tap and weight trimmed to 144kg.

Pops' new bike – the XR51 – arrived in Britain with a compact aluminium-zinc alloy frame that shortened the wheelbase by 55mm, steepened the steering head and was fitted with a 16in front wheel to exploit Britain's good range of rubber for the smaller hoop. The Yoshimura engine was surprisingly close to stock, relying largely on revised cam profiles and

34mm Mikuni flat-slides to add horsepower. Other mods included a dry clutch, four-pot Brembo front discs, and a heftier swinging arm.

10 March 1985: the day had to come, and it belonged to Freddie Spencer. After taking the F1 national, Freddie bestrode an HRC-supplied VF750R to win the first Superbike Daytona 200, and lead Wes Cooley, Jeff Haney and Ron Haslam in a 1-2-3-4 for Honda, bringing to an end Yamaha's 13-year winning streak. Spencer came through the field after pitting early to check on a mythical oil leak, while Cooley's bike finished with transmission woes and Haslam's went off-key around half distance. Yamaha did well. FZ750-mounted Canadian Reuben McMurter and Jim Filice staged an absorbing scrap for fifth that went Murter's way, and Sam McDonald looked very fast until his factory Yamaha's clutch let go after seven laps. Meanwhile Wayne Rainey, back from Europe and still with Yamaha, broke a collarbone in practice when his FZ750 broke an oil line.

PRODIGY

Suzuki had a tough time. It would be another year before the GSX-R750 went on sale in the US, and despite finding another mesmerisingly talented youngster in Texan Kevin Schwantz, the team had to wheel out the air-cooled GS again. Incredibly, Schwantz qualified third for the big race and thought he might run second on the day, but was stopped on the line by a broken clutch hub. He'd still impressed everyone. Yoshimura team man Suehiro Watanabe reckoned Schwantz was riding the old bike at 120 per cent of its capabilities.

A month later, at Willow Springs, the old air-cooler held together while "20-year-old prodigy" Schwantz demolished the opposition in both races, each time leading home the Merkel and Cooley Hondas. The pendulum swung against him at Sears Point, however, where he fell from his Ducati during practice for the Battle of the Twins race, breaking a collarbone. In a crash-strewn Superbike race, Cooley was undeniably the big loser, going down in the fast turn 1 with Jimmy Filice's Yamaha, breaking both legs and a hip, and rupturing his spleen. Filice was unhurt. Merkel went on to win from Todd Brubaker's Honda and did it again three weeks later at Elkhart Lake, this time with John Ashmead astern of Brubaker. Four rounds down, Merkel 56, Brubaker 43, Glenn Barry (Honda) 31.

Filice and McDonald brought their Yamahas into fifth and sixth at Elkhart Lake, solid results for Yamaha's fledgling effort, despite a late gear change problem for Filice. Race kits were coming to the UK as well, with roads ace Sam McClements among the first to get one. The kit ramped up power to around 130bhp at 13,000rpm, and included crank, rods, high-comp pistons, overbored carbs, ignition, exhaust, a high-flow fuel pump, and the obligatory oil cooler. This was only the start for Yamaha: something called an FZR750R Genesis was also coming, using an FZ engine in a new 'Deltabox' aluminium frame like that used in Eddie Lawson's world title-winning YZR500. The developmental bike also merited factory suspension, and was likely to be ridden by Kenny Roberts and Tadahiko Taira in the Suzuka 8 Hours.

The trump card for the '85 season again came from Honda. The RVF750 (NW1A) made its debut at the Le Mans 24-hour in April. There, both Rothmans-backed factory bikes led early, but broke engine mounts and were withdrawn while Guy Bertin, Bernard Millet and Philippe Guichon won on their private GSX-R750, giving the new Suzuki its first international victory. But the new Honda – lower, lighter and leaner even than the RS750R – was already winning hearts and minds, revised porting and a new exhaust system contributing to the engine's better torque and stronger, freer-revving top end: power was now estimated at 130bhp at 12,500rpm. The bike dazzled with its design and components, which included Showa factory suspension and hush-hush weight-trimming; but the heart of the matter was a new frame that anchored steering head to swinging arm pivot with twin 90 x 40mm aluminium spars, using the engine as a stressed member.

Back in the US, Schwantz and the sprinkling of Yamahas tried to stem the Honda tide in AMA Superbike, though in Britain four-stroke honours were split more evenly. As the season got under way, it seemed nothing would stop Mick Grant in Superstock. He won the first four rounds of the series for Suzuki, at Brands, Donington (twice) and Mallory, with Marshall striving to keep him in sight on his Honda Britain VF750F. In its third season the Honda V4, now in Rothmans colours, wasn't quite the competitive force it had been, and with Gardner now committed to GPs Marshall had his hands full fending off the developing Yamahas of Keith Huewen and Kenny Irons and Paul Iddon's Suzuki. But Grant's GSX-R was the big problem: "it's too quick for my Honda," said Marshall. Four rounds down: Grant 60, Marshall 44, Huewen 28, Parrish 22.

In TT-F1, roles were dramatically reversed. Marshall, still on his '84 RS750R, won the first three rounds of the series, leading from start to finish at Thruxton while new team-mate Roger Burnett fought through to finish second from Grant. The Honda pair did the same at Donington as Grant and Parrish fell at Park Chicane, letting Tony Rutter's F1 Ducati into an unexpected third, and then Marshall blasted past early leader Grant to win comfortably at Snetterton, Burnett finishing third behind Grant. Three rounds done: Marshall 45, Burnett 34, Grant 22.

As well as proving peaky and being up to 15bhp short of the figures posted in early season tests, the TT-F1 Suzukis had reliability problems, particularly with conrods. "They'd snap," recalls Paul Boulton. "As you shut the throttle at high rpm and took the compression pressure out of the cylinder, bang. It was often number three, and of course the broken rod went round and cut the crankcases like a buzz saw – and, more often than not, damaged the dry clutch. So it trashed your motor, basically."

There were exceptions. As expected, Joey revelled in his first ride on an RVF750 in the F1 TT, laying waste to the opposition to win by more than

Back on a four-stroke at a major race after three years of GP two-strokes, Eddie Lawson steered his factory Yamaha FZ750 Superbike to a comfortable win in the 1986 Daytona 200. Wayne Rainey (6, Honda) struggled with tyre wear. (Courtesy Bauer Media)

five minutes, and post a new lap record at 116.43mph into the bargain. Tony Rutter slotted his GSX-R750 into second place on the final lap to complete a fuss-free run after more fancied bikes had expired, Grant's Heron GSX-R750 and Marshall's '84 RS750R among them (both with gearbox ailments). But the greatest triumph of all went to Sam McClements by putting his kitted FZ750 into third place after being shipwrecked. Sam, Joey and Robert Dunlop, along with eight bikes, had sailed from Northern Ireland to the event in a fishing boat, which ran into trouble and sank. Five bikes were salvaged, including Sam's Yamaha.

Joey also took the Senior TT, this time leading Rothmans Honda team-mate Marshall's RS500 home, and at a wet Assen made it two from two in the TT-F1 world title. Grant looked good too, and while both leaders suffered from hefty slides as the track began to dry towards the end of the race, Grant got through without a fuel stop, and chipped away at Joey's lead, though not quickly enough. Mark Salle was third, his GSX-R750 on intermediates, after Marshall (dropped valve) and Steve Parrish's RD500LC (broken power valve) had looked promising.

After Assen, Marshall was dropped from the world title campaign. "With two mechanical failures in as many races we're running out of parts for his RS750R," said Rothmans Honda team boss Barry Symmons. Marshall would instead concentrate on the British TT-F1 title.

Joey surged on. At Vila Real he caught early leader Graeme McGregor's Heron GSX-R750, getting clean away after the fuel stops with Grant third after Suzuki-mounted Andy McGladdery's gearbox packed up. At Montjuich, Joey won while McGregor and Tony Rutter suffered serious injuries after crashing on oil dropped when McGladdery's Suzuki put a rod through its cases. McGladdery later said he'd seen no oil flags until after the pile up. Rutter was in a coma on the Monday after the event, McGregor diagnosed with broken ribs and internal bleeding. Grant retired with brake problems. With four rounds done, the title was as good as Joey's: Dunlop 60, Grant 22, Rutter 18.

Back in the US, Flying Fred was still on top for Honda, although not quite having things all his own way. At Loudon he ran the race at qualifying speed to get away from John Ashmead and McDonald's Yamaha. John Bettencourt didn't score, crashing in practice, breaking fingers and putting himself out for Pocono, where Merkel won again, getting away to leave Ashmead fending off Filice until the Yamaha man dropped it on the last lap, letting Glenn Barry into third.

Merkel put himself out of Laguna Seca by crashing in practice while sparring with Schwantz. Brubaker also fell, and with McDonald recovering from a fall at Pocono, and Schwantz sidelined by a rod appearing through the GS700's cases, Ashmead took the lead and held it, despite being pressed by Filice and McMurter's scrapping Yamahas. As he was still limping at Mid Ohio, Merkel sat out the race while early leader Filice's Yamaha first vibrated, then blew. Bettencourt led, Randy Renfrow gave chase but missed a gear and then lost his drive chain. Yamaha-mounted McMurter slipped into second with Brubaker completing the podium. Eight rounds done: Merkel 96, Bettencourt 68, Ashmead 65, Brubaker 63.

In British racing too – in Superstock, at least – Mick Grant's dominance seemed to be going the same way as Merkel's. When the circus reconvened at Snetterton, the headlines went to Marshall, who used his RS500 to bag his fifth national championship; but in Superstock the going got no easier for Honda, despite being allowed to use selected hot-up bits in a bid to make the VF more competitive. In the event, Burnett brought the first Honda home in sixth, well behind Huewen and Irons, who took the first two spots for Yamaha, and Suzuki-mounted Salle, who won an 11-bike battle for third. At Cadwell Park a privateer won again. Trevor Nation put his Suzuki in front at the Hairpin on the first lap and stayed there. Marshall gave chase, passing Salle's ill-handling Suzuki and then Burnett, but at the flag he was seven seconds adrift of Nation. Grant trailed into fifth behind a rehabilitated McGregor, but there was no such consolation for Huewen, who lacked the intermediates the going required.

Grant got back onto the podium with an unhurried win at Oulton Park after passing early leader Marshall. Parrish tried a late charge, putting his FZ past Marshall, but ran out of time and finished second. Seven rounds done: Grant 99, Marshall 78, Parrish 54, Huewen 50.

Honda enters …

Now on full-time GP duty, Wayne Gardner's appearances elsewhere were few and far between, but in July he did his bit to cement the RVF750's growing reputation with one of the rides of his career at the Suzuka 8 Hours. Regarded by Honda as one of the four most prestigious events on the calendar – along with Daytona, the TT and the Bol d'Or, the 8 Hours had become the event where the four major Japanese factories revealed some of their latest technology, and hired the world's best to put it to the test in what was effectively an eight-hour sprint race. And in 1985, Gardner and co-rider Masaki Tokuno went head-to-head with KR and Taira on Yamaha's new FZR750R.

Roberts qualified fastest but Gardner led early, while KR, needing a pusher to start the FZR, fought up to sixth in the first hour. Tokuno lost the lead to Roberts during his first stint but Gardner got it back. Roberts again passed Tokuno, but Gardner saved the day by riding the last two hours himself, and though the Yamaha was slightly faster, Taira rode the last session and lost ground under pressure – and then the Yamaha dropped a valve with half an hour to go. Gardner won from Baldwin and Dominique Sarron's RVF (equipped with a single-sided swinging arm deigned by Guy Coulon), and was mobbed by a good proportion of the estimated 250,000 crowd. He collapsed with heat exhaustion and had to be given oxygen. No such problems befell Crosby and Schwantz, who at least had a trouble-free run into third on their underpowered GSX-R750.

His first major ride on a four-stroke left King Kenny a touch underwhelmed. "It makes a lot of noise but it won't light up the tyre," he told Mat Oxley in *MCN*. "I can get the FZR into a turn okay, but I don't know where I'm coming out. It's competitive but it's got to be lighter and more powerful."

A week later, Joey gave the RVF its first appearance in mainland Britain at a sodden Silverstone TT-F1 race. He led from the start but retired a lap later with a cracked exhaust leading to a worsening misfire. "I'm glad of it," said Joey. "There's no way we should be riding in these conditions." Criticism indeed. Marshall collected the 15 points and Parrish led Grant and McGregor home after a mighty scrap for second. The Heron Suzuki team did better still at Scarborough. While Rothmans Honda took the weekend off, McGregor led from flag to flag and Grant ran third behind Trevor Nation's Suzuki despite losing second gear. Five rounds done: Marshall 60, Grant 42, Burnett 34.

Joey duly took his fourth TT-F1 world title on home ground at Dundrod, bagging the 250 and 500 races as well. He hardly broke sweat, refuelling without losing the lead. Grant and McGregor finished second and third, offering more evidence that Suzuki was overcoming its reliability problems, aided by experimentation with oil; though not its lack of power – to which, team boss Rex White told Gary Pinchin for his excellent book, *Suzuki GSX-R750*, the "biggest contributing factor" was a shortage of top-line Mikuni carbs from Yoshimura. Joey wrapped up his season at Hockenheim, making it six from six and losing the lead to Ernst Gschwender's Suzuki only at his fuel stop. Who would stop him? Final points: Dunlop 90, Grant 40, McGregor 32.

Yoshimura hadn't contracted to do the full AMA series but might have wished otherwise after Schwantz took back-to-back rounds at Seattle and Sears Point. Merkel, still in pain from his Laguna Seca crash, didn't start at Seattle, leaving Bettencourt and Brubaker to stack the podium for Honda. Fred was back at Sears Point and though still uncomfortable, finished second from Brubaker and then took the title with wins at Brainerd and Daytona. The fans went home to muse on the prospect of Schwantz and Rainey joining the action full-time in 1986. Final points: Merkel 125, Bettencourt/ Brubaker 105, Barry 99.

In September, Andy McGladdery was out of action with a broken wrist from a fall at the Ulster. While cooling his heels he visited Tony Rutter, convalescing after his Montjuich fall, and found him in a neck brace, recovering from a double fracture to the spine and damage to one eye. "It's a miracle he survived," said McGladdery. Rutter hadn't ruled out making a comeback.

Superstock resumed at Scarborough with Nation taking the eighth

Down payment: in 1986 Marco Lucchinelli won the Misano round of the TT-F1 world title, and the Daytona Battle of the Twins race on Ducati's 851cc TT-F1 Pantah. (Courtesy Ian Falloon)

round – and his second win – by fending off champion-elect Mick Grant and McGregor. Grant's only real challenger for the title was back in action at Thruxton the following weekend, and while Mark Salle cut through the field to get his Suzuki home first from Parrish, Marshall managed third – with Grant in his shadow.

Marshall consoled himself by taking the King of Thruxton title (on Gardner's NS-engined triple) and then went to Cadwell and won the British TT-F1 title with a round to spare. On his home turf, Marshall was, according to team-mate Burnett, "better than ever" and made it five wins from as many starts to lead a Honda 1-2 with Grant third; but then it all went sour. While practising at Brands for the Powerbike International, Salle dropped his RGB and was struck by several of the riders following. He died, just 28, from "massive head injuries" and left a widow, Sharon.

Marshall finished as he had started in TT-F1 and led the Brands final round from start to finish while Burnett muscled through to follow him home from Grant, McGregor and Nation. Final points: Marshall 90, Grant 62, Burnett 58, McGregor 45, Parrish 44.

Needless to say, the Honda crew didn't have such an easy time in the *MCN* Superstock finale, and while Nation broke free of a mighty scrap for his third win of the year, scraping home from Rob Mac and Burnett, Marshall was sixth and just in front of Grant, who took the final chequered flag of his career and with it the inaugural *MCN* Superstock title. Final points: Grant 119, Marshall 90, Parrish 78, Nation 66, Huewen 65.

Grant hadn't wanted to do Superstock initially. "But I won the first four rounds, so it suddenly became a nice idea; and we won those because we got the first GSX-R into Europe, I think. They'd put 16in wheels in it and a few bits off the RGs. It was a cracking motorbike. It had no vices, it was just a nice floppy old thing that went well."

Help in Superstock was coming for Honda. At the Bol d'Or, where the threat of the Yamaha FZR collapsed with a broken primary drive and Gerard Coudray, Patrick Igoa, and Alex Vieira took their RVF to Honda's tenth Bol win, the VFR750F, the latest and sweetest of Honda's V4 dynasty, was launched. According to some, the newcomer owed more to the RVF than the old sports-tourer VF750F, and certainly the gear-driven cams and valve train were new, along with the 1.2kg lighter piston/rod assembly and the new 180-degree crank, all housed in narrower cases, even if it was the same 70 x 48.6mm 90-degree dohc V4. Most welcome of all, perhaps, was the twin-spar alloy frame that looked much akin to the RVF's, albeit with smaller, 60 x 28mm main spars. The other major figure was 105bhp.

Honda's twin-spar alloy frame was no longer the only game in town: the Harris bothers offered one for the FZ Yamaha engine, with suspension units supplied by Dutch outfit White Power, a steering head adjustable on eccentrics, a 17in front wheel, and overall geometry akin to a 500 GP bike. Best of all, a complete bike could weigh as little as 150kg.

Close season team movements included a complete rider change at

Heron Suzuki: Grant had retired, McGregor returned to George Beale and McElnea went GP racing with Yamaha. The team signed Paul Iddon, and it looked for a time as though Marshall might join him. Though still disappointed with Honda's handling of his 1984 TT-F1 world title bid, he re-signed for the Rothmans outfit, again with wing man Burnett. Elsewhere in Honda world, Wayne Gardner, seeing off Rob Mac and Mal Campbell as 1985 ended to claim his third Swann Series, was committed to GPs in 1986, and Ron Haslam had signed with Elf for the same purpose.

Although the British Championship ran to a dozen rounds in 1986, *MCN* Superstock was just as lucrative, paying £2300 per round compared with the national title's £2000 even. And the series was changing: two-strokes were now out, minimum weight was up from 159kg to 170 and engine kit bits were now banned: Honda would "have to rely on the power on its new 750," *MCN* briskly pointed out – though modification of stock parts would be allowed, and suspension and exhausts could be changed.

Meanwhile, as British TT-F1 dwindled to a five-race championship for 1986, the world championship approached its zenith with eight rounds, with new races at Mugello and Imatra. But change was coming: Steve McLaughlin's Superbike plan came one step closer to reality at Heathrow Airport where reps from the ACU, the AMA, the Motorcycle Federation of Japan, and the Japanese factories met to discuss just one point – that 500cc GP racing was pricing itself out of existence, and that a new world championship was needed.

The meeting developed in outline a hybrid championship to replace

After Wayne Gardner beat a quality TT-F1 field at the 1986 Suzuka 200 on Honda's trick VFR750F-based NW6X, Geoff Johnson rode to second places in the F1 and Senior TTs. (Courtesy TTracepics.com)

TT-F1 but using TT-F1 engines and AMA Superbike frame regulations, to be run on a combination of short tracks and road circuits, with riders permitted to drop a round if the TT wasn't to their liking. The idea would be presented at the FIM spring congress. "It's the end of F1 but a new development class for the world," said ACU director Bill Smith after the meeting. The class would be known as TT-Superbike, and, miraculously, by March there was an official calendar of nine rounds for 1987, with more to come; at one point, McLaughlin was talking to 19 countries, all of them wanting a round.

Factory style

In the US, Rainey signed a two-year contract with Honda for Superbike and F1 as Baldwin joined KR's Lucky Strike Yamaha GP team. Rob Muzzy was recruited to look after Rainey's bikes as AMA Superbike Production celebrated its 10th anniversary. As Daytona drew closer, however, it seemed unlikely Freddie Spencer would lead AHM's effort. In February he was in hospital with a mystery virus believed to be related to the sinus trouble that had laid him low and cost him 6kg in bodyweight. Eddie Lawson, on the other hand, was fighting fit, and took to his FZ750 with enthusiasm and purpose.

Rainey and Merkel now had Honda's latest contender for Superbike, the VFR750F-based NW6X. Said to give 135bhp, the newcomer looked more like a stocker than ever, but ran magnesium-body 32mm flat-slide Keihin carbs and factory Showa 43mm forks as well as HRC magnesium wheels and a GP-spec swinging arm. The engine included the usual performance-boosting features: oversize titanium valves, pistons raising compression from 10.5 to 11.5:1, a ported head, cams giving more lift and duration, and a 1mm overbore, taking capacity to 770cc. There was also a 360-degree crankshaft rather than the stocker's 180, giving better torque out of corners at the expense of smooth running.

America got its first look at a competition GSX-R750 via the Yoshimura Daytona effort, with bikes for Schwantz, Japanese Satoshi Tsujimoto and Kork Ballington (running the British team's new Skoal Bandit sponsorship). Unlike the Hondas, the GSX-Rs needed ballast to reach the AMA's minimum weight, but the numbers seemed similar. The 771cc engine was said to deliver 131bhp at 12,000rpm with 12.5:1 compression, and breathing through 36mm flat-slide Mikunis. Forks were 43mm factory Kayabas, a Fox rear unit and three-spoke mag wheels (18in front for Schwantz and Tsujimoto, 16in for Ballington). Schwantz's bike also had a new titanium exhaust system with 'power' chambers linking pairs of its short headers, which he said helped him get off corners better.

It was Yamaha's 130bhp, 17in front wheel FZ (factory designation 0U45) supplied for Lawson (and Baldwin) that made the running, however. Getting some early practice for his tilt at the '86 500cc world championship, Lawson led from the flag, keeping his nose in front while Rainey fought wheelspin, diving into the pits for an unscheduled tyre change as early as lap 11.

Schwantz, promoted to second after Rainey's stop, had problems with the GSX-R's chain jumping its sprocket so nursed it home. Reigning AMA Superbike champion Merkel got third after Baldwin (dropped valve) and Tsujimoto (blown motor) stopped, and Rainey recovered to finish fourth.

Britain got its first glimpse of America's new breed three weeks later at the Transatlantic Trophy. After a talent-laden US team led by Roberts and Spencer gave the UK a hiding in 1984, the home side got back on top a year later, RS500-mounted Gardner winning three races of six. So the score stood at 10-5 to the UK as Merkel's talented newcomers arrived, most of them to ride British-supplied bikes. The Transatlantic Trophy was now Britain's first toehold for Superbike: following a chat between Steve McLaughlin and Donington MD Robert Fearnall at the French GP, the Easter series would run technical regulations similar to those outlined for the proposed TT-Superbike World Championship.

The three-day Donington party was won by the Brits 314-214, though

Elbows out Superstock action at Mallory in 1986: Trevor Nation (Suzuki GSX-R750) leads Neil Robinson, Kenny Irons and Keith Huewen. Nation won the race, Irons the title. (Courtesy Bauer Media)

Schwantz took four of the eight races, and Merkel two, while Britain packed the places. Had Ron Haslam been given a more competitive ride for the weekend the balance might have been different, but on Friday he was out on a street VFR750F and pulled out of race two suffering an embarrassing lack of power and cornering clearance. He tried Marshall's VF750F Superbike on Monday after Reg had crashed in a supporting race, dislocating a hip, but went back to his stocker for the last race of the eight and finished a staggering third. The Americans, meanwhile, had the miserable weather to master. Schwantz had never before ridden in the wet, but adapted quickly to give what *MCN* described as "an acrobatic performance" – and on an ex-Tony Rutter GSX-R he hadn't seen before. His factory GSX-R was missing, said Kevin, because "I broke too much stuff at Daytona." Schwantz, never short of friends in the UK, gained one in particular who watched, captivated, as he and Merkel slipped and slithered their way into the records books that miserable Easter – Barry Sheene. Impressed by what he'd seen, Sheene arranged a trial for Schwantz on the Castiglioni brothers' Cagiva GP bike.

For a time, that was as good as it got for Schwantz. Back in the heat of the Camel Pro Road Race Championship (for 1986 combining points from F1 and Superbike), he scrapped with Rainey at Sears Point but both were penalised a lap for passing under a yellow flag, the win going to Merkel from Shobert. At Brainerd Schwantz went over the high side while scrubbing in tyres, breaking a collarbone. Rainey led from start to finish with Merkel coming through the field for second. Canada-based Kiwi Gary Goodfellow was third on a largely stock GSX-R. Yamaha's contracted riders, Filice and John Kocinski, stayed at home, making sure they weren't running the suspect kit rods recently discovered. Schwantz wasn't fully fit for Elkhart Lake, so watched Rainey win again from Merkel and, this time, Dan Chivington's Yamaha. Superbike points after four rounds: Merkel 65, Rainey 51, Goodfellow 31, Shobert 27 … Schwantz 16.

Joey Dunlop began his TT-F1 world title defence at Misano for the new Italian round. His new RVF, though still using VF cases, adopted the Coulon single-sided swinging arm and a new, better-breathing exhaust. In his book, *Honda's V-Force*, Julian Ryder says power was ramped up to 137bhp, and dry weight trimmed to 152kg, but Joey still got a shock at Misano from Marco Lucchinelli's F1 Ducati, which ran an experimental 851cc 97bhp Pantah engine and a rising-rate rear end. It was good enough to put Lucky into a commanding lead before a broken pipe and a badly worn rear cover slowed him. Joey came back, closing to within striking distance as they began the last lap. But then the Honda ran dry and Lucchinelli was gone, winning from the Suzukis of Anders Andersson and Robbie Phillis, while the British Skoal Bandit Suzuki pair, Paul Iddon and Chris Martin, both went out with crank failure.

Joey and Iddon had a better weekend at Hockenheim, the Honda man coming away with a win after twice coming from behind, while Iddon did the 97-mile race on one tank of fuel to bag second. Andersson and Peter

Rubatto made it a good day for Suzuki with third and fourth, while Kenny Irons, now alongside Parrish in the Loctite Yamaha outfit, was fifth despite clutch trouble.

Joey was on top again at the F1 TT, winning with almost a minute's clean air behind him. An intriguing duel developed for second place between Andy McGladdery's Suzuki and Geoff Johnson, riding an HRC NW6X that came his way after Gardner had used it to thump a TT-F1 field at his second home, Suzuka. To their rear, Roger Marshall, riding Joey's '85 race-winning RVF, gave chase, but by lap four was stopped with an ailment initially diagnosed as bent valves. As Johnson pulled clear of McGladdery's Suzuki – which began cutting out as early as the second lap – John Weedon got his kitted RG500 Suzuki roadster into fourth. Johnson did it again in the Senior, running his NW6X into second (now with suspension tweaked by Ron Williams to help keep the front end down) behind Roger Burnett's RS500, while RVF-mounted Joey, beset with handling problems, was fourth astern of Barry Woodland's RG. Still, he was on top in the world title chase, and took his third win at Assen after early leader Neil Robinson's Suzuki lost its chain. Schwantz, taking a look at continental Europe, was second on a kitted RG500 with Iddon third from Irons – but there was no denying who was in charge after four rounds: Joey 45, Andersson 28, Iddon 22.

The abbreviated British Shell/ACU TT-F1 title got going at Thruxton, where the uncertain weather made tyre choice a lottery. Ray Swann got it right and splashed home first on his Kawasaki from Nation's Suzuki. A week later at Mallory Park, newcomer Mark Phillips got Suzuki's first win on his Padgetts' RG500 from Iddon and Irons. At Donington, Irons was in charge, leading home Parrish for a Loctite 1-2, with Nation and Robinson third and fourth for Suzuki. Kiwi Richard Scott, now riding the fabled NW6X thanks to Rothmans Honda team boss Barry Symmons, was fifth – and won the opening leg of the British 1300cc Championship on the bike. Three rounds done: Nation 30, Irons 25, Phillips 21.

SUPERSLICK

Superstock, now co-backed by braking specialists EBC, opened in coin-toss conditions at Brands, with Roger Burnett putting his VFR in front, then decking it while GSX-R jockeys Nation (with a Metzeler road tyre on the back) and Mellor led as Marshall (slicks) and Huewen (intermediates) struggled over third. Come the last lap, Nation got through Clearways better, with Marshall securing third at the same spot.

Previewing the series, *Motor Cycle News* said Superstock preparation was largely about uprated suspension – White Power rear units were popular – wider rims and brakes. Kenny Irons said his FZ didn't like "really tight circuits" though it was more stable than most GSX-Rs. His cylinder head had been skimmed, he said, to compensate for the Yamaha's extra weight. Honda Britain, too, boosted its effort for '86, with Barry Symmons offering workshop space and parts to Ron Grant and his runner, Richard

Scott. Their effort would run in parallel with Honda Britain's official effort, and their VFR now had "permitted bits from the VFR race kit bolted on," including carburettors, a larger radiator and a 4-2-1 exhaust.

Nation did it again at Mallory Park after a classic scrap with Irons, Robinson, and Huewen. While the Hondas overheated during the delayed start, Nation got in front at the hairpin to win, as Irons passed Robinson for second. Irons pulled one back at Snetterton, beating Huewen by a wheel, while Nation crashed out of third on the last lap, letting Scott in on the best of the Hondas. Of the Rothmans bikes, Burnett pulled out in pain from a fall, and Marshall was eighth. "Development is slow," said Burnett, though the lighter, trimmer Honda Britain VFRs now followed the example set by Ron Grant, running oversize pistons and re-profiled cams. Three rounds down: Irons and Nation 32, Huewen 28, Mellor and Scott 21.

In the US, Honda was still dominant. Through the middle of the season Rainey took three straight Superbike wins: at Loudon he was "long gone" by the end of the opening lap, with Merkel getting the best of a five-way scrap for second, and VF-mounted Shobert third. Rainey and Merkel ran 1-2 again at Pocono with Schwantz third, and at Laguna Seca Rainey again ran away with Shobert this time second, while Merkel, starting from the back of the grid after a practice fall, worked up to third. Schwantz had run as high as third before his third engine of the weekend blew, on the start-finish straight. Seven rounds down: Rainey 111, Merkel 110, Shobert 56, Goodfellow 50.

Joey was also doing the job for Honda. Although in pain from ribs broken in a car crash, Dunlop finished fifth in the Jerez round of the TT-F1 world title, keeping the title lead while Paul Iddon scored Suzuki's first TT-F1 win of the 750 era from Graeme McGregor's Ducati. A week later at Vila Real, Joey was at his unstoppable best, taking 1.5 seconds off the lap record while pulling clear of Iddon, who, like third place man Anders Andersson, was making his Vila Real debut. Six rounds done: Joey 66, Iddon 49, Andersson 46.

Next it was Gardner's turn for Honda. Taking a break from his GP campaign, he claimed his second successive win in the Suzuka 8 Hours, this year paired with Dominique Sarron on a new, VFR-based RVF with the new sportster's six-speed 'box. The more compact lump was further forward in the frame to give better weight distribution, had a longer swinging arm and an engine, rated at 135bhp, said to offer better mid-range. It certainly was good enough to keep the KR/Mike Baldwin FZR at bay until Baldwin crashed with two hours to go. Second at the flag were Aussies Kevin Magee and Michael Dowson on an FZ750, ahead of the Yoshi Suzuki shared by Schwantz and Tsujimoto.

The AMA Camel Pro Road Race title wound down at Mid-Ohio – where Merkel won from Schwantz and Dan Chivington's FZ750 after Rainey high-sided on a cooked rear tyre – and concluded at Road Atlanta. There Rainey and Schwantz entertained a sparse crowd until, said Schwantz, "it jumped

Lucchinelli went to Daytona in 1987 and won the Battle of the Twins race again, this time with the first of Ducati's water-cooled, eight-valve dohc 851s. (Courtesy Ian Falloon)

out of gear going into turn 6. I ran 'er in there but there was no motor to slow 'er down." Down he went, giving Rainey a comfortable win – and Merkel, in second, his third Superbike title and first Camel Pro Road Race Championship. Final Superbike points: Merkel 148, Rainey 131, Ashmead 57, Shobert 56.

At the same meeting, Kork Ballington won the AMA's last-ever F1 race, getting his Bob McLean RS500 home from title-winner Randy Renfrow's RS. From now on, it was Superbikes all the way.

Joey, meanwhile, had landed his fifth TT-F1 world title. In Finland he won comfortably from Iddon despite blowing two engines in practice. He used an '85-spec five-speeder for the race, passing leader Neil Robinson's Suzuki, who slipped to third after being caught on a badly worn rear cover. Robinson got it right at the Ulster, however, and led from start to finish while Iddon crashed at the hairpin, and Joey, caught up in the ensuing traffic jam, worked his to second from McGladdery's 'Growler' Suzuki. Final points: Joey 93, Iddon 58, Andersson 58, Robinson 41.

The racing done, speculation mounted over the future of Rothmans Honda. Team boss Barry Symmons said the Ulster might have been Joey's last as a factory man, as Rothmans might withdraw from TT-F1 over a lack of media interest. Honda too, was changing course: a sharp rise in the value of the Yen – 43 per cent in 1985 – was making GP bikes and street V4s prohibitively costly to produce, and steel-framed CBRs were just around the corner.

Back in the turbulent waters of Superstock, Irons looked like a winner in the Cadwell Park fourth round until getting it wrong at the hairpin in wet going, letting Huewen and Richard Scott's quickening VFR through to take first and second. But Irons made up for it with successive wins at Oulton Park, Thruxton, Scarborough and Donington. After finishing second at Oulton, Scott ran Irons close over the bumps at Thruxton, while at Scarborough Irons ran away when Nation and Huewen crashed, and Phil Mellor got second. At Donington, Irons fell in practice but got home clear of Huewen for number four. He looked like making it five at the series Brands Hatch finale and chased Huewen's Suzuki until a couple of major slides made him roll it off and settle for fifth – and the title – while Scott, Iddon and John Lofthouse chased Huewen home. Final points: Irons 118, Scott 105, Huewen 91, Nation 76.

McGladdery joined the walking wounded when he broke two ribs in an Oulton Park Superstock melee, but was there when it mattered in the Scarborough round of the Shell British TT-F1 title. He took the lead when Irons' motor blew at Memorial Corner, and won comfortably from Huewen, Mellor and Phillips. But the racing faltered at Scarborough as

Kevin Schwantz and Wayne Rainey (pictured at Brands) were still developing their rivalry at the 1987 Transatlantic Trophy. Between them they won all nine races. (Courtesy Mortons Media Archive)

word filtered down of Neil Robinson's death, the ugly result of a Quarry Hill practice crash. He was 24.

At the Silverstone national, Iddon took up the running, putting his Skoal Bandit Suzuki into first from Scott's Honda, Parrish, and Irons, with Phillips sixth and looking strong for the title after Nation fell heavily at Scarborough. Sure enough, at Cadwell Park Phillips took his second win of the series. Irons led early while Phillips outbraked Nation for second and then passed the Loctite Yamaha at Park Corner. Game over: Phillips 49, Irons 45, Nation 41, Parrish 38.

The future of TT-F1 remained a source of confusion. In Britain it seemed to have no future at all: the domestic title was dropped for 1987, the ACU reporting that "circuit owners just aren't interested in running F1" and encouraging would-be TT-F1 runners to join the new, effectively formula libre Shell Super One class for 1300cc four-strokes and 500cc two-strokes. Yet as far back as May, and in spite of its backing for TT-Superbike, the FIM granted a reprieve for the class at world championship level beyond the end of the 1987 season, after the Japanese factories suggested they wanted it to continue. At a meeting in the Isle of Man, riders and entrants too, made clear their support for TT-F1. "It's about time sponsors and riders were consulted on major issues," Bill Smith told *MCN*. "The competitors who supported F1 and F2 when they were introduced have been kicked in the teeth."

Another meeting of competitors at the Dutch TT (with the vice-president of the FIM's Road Race Commission, Adrien Veys) added fresh impetus to the argument, and whispers from Geneva now had it that TT-Superbike would begin in 1988, giving another year for competitors to prepare and for TT-F1 to wind down. Then, after meeting riders again at Imatra, Dutch FIM delegate Jo Zegwaard went to the FIM Autumn Congress in Sicily and suggested not only that TT-F1 continue, but that it should include 1000cc twins and exclude two-strokes. The class was growing in popularity in Europe, he said, and provided work for small businesses such as frame makers. TT-Superbike could, he added, be more costly than the "hyper-expensive 500 GP class." The ACU even came up with a plan to replace the existing and only moderately successful European championships with TT-F1 classes.

In October, MCC (McLaughlin, Carter, Cox) ran its first meeting, the International Superbike Masters at Calder Park in Melbourne. Mal Campbell won overall after Merkel won the first race and fell in the second. Meanwhile, the FIM congress ruled that TT-Superbike would begin in 1988, and TT-F1 would stay indefinitely, with Superbike to be run on short circuits and F1 keeping the road venues.

The Superbike tech regs were finalised at the same meeting. These were much as before, though permitting changes of forks and swinging arm – so long as they were of the same type – and requiring stock carburettors. Homologation was on a sliding scale: 1000 units for manufacturers turning out more than 100,000 bikes per annum; 500 for factories making 50-100,000 and 200 for smaller marques.

ONLINE

Steve McLaughlin had hoped to have at least his end of TT-Superbike wrapped up by now. In the autumn of '86 he convened a meeting at a London hotel that was hosted by the ACU. He'd invited Michihiko Aika from HRC, Mitsuo Itoh from Suzuki, Neville Goss and Bill Smith from the ACU, Bill Boyce of the AMA and people from the TT committee and more federations, including Japan's.

"They were there to sign an agreement," explains McLaughlin. Unexpectedly though, Goss had criticisms of the TT-Superbike plan, and while there were no witnesses to the heated exchange that later took place between he and McLaughlin, TT-Superbike died as a result. There was, however, still a series sanctioned by the FIM, a calendar that promised meetings at circuits around the world, and a contract that, along with much else, required MCC to provide the FIM with a $100,000 guarantee. At the turn of the year, Daytona pulled out of the series. "So now I have no money," says McLaughlin. "I'm up shit creek, but I get a call from a New Zealand outfit called Global Sports & Promotions, and after a meeting in Los Angeles I'm on a plane to Auckland." The flight was the first of a dozen or more, but

Bimota added its twin-spar alloy frame to Yamaha's FZ750 engine and called it the YB4. Virginio Ferrari (pictured) rode it to win the 1987 TT-F1 World Championship, ending Joey's five-year reign. (Courtesy Elwyn Roberts)

amid them Sports Marketing Company (SMC) was born. McLaughlin had a backer and the championship was under way again – but now it was just Superbike. An 8-5 FIM vote endorsed the future of the World Superbike Championship (WSB) on short circuits. Luigi Brenni told TT Chairman Peter Hillaby he hoped TT-F1 would retain world championship status; at any rate, an eight-round title was scheduled for 1988.

The finances and format of WSB were taking shape. "There would be two 100km races per round, and SMC would put up $100,000," McLaughlin recalls. "Prize money of $25,000 would be divided among the first three riders and $7500 for the next 10, with a fixed travel fund to cover costs: a two-bike team finishing in the top 13 was guaranteed $15,000 for a weekend – and there was an additional travel fund for races outside Europe."

1986 ended with plenty of comings and goings in British racing, among them the disbanding of the Honda Britain team. Burnett would join Honda's GP effort and Joey would again be contesting the TT-F1 world title, backed directly from Japan – though there would be no RVF for 1987, but instead a new, VFR-based NW6B. "Joey's bike will be the most potent F1 bike ever," said Symmons. Steve Parrish, meanwhile, announced his retirement and recruited Keith Huewen and Trevor Nation to fly his Loctite Yamaha colours in Superstock and TT-F1. Skoal Bandit Suzuki first dropped Paul Iddon, persuading Marshall and Irons to ride its new XR55 TT-F1 bike and Superstockers, but then reinstated him when Irons moved to the Suzuki GP team.

In the US, Honda released Fred Merkel and concentrated its road race effort on Wayne Rainey, with Rob Muzzy and Sparky Edmonston again behind him (Merlyn Plumlee had a job in Colorado). Schwantz re-signed for Suzuki with AMA Superbike as his priority, but squeezing in as many GPs as he could on the new XR72 V4. Tsujimoto would join him for Daytona and then stay on for the Camel Pro Series.

Also in the US, KMC was offering race kits for the new GPX750R – or 'Ninja' in US parlance – comprising cams, pistons, rods, carburettors, valve springs, a beefier clutch and close-ratio gears. Altogether, 50 kits were available at $2999 or, when they came to the UK, £2127.50. In the Yamaha camp, Filice would be campaigning one of Yamaha's US-only aluminium-framed FZR750Rs – if they were homologated in time. Mitsui, Britain's Yamaha distributor, considered the 107bhp 750 altogether too salty at £6000, and thought it would be competing for sales with the newly launched FZR1000. Still, a tweaked FZ750 for the UK market would be 20kg lighter than the '86 model with a lighter piston/rod assembly, an exhaust cam re-profiled to bump mid-range, a new 4-1 exhaust, and fuel-injection.

Meanwhile, Ron Grant did his bit for Honda by building three VFR-based bikes inspired by the NW6X for the UK's Transatlantic Trophy entrants, Haslam, Richard Scott, and Simon Buckmaster. As well as trick American cams and close-ratio 'boxes they would have the all-important 360-degree crank. Scott rode the Honda Britain NW6X after Geoff Johnson did good things on it at the TT, and, as the season wore on, Symmons and Grant had a peek inside and found the non-stock crank. "It certainly worked," recalls Scotty. "The bike jumped off corners much better than a stocker." The change got Grant thinking, and he spoke of racing Triumph twins in the US during the '60s, when they'd swap between 180- and 360-degree cranks to suit the torque requirements of particular tracks. So Symmons had three stock cranks converted, one of which was fitted to Scott's Superstock bike for the final round of the '86 series at Brands – and now Grant began offering £1000 cut-rotate-pin-weld crank conversions for private runners in TT-F1 or Superstock. "The rules say you can lighten, polish and modify any standard part," Grant explained to Road Racing Monthly. "We allowed the modified cranks because it will put the Honda with the Suzuki and Yamaha in the title fight," said Superstock's chief scrutineer Rod Scivyer.

Suzuki was less than pleased, however. Team boss Rex White said the team would pull Phil Mellor from Superstock if the plan went ahead. "We could have got Scott's VFR chucked out last year," he told Motor Cycle News, "but decided not to as long as there was no loophole for 1987." Suzuki took legal advice. Superstock organisers said the provision existed to make the VFR competitive with the other 750s. Meanwhile, Scott's '86 TT-F1 bike had gone to Andy McGladdery to use in the world title.

Freddie Spencer was back for Daytona and apparently recovered from his sinus and wrist problems. At any rate he made short work of Lawson's lap record in tyre tests, and was a warm favourite to win until he hit a crashed bike in qualifying and fell, cracking a collarbone and shoulder blade. He said he hoped to be fit for the Japanese GP. In his absence, Schwantz and Rainey resumed their acquaintanceship, enjoying their new radials (Michelin and Dunlop respectively), getting away from Tsujimoto and, scrapping for fourth, FZR-mounted Reuben McMurter, Roger Marshall's ballasted GSX-R, Andersson and Doug Polen, also Suzuki-mounted. Schwantz held the lead through the first stop but was put offline by a backmarker and fell at the chicane. Marshall stopped with an oil leak and Andersson crashed, but Rainey swept on, winning from Tsujimoto, Polen and McMurter, who rode most of the race without a clutch.

Apart from offering an early glimpse of the rivalry maturing between Rainey and Schwantz, Daytona 1987 was also the year of the Ducati 851, Ducati's new water-cooled eight-valver. Lucchinelli had won the 1986 Battle of the Twins race on the last of the old 750cc Pantah engines, supplanted at the 1986 Bol d'Or by the 748ie, the prototype eight-valve water-pumper built up from the Pantah's cases and using the F1's cylinder dimensions at 88 x 61.5mm. The 748's cylinder heads used 34mm and 30mm valves at a 40-degree included angle, with trademark desmodromic actuation and fuel-injection from Weber-Marelli. Mounted in a steel space frame, it made 94bhp and proved good enough to propel Lucchinelli, Virginio Ferrari and Juan Garriga to seventh at the Bol before rod failure stopped them. The bike was designed by Gianluigi Mengoli and developed by Massimo

Keith Huewen added the 1987 MCN-EBC Superstock title to Yamaha's growing list of successes, winning the Cadwell round with a damaged shoulder and taking the series with a round to spare. (Courtesy Bauer Media)

Bordi. By Daytona it had grown to 851cc (92 x 64mm), had bigger, sturdier cases, a six-speed 'box, compression ramped from 11 to 12:1, one of the uglier handmade aluminium frames on view, and, bottom line, 120bhp at 11,000rpm and 165kg. Lucchinelli put in a second commanding win and confirmed that there might be life beyond 750cc inline fours in Superbike.

Rainey and Schwantz resumed their struggle against the background of the Transatlantic Trophy, in 1987 back at Brands on Good Friday, then at Donington's new GP circuit, with three races each on Easter Sunday and Monday. Grumbles from deflated Brits, about unfamiliarity with the series' AMA Superbike rules, about Schwantz's XR55 with its trick 43mm Showas and titanium exhaust, about Rainey's $20,000 magnesium flat-slide Keihins, might have been warranted so far as they went. But while Ron Haslam's bike wasn't what it might have been, Kiwi Gary Goodfellow scored seven podiums for the US on unfamiliar circuits, with a bike as unlike factory kit as any ridden by the Brits; and in his performances for the UK, Kiwi Richard Scott showed himself cut from the same cloth. The simple truth of the matter was surely that America's great champions of the '90s came to Britain surging towards their towering best, Rainey's composed mastery overlain with a veneer of steel that enabled him to meet the eccentric showmanship of Schwantz's genius. Rainey's five wins, two seconds and a third and Schwantz's four wins and five seconds brooked little argument. That Schwantz outbraked himself at both Druid's and Melbourne only added to his raw-edged allure.

And that was just the beginning. AMA Superbike resumed at Road Atlanta where Rainey got away first. Schwantz gave chase, and by lap five they were 15 seconds clear of Shobert in third; three laps later Schwantz was past Rainey, but then ran off at turn 3, giving Rainey the win. Schwantz fought back past Shobert for second but couldn't close the gap to Rainey. "He was working the suspension real hard, and he couldn't get out of the corners good," Rainey told *Cycle News*. Major changes to Schwantz's bike for the year included double-thickness top frame tubes, Carrillo rods, and revised air ducting. The factory Suzuki and Honda each nudged past 135bhp.

At Brainerd, Schwantz crashed at blistering speed in Saturday practice, losing the front end. A first-aid man raced to his aid and did the usual concussion check: "Is it Saturday or Sunday?" he asked. "I slid that far," answered an unruffled Schwantz, "it could be Sunday." Tsujimoto crashed his GSX-R in the melee and wasn't so fortunate, breaking an ankle and hurting his back. In the race Rainey got out early and stayed there, Schwantz settling for second from Shobert and Dan Chivington's Honda. A fortnight later Schwantz won at Loudon, pulling a 10-second break early on Rainey then easing off. Shobert was again third, beating Polen out of a six-bike scrap. Schwantz's fight-back had begun. Four rounds down: Rainey 76, Schwantz 53, Shobert 39, Polen 34.

ITALIAN JOB

Fred Merkel was missing from AMA Superbike in 1987, opting instead to run a privately backed VFR750F, again prepared by Ron Grant, in the TT-F1 World Championship against Joey's NW6B and the new Suzukis, which, like the Americans,' using a stiffened chassis and Carrillo rods to improve reliability. The opening round at Misano fell to Skoal Bandit teamster Iddon, with Marshall close behind until he crashed with oil on his back tyre. Anders Andersson fell while Merkel ran into second from Joey, who battled suspension problems. Merkel didn't start in Hungary after breaking a crankshaft – apparently the heat treatment used in the 360-degree conversion played havoc with the hardening, and teeth were shearing from the central pinion. Meanwhile, Joey crashed in practice – the first time he'd jumped off an F1 bike – as did Marshall and Iddon during the race, leaving Virginio Ferrari to lead Davide Tardozzi in a 1-2 for Bimota's FZ750-powered YB4s from Andersson while Dunlop, ill-suited to Hungaroring's twists and turns, was eighth.

But Joey was back on top at the F1 TT, taking his fifth win in a row and posting another lap record. While Marshall battled fuel starvation, Andersson a misfire and Iddon retired with worn sprocket, Dunlop finished almost a minute clear of Phil Mellor's Suzuki and Yamaha-mounted Geoff Johnson. Then, as the week ended, he took to his RS500 to win a rain-shortened Senior TT – his tenth win on the Island.

When Superstock got going, Yamaha began to dominate: 19-year-old newcomer Terry Rymer won at Brands, where Loctite boys Huewen and Nation filled the podium, and at Mallory Park from Roger Hurst's Yamaha

Kawasaki made a limited return to four-stroke racing in 1987 with Superbikes based on the GPX750R. Australian Robbie Phillis (shown here leading Mick Doohan's Yamaha) claimed some of its earliest successes. (Courtesy Ian Falloon)

and Huewen again. The pick of the Suzukis was Mellor's. After fifth places at Brands and Mallory he dead-heated at the Donington third round in a desperate drag to the line with Nation, with Huewen third from Rymer and McGladdery's Honda – so far, the only one to make the top ten, anywhere. Three rounds down: Rymer 42, Huewen 32, Nation 28.5, Mellor 25.5.

Honda was still on top in AMA Superbike, however. After crashing in practice, Schwantz outbraked Polen into turn 5 at Elkhart Lake and won comfortably. Yet Rainey, battling an out-of-round front tyre, pushed Polen back to third. Filice, meanwhile, having dodged the sour rods that threatened to derail his FZR earlier in the year, broke a finger in a Loudon fall and didn't start at Elkhart Lake.

Both front-runners faltered at Laguna Seca, where the two races paid points on the aggregate result. In the first, Schwantz rocketed away while Rainey worked through the field but then pitted to replace his blistered rear tyre. Schwantz too was sliding more than normal – a high track temperature being the problem – but hung on to win from Polen, Shobert and Filice with Rainey 12th. Schwantz looked like making it two but lost the front end at turn 9 and a struggling Rainey won from Shobert and Filice. Schwantz won again at Mid Ohio, pulling away from Rainey and Filice, but Rainey's consistency was paying off. Seven rounds gone: Rainey 118, Schwantz 94, Shobert 81, Polen 60.

In TT-F1, all Joey's good work at the TT was undone at Assen when he and Merkel collided, sidelining them both. Meanwhile the Bimotas put in another team exhibition, Ferrari making a last-lap pass to win from Tardozzi, Marshall, and Iddon, and overtake Joey at the top of the table. The Ulster GP round was abandoned when Klaus Klein crashed in filthy weather and died after being thrown into a hedge. Ferrari had already gone, walking out after seeing Kiwi Glenn Williams lying in the road after crashing at Windmills. "It's a nightmare," said Ferrari. "The bikes are too fast for this course." With the Japanese round going to the regional specialists, Yamaha-mounted Kevin Magee winning from Yukiya Oshima's Suzuki and Mick Doohan's Yamaha, the points stayed as they were after Assen: Ferrari 30, Joey 28, Peter Rubatto (Suzuki) 26, Tardozzi 24.

The Honda RC30 became the only game in town for Superbike in 1988. Mal Campbell (leading) and Gary Goodfellow illustrate the point at Oran Park, Sydney. (Courtesy Phil Aynsley)

Magee and Yamaha were also on top in the Suzuka 8 Hours, finally breaking the Honda-Suzuki duopoly after nine factory Hondas had gone out, leaving the FZR750R Magee shared with Martin Wimmer to duel with the Gary Goodfellow/Katsuro Takayoshi GSX-R750 in the closing laps. Magee challenged for the lead with minutes left, and Takayoshi ran wide under pressure, letting Magee through to win by just 1m 20s and claim Yamaha's first win in the 8 Hours.

While Suzuka sweltered in 35-degree heat and 50 per cent humidity, the Superstock circus reconvened at Knockhill, north of Dunfermline – though without Trevor Nation, who broke a collarbone in practice. Mellor, Rymer and McGladdery made up for it, with Teessider McGladdery giving Honda its first Superstock win from Mellor while Rymer found neutral at the wrong moment and went down. A week later at Snetterton, McGladdery almost made it two, being pipped by Roger Hurst's Yamaha at the line, while

Huewen boosted his title prospects with another third. Before Cadwell's
sixth round Huewen put in a full day's practice braking for the hairpin. It
paid off: he broke from the first-lap melee and stayed ahead to lead home
a youthful Jamie Whitham, who'd battled long into the race getting past a
convalescent Nation. At Thruxton it was Mellor's turn, passing Rymer early
and pulling away to win from the Yamahas of Gary Noel, Rymer and Nation.
McGladdery, meanwhile, was out after clouting his right knee on a bank
during practice for the ill-fated Ulster. Points after seven rounds: Huewen
66, Rymer 60, Mellor 56.5, McGladdery 52.

Schwantz tried but failed. He won the last two AMA Superbike races,
but second at Memphis and sixth at Sears Point were good enough for
Rainey. Both had their problems: Rainey overheating in Tennessee while
Schwantz fought through from the back row in California after jumping the
start in his heat. Where Rainey had never finished a round outside the top
six, Schwantz struggled to make up the points he lost in falls at Daytona
and Laguna Seca: Rainey was champion again. Final points: Rainey 143,
Schwantz 134, Shobert 94, Polen 71. Filice ended the season on a high note,
running fifth at Memphis and second at Sears Point. The FZR was maturing
nicely after early problems, and the 0W01 would soon be on its way. But
Honda had one last trump in its hand.

Ferrari and Tardozzi again did their double act in the Hockenheim round
of the TT-F1 world title, pulling away to make Joey's VFR look asthmatic.
Ernst Gschwender got his Suzuki into third, beating Joey home and giving
Ferrari a nine-point break at the top of the table. The series ended with
Britain's second round, at Donington, where Honda recruited Merkel

*First blood to Bimota: Davide Tardozzi won the opening World Superbike race at
Donington on the now fuel-injected YB4EIR. (Courtesy Phil Aynsley)*

and Australian Paul Lewis to back Joey while Bimota added Fausto Ricci and Fabrizio Pirovano. Joey got additional firepower in the guise of the RVF Dominique Sarron shared with Jean-Louis Battistini and Jean-Michel Matteoli to win the Bol d'Or. Alas, clutch slip dropped him to third while Ferrari kept Joey in sight, finished seventh and collected the title. The race, meanwhile, came down to a spirited scrap between Skoal Bandit team-mates Iddon and Marshall, the laurels going Iddon's way by virtue of using 36mm carbs borrowed from Andersson that pumped mid-range and reduced fuel consumption, allowing Iddon to run the race without stopping. "Donington isn't quick enough for my big carbs," he said. "Roger broke the lap record several times trying to catch Paul," explains Paul Boulton, Iddon's mechanic in '87. "I'd bitten my nails back to my elbows by the end of race." Final points: Ferrari 49, Joey 46, Iddon 43, Tardozzi 36. After all its tribulations the GSX-R's original 48.7mm-stroke engine finished a winner.

Marco Lucchinelli claimed overall victory at the Donington WSB round for Ducati's further refined 851 EVD. (Courtesy Ian Falloon)

"137bhp at the back wheel from an oil-cooled 750 is pretty good, even by today's standards," says Boulton.

The season closed with Suzuki on top in Superstock as well, Jamie Whitham taking the Mallory round on a borrowed Skoal Bandit bike and then breaking free of a 10-bike dogfight in the Brands Hatch finale to win from Des Barry's Yamaha and Nation's Loctite FZ. After finishing second to Whit at Mallory, Huewen crashed hard on the first lap at Cadwell. But the race was red-flagged and he made the restart, borrowing Nation's bike to win both race and title with a broken shoulder and rib. Three weeks later he ran home a no doubt painful fifth, his job superbly done. Final points: Huewen 101, Hurst 66, Mellor 61.5.

The culmination of Honda's production V4 programme was glimpsed in July. The VFR750R, factory code RC30, was on its way in modest numbers: initially just a few hundred, but then the 2500 needed for homologation as Honda decided to throw its weight behind the new World Superbike

Championship. At its heart was a 70 x 48.6mm 90-degree dohc, 16-valve water-cooled V4, but beyond that it diverged sharply from the established VFR750F. The 360-degree crank was back, mounting titanium rods (a first in a road bike). Compression ratio was 11:1, the valves were disposed in a narrower included angle than the VFR-F's, and the gear-driven cams ran in needle-roller bearings. Carbs were 38mm Keihin CVs. Power output for the roadster was given as 112bhp at 11,000rpm (12,500rpm redline), delivered via a wet, multi-plate clutch to a six-speed 'box. The radiator even channelled water through the oil cooler. The chassis mounted Guy Coulon's Honda France single-sided swinging arm. Wheels were 17in and dry weight a claimed 185kg. Everything was trim, tidy and tiny, with rake at 26 degrees and wheelbase 1470mm. Forks were 41mm Showa. The asking price, at £8500 in the UK, was stellar for the time but dealers were still turning customers away.

Meanwhile, as Suzuki announced its new short-stroke (73 x 44.7mm) GSX-R750 with a new gas-flowed head, and reworked exhaust system, Ducati revealed its WSB 851 homologation model, the 'Tricolore,' with its 'Superbike Kit' that gave 120bhp at 10,000rpm, a chrome-moly frame and Marzocchi M1R forks. It was priced at £10,500. Before Christmas, Honda announced its race kits for the RC30, for Production and Superstock, with a third level, for WSB/TT-F1 priced at £3857, including carburettors and a full exhaust system.

GOING SOLO

The frocks had been ordered and the band booked; but what kind of dance would there be? Midway through 1987 ACU stalwart Bill Smith mused aloud on the idea of a fresh compromise, "leaving F1 as it is and letting the Americans [and Asia] go ahead with Superbike," then running a series of regional qualification races and ending the season with a head-to-head contest between the two classes "somewhere like Dubai." But soon afterwards Luigi Brenni, the head of the FIM's Road Race Commission, suggested that TT-F1 should perhaps put its own house in order, that in the light of the appalling events at the '87 Ulster GP, better safety standards were needed.

Yet the participation from Bimota at factory level during the 1987 TT-F1 world series – surely tailor-made for a high-profile chassis company seeking a promotional medium for its products – added to solid support from entrants and riders, emboldened TT-F1 supporters to repackage the class again, now as a supporting event at European championship meetings with reduced homologation numbers to attract smaller manufacturers, and with the TT as the only pure road circuit on the calendar.

In October, McLaughlin convened a meeting in the UK to discuss his own form of compromise. Peter Hillaby and Colin Armes from the ACU attended, together with Barry Symmons from Honda Britain. The central point of discussion was a reworking of TT-Superbike, based largely on that

V4 vindication: on his Oscar Rumi-backed, Ron Grant-prepared RC30, Flying Fred Merkel claimed the first World Superbike Championship – and the second. (Courtesy Phil Aynsley)

advanced by the ACU three years earlier, the initial objective being a hybrid series that over the course of a couple of seasons would become largely Superbike, but including the TT as a key round. McLaughlin went to the FIM congress ready to present his modified proposal, and counter TT-F1's defenders who were already in Paris to drum up support.

McLaughlin still had problems to overcome. He had already had to find private sponsorship to bolster Hungarian and Portuguese bids to hold rounds, and had to defuse attempts by former allies first to undermine, then to hijack the series, compelling him to outmanoeuvre the rebels by rewriting, overnight, the final presentation for the FIM. But the 1988 World Superbike Championship was ratified in Paris as planned: there would be nine rounds, beginning at Donington in April and ending at Manfeild, New Zealand six months later. Yet even now, with TT-F1 and WSB apparently destined to run along parallel lines in seasons ahead, talks were arranged between Sports Marketing and TT-F1's backers. "Obviously we would like to find common ground," said Bill Smith. "But virtually everyone accepts there is only room for one series, if not in '88 then in '89."

A month later, the two series were going their separate ways again. "Superbikes are go," McLaughlin told *Motor Cycle News*. "All those people who said we would never make it are going to see what the series is all about." The die was cast.

Fred Merkel and Joey were ready, their RC30s coming via Italy and

Honda Britain respectively; Fabrizio Pirovano had signed for Yamaha; Paul Iddon was talking to Bimota and Lucchinelli would ride the Ducati 851 EVD he and Massimo Bordi had lobbied hard for. Bimota was ready, its new, fuel-injected YB4IER having acquitted itself well on debut at Vallelunga; and Honda was almost ready. While Kevin Magee won the '87 Swann Series on Marlboro Yamaha's FZR1000 Superbike, Mal Campbell had stolen a win at Calder on the most exotic of them all, the oval-piston 160bhp NR750.

Campbell had taken his NW6A to the 1986 Australian Superbike Championship, the last before endurance races took centre stage. At the start of 1988 he was due to campaign the Honda team's RC30s in the Shell Superbike Series – and there met with trouble, at least in the short term. A spate of crank and big-end failures dogged the RC30's early competitive appearances. "It was rings, basically," recalls Clyde Wolfenden, then handing over to Mick Smith as manager of Team Honda Australia. "This was really the first bike they'd put single-ring pistons into and they just went too light on ring tension. Compression pressurised the sump and pumped oil out of the engine into the catch tank. You'd do about ten laps and have no oil left in the engine." There were other explanations, including poor bottom-end oil pressure and inadequate clearances between adjacent big-ends. "We got down to running production engines eventually," recalls Mick Smith, "supplied by Trevena Honda in Adelaide. But soon Honda sent new rings and then pistons, and that solved the problem."

The season began as usual at Daytona, where Schwantz rode the new short-stroke GSX-R to its first win before he headed for Europe to keep another appointment with Rainey. Meanwhile the Superbike circus moved to Donington Park where, on a typically blustery early spring Sunday, Roger Burnett put his Honda Britain RC30 on pole for the first race of the first World Superbike Championship. Next to him on the front row were Tardozzi's Bimota and Lucchinelli's Ducati EVD. Clutches lifted and gears selected, revs rose and moments later Burnett, Merkel, Pirovano's FZR and Tardozzi were charging towards Redgate. For the moment, the talking was over. Superbike was about to go global.

World Superbike took some 15 years to realise. Mr Superbike – Steve McLaughlin – found a sense of humour useful. (Courtesy Steve McLaughlin)

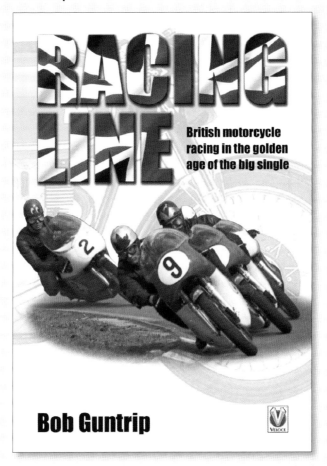

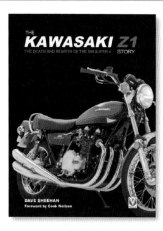

The Kawasaki Z1 Story –
The death and rebirth of the 900 Super 4
How the smallest of Japan's Big Four motorcycle manufacturers nearly beat the world's biggest to become the first to the market with a Four, and how Honda's CB750 debut almost spelled the end for the Z-1 ... before Kawasaki stunned everybody with something bigger, faster, and better!

ISBN: 978-1-845848-07-1
Paperback • 21x14.8cm
256 pages • 135 pictures

Honda NR500/NS500 –
The trials of regaining the Motorcycle World Championship

Honda's 4-stroke heritage allowed world motor cycle racing and sales domination. However, in the 1970s, 2-strokes dominated racing, damaging 4-stroke sales.
A winning 4-stroke Honda GP racer was needed, but it was a glorious failure. Finally, Honda went 2-stroke, and the resulting NS500 Honda eventually met success in 1983.

ISBN: 978-1-787115-77-4
Hardback • 21x14.8cm
192 pages • 20 pictures

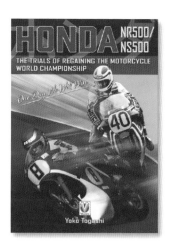

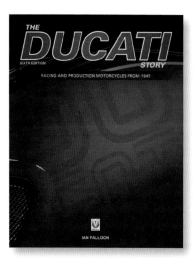

The Ducati Story –
Racing and Production motorcycles from 1945
Ian Falloon's authoritative history of the marque – expanded and brought up to date for this 6th edition – tells the inside story of Ducati's chequered path to glory, and describes every model, from the original 48cc Cucciolo to today's exotic Superbikes.

ISBN: 978-1-787110-85-4
Hardback • 27x21cm
• 361 pages • 349 pictures

For more information and price details, visit www.veloce.co.uk

Motorcycle Racing with the Continental Circus
– 1920 to 1970

A fascinating history of Continental motorcycle racing, from the pre-war period through to the 1970s, this book details the British riders and privateers from around the world, who earned their living competing in races and events on the circuits of Europe – for the racers an exciting and nomadic existence, known as the 'Continental Circus.'

ISBN: 978-1-787112-74-2
Hardback • 25x20.7cm
96 pages • 92 colour and b&w pictures

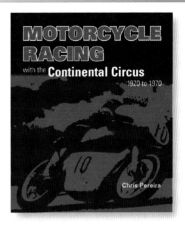

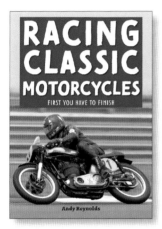

Racing Classic Motorcycles –
First you have to finish

The life of a classic motorcycle racer, who was fortunate enough to ride the best classic machines of the time at the highest level, and on some of the best-known courses in the world. Told in his own words, this book recounts his successes, friendships, and hardships, and gives a great insight into the world of motorcycle racing.

ISBN: 978-1-787114-81-4
Paperback • 21x14.8cm
• 240 pages • 57 pictures

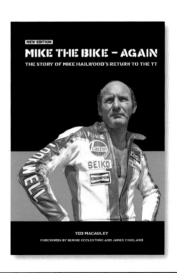

Mike the Bike – Again
The story of Mike Hailwood's return to the TT

An inside look behind the scenes at the top-secret planning, build-up, and spectacular success of Mike Hailwood's amazing comeback in 1978, 20 years after his debut at the age of 18. Written by his manager and friend, Ted Macauley, it is also a tribute to a remarkable man.

ISBN: 978-1-787113-13-8
Paperback • 21x14.8cm
• 112 pages • 40 pictures

• email: info@veloce.co.uk • Tel: +44(0)1305 260068

INDEX